THE
ROAD
I TRAVEL

To order additional copies of
The Road I Travel, by C. Raymond Holmes,
call **1-800-765-6955**.

Visit us at
www.reviewandherald.com
for information on other Review and Herald® products.

THE ROAD I TRAVEL

MY JOURNEY ALONG THE NARROW WAY

C. RAYMOND HOLMES

REVIEW AND HERALD® PUBLISHING ASSOCIATION
Since 1861 | www.reviewandherald.com

Copyright © 2011 by Review and Herald® Publishing Association

Published by Review and Herald® Publishing Association, Hagerstown, MD 21741-1119

Review and Herald® titles may be purchased in bulk for educational, business, fund-raising, or sales promotional use. For information, e-mail SpecialMarkets@reviewandherald.com.

The Review and Herald® Publishing Association publishes biblically based materials for spiritual, physical, and mental growth and Christian discipleship.

The author assumes full responsibility for the accuracy of all facts and quotations as cited in this book.

Unless otherwise noted, Bible texts in this book are from *The Holy Bible*, English Standard Version, copyright © 2001 by Crossway Bibles, a division of Good News Publishers, Used by permission. All rights reserved.

Scripture quotations marked NASB are from the *New American Standard Bible,* copyright © 1960, 1962, 1963, 1968, 1971, 1972, 1973, 1975, 1977, 1995 by The Lockman Foundation. Used by permission.
Texts credited to NIV are from the *Holy Bible, New International Version.* Copyright © 1973, 1978, 1984, International Bible Society. Used by permission of Zondervan Bible Publishers.
Texts credited to NKJV are from the New King James Version. Copyright © 1979, 1980, 1982 by Thomas Nelson, Inc. Used by permission. All rights reserved.
Bible texts credited to Phillips are from J. B. Phillips: *The New Testament in Modern English,* Revised Edition. © J. B. Phillips 1958, 1960, 1972. Used by permission of Macmillan Publishing Co.
Bible texts credited to RSV are from the Revised Standard Version of the Bible, copyright © 1946, 1952, 1971, by the Division of Christian Education of the National Council of the Churches of Christ in the U.S.A. Used by permission.
Texts credited to RV are from *The Holy Bible*, Revised Version, Oxford University Press, 1911.

This book was
Edited by Russell Holt
Copyedited by Soraya Homayouni and James Cavil
Cover designed by Haley Trimmer
Cover photo fotolia.com
Typeset: Bembo 11/13

PRINTED IN U.S.A.

15   14   13   12   11   5   4   3   2   1

Library of Congress Cataloging-in-Publication Data
Holmes, C. Raymond, 1929-   .
   The road I travel : my journey along the narrow way / C. Raymond Holmes.
      p. cm.
1. Christian life—Adventist authors. 2. Spirituality—General Conference of Seventh-day Adventists. I. Title. II. Title: My journey along the narrow way.

   BV4501.3.H665 2011
   248.4'86732—dc22

                                      2011007357

ISBN 978-0-8280-2581-2

DEDICATION

To all the spiritual friends
who have been my companions along the road I travel.

ACKNOWLEDGMENTS

Special thanks to Israel Ramos for suggesting the title;
to Ron du Preez for critiquing the manuscript
and writing the Foreword;
and to Jay Gallimore and Al Newhart
for their prayers and persistent encouragement.

CONTENTS

PREFACE

W riting this book has been an answer to prayer. For most of 2008 I struggled with a sense of sadness that was almost overwhelming at times. Not that it could be called depression, which is characterized by inactivity and difficulty in thinking and concentrating. I was busy enough and certainly had no difficulty thinking and concentrating. Ever since retirement from the faculty of the Seventh-day Adventist Theological Seminary at Andrews University, I have been happily serving, part-time, as "senior" pastor of a small Seventh-day Adventist congregation in Bessemer, Michigan, just one mile from the Lutheran church I pastored in the 1960s!

However, my only sister died from a rare liver disease in September 2007. A year later I was still grieving, and the sense of sadness was getting to be too much. Waking up very early in the mornings, around 3:00 or 4:00 a.m., I spent the sleepless time in prayer, asking God to relieve me somehow. After a few days I received two books in the mail, gifts from a friend. One, titled *Faith Undone*, was an exposé and critique of the contemporary phenomenon known as the "emerging church."[1] The other was titled *A Time of Departing*, in which the author discussed how mystical practices are finding their way into Christian churches through what is called the "spiritual formation movement."[2] Both books were very critical of the theology of Rick Warren and his books *The Purpose Driven Life* and *The Purpose Driven Church*, as well as Richard Foster's book *Celebration of Discipline*.

I read both the books sent to me, carefully underlining and making notes. When I was finished, I thought, *These people are stealing our language! We need a book about spirituality from a biblically sound Seventh-day Adventist perspective*. Furthermore, in light of the fact that I had taught a course on spirituality at the Seventh-day Adventist Theological Seminary in the 1980s and 1990s, I thought, *Maybe I ought to do it*. You probably have already guessed what happened. My sadness disappeared. Gone! Replaced by a sense of elation and purpose. God does answer prayer! Sometimes it

11

takes time, but He hears, and He answers. I hope that the final product is worthy of His attention and yours. Now you know what I did during the 2008-2009 and 2009-2010 Michigan winters.

Before you read further, I want to make clear my position on the authority of the Bible as God's Word. I believe that the Bible is the inspired and infallible revelation of God, who is its author. This belief was a primary reason for my transition from the Lutheran to the Seventh-day Adventist Church. All teaching and practice in the church must be tested against the Bible. Also, all Christian experience must be so tested. Human experience and human claims do not test Bible truth. Neither the inner life nor Christian experience are the ground, or source, of truth. However, genuine Christian experience does authenticate and demonstrate biblical truth in the life. It is my firm conviction that biblical arguments are persuasive and take precedence over scientific, cultural, psychological, sociological, philosophical, phenomenological (particularly the so-called *collective unconscious*), and experiential arguments.

The basic premise of this book is that salvation comes from the experience of faith in the living Word, Jesus Christ, and in the written Word, the Bible. This faith will be referred to throughout this book as "believing faith." The source of that faith is God, who reveals Himself to us in His Word and comes to us in the person of His Son, Jesus Christ. This is the central truth of that faith. Saving faith is based not on human reason or experience but on the promises of God's Word. However, it is not possible to talk about spirituality without talking about the experience of faith, about the relationship between objective truth and the subjective experience of that truth. I have written from the perspective of that experience, because without the inner dimension, faith would be a lifeless form of rationalism, a dead and meaningless orthodoxy. Please read what is written in the following pages in the light of this conviction.

I consider myself a theological centrist who is dismayed by those who push a "felt needs" agenda ahead of the will of God as revealed in the Bible—those who make the same drastic mistake Luther sometimes made in putting natural law ahead of divine law. I am talking about the left-leaning theological activists who are doing a hatchet job on Protestantism in America and elsewhere by capitulating to the demands of culture. These individuals have been successful largely because of their confidence that those who listen to them have no clue, because of a lack of Bible study and a misinformed confidence in pulpit pronouncements and in the actions of church councils and assemblies.

To withstand such pressure, strong internal convictions are required. Believers are constantly being hammered by theologically liberal elites to "grow" and "evolve" in their thinking away from the biblical text toward more eclectic positions. But we need not look to other world religions, to the New Age, or to the emerging church for guidance if we have our spiritual eyes fixed on the Christ revealed in the Bible. There, and there alone, do we find the clearest and most reliable insight into truth and the authentic experience of believing faith, which the Spirit of Prophecy affirms and corroborates.

Working on this book for more than a year has more sharply clarified the motivation for doing so. It is to encourage Seventh-day Adventist Christians to stay true to the message and mission of their church come what may. Part of that motivation is my suspicion that the reason some Seventh-day Adventists have been attracted to New Age and emerging church ideas has been a lack of emphasis, in the Adventism they have known, on the reality of the inner life of faith—a lack of emphasis on a believing faith, on a faith that believes right doctrine is supposed to produce a vibrant and meaningful belief experience that will stand the tests of life. Jesus said, "I am the way, and the truth, and the life" (John 14:6). He is the way we take and follow. He is the truth that is foundational to our faith. He is the life we live as disciples. What is needed is not doctrine alone, but Jesus Himself. Doctrine and the experience of faith cannot be divorced from each other. The apostle John warns and appeals: "Watch yourselves, so that you may not lose what we have worked for, but may win a full reward. *Everyone who goes on ahead and does not abide in the teaching of Christ, does not have God. Whoever abides in the teaching has both the Father and the Son.* If anyone comes to you and does not bring this teaching, do not receive him into your house or give him any greeting, for whoever greets him takes part in his wicked works" (2 John 8-11).

I hope the reader will not be disappointed that this book is not primarily polemical. Although there is a place for works that analyze and critique, I did not want to spend all of these pages arguing the pros and cons of differing views of spirituality. There are ample polemical sources available—including the two books mentioned above, plus *Who's Driving the Purpose Driven Church?* by James Sundquist.[3] For those who want to consult an Adventist resource on the emerging church, the Summer 2008 issue of *Adventists Affirm*[4] is an excellent source. What I want to do in this book is to explore the reality and meaning of spirituality from a thoroughly biblical Adventist perspective, with the accent on the way in which believers give expression to *what* they believe by *how* they live. I have confined myself to a discussion of spirituality, not spiritualism. Therefore, this book is more like a pastoral letter to those who have remained, or are determined to remain, faithful to the message and mission of the Seventh-day Adventist Church. It is not a theological treatise, although there is theology in it. Some of it may even sound sermonic, for which I do not apologize. I am a preacher, after all.

There is no possible way I could write this book without personal references. So I have used the narrative mode of expression, seeking understanding through the power of story. Why? Because the subject of this book could not be talked about exclusively in an objective, intellectual, cerebral way. Such an approach would be dull and uninteresting to some readers, and, more important, it would be out of character with the subject, as ensuing chapters will demonstrate. After all, spirituality cannot be talked about apart from the subjective dimension. To be sure, spirituality has theological and doctrinal components, which are referred to in context; but before it is anything else, spirituality is the kind of personal experience identified as believing faith. I have done my best to explain what I mean by that term. The narrative mode also provided the opportunity to be somewhat autobiographical and reflective of the Adventist style of my own spirituality. What I have written is the result of study, experience, and observation.

When I discussed the concept of this book with one of my colleagues, he counseled me to identify my audience, those to whom it would be addressed, in order to be guided in expressing my thoughts. But as I wrote, I discovered that the audience I had in mind was a mixed one. You will find, in the pages that follow, material meant for any reader, especially for the thoughtful Seventh-day Adventist Christian. But you will also find material meant specifically for preachers and students of preaching. I don't think you will have too much trouble sorting it all out and applying it relevantly and perceptively.

At the end of each chapter you will find questions designed to help you reflect on the content of that chapter, not only conceptually but perceptually. Not just with your head but with your heart. I pray the exercise will prove valuable in the ongoing process of developing a believing faith and spirituality.

"The Christian life is a battle and a march. But the victory to be gained is not won by human power. The field of conflict is the domain of the heart. The battle which we have to fight—the greatest battle that was ever fought by man—is the surrender of self to the will of God, the yielding of the heart to the sovereignty of love."[5]

[1] Roger Oakland, *Faith Undone* (Silverton, Oreg.: Lighthouse Trails Publishing, 2007).
[2] Ray Yungen, *A Time of Departing* (Silverton, Oreg.: Lighthouse Trails Publishing, 2002).
[3] Bethany, Okla.: Rock Salt Publishing and Bible Belt Publishers, 2004.
[4] Volume 22, number 2. Write to P.O. Box 36, Berrien Springs, Mich. 49103.
[5] Ellen G. White, *Thoughts From the Mount of Blessing* (Mountain View, Calif.: Pacific Press Pub. Assn., 1956), p. 141.

FOREWORD

At last—a thoroughly Adventist approach to the vital necessity of genuine scriptural spirituality!

For decades a variety of conservative Seventh-day Adventists have shared their concerns and criticisms with me regarding fellow Adventist thought leaders, who have been actively promoting and practicing something labeled "spiritual formation" or its related activities. Yet I do not recall that any of these worried "watchmen" ever suggested or supplied a superior alternative. Ellen White noted, "As we seek to turn men from their self-indulgent efforts to secure happiness, we must show them that we have something better than that which they are seeking."[1] Furthermore, she stated: " 'Something better' is the watchword of education, the law of all true living. Whatever Christ asks us to renounce, He offers in its stead something better."[2]

In this autobiographical account C. Raymond Holmes provides this much-needed "something better." True, it is *not* a comprehensive consideration of all the possible biblical passages that may relate to the issue, nor is it a thoroughly theological tome on the topic nor a full-fledged refutation of the fundamental fallacies of the mystical methods emerging among some professed Christians. Instead, this book is a profoundly personal story of the author as he has enjoyed his journey with Jesus over the past many decades.

But it is much more than simply a subjective, sentimental story. Those who choose to join Holmes in *The Road I Travel* will encounter more than merely a trip down memory lane; they will be transported to new heights of authentic biblical spirituality, into a richer and fuller experience with Jesus Christ. Holmes rightly recognizes that while it may not ever be possible to accurately *define* genuine Christian spirituality, this vital aspect of the believer's life can be adequately *described*. So he invites the reader to join him on his spiritual safari as he travels from the past to the present.

Traditionally, Seventh-day Adventists have been known as the "people of the Book," because of our appropriate insistence that all doctrines must be founded firmly upon the Word of God—the Bible. Indeed, this correct emphasis has convinced many to join the ranks of the remnant church. All too often, however, this emphasis on the objective and intellectual aspects of our religion has come at a very heavy price. Ellen White lamented:

"As our numbers are increasing, broader plans must be laid to meet the increasing demands of the times; but *we see no special increase of* fervent piety, of Christian simplicity, and *earnest devotion*. The church [the members] seem content to take only the first steps in conversion. They are more ready for active labor than for humble devotion, more ready to engage in outward religious service than in the inner work of the heart. Meditation and prayer are neglected for bustle and show. *Religion must begin with emptying and purifying the heart, and must be nurtured by daily prayer.*"[3]

Just as true faith will be manifested through spirit-filled action, "right doctrine," Holmes maintains, "is supposed to produce a vibrant and meaningful belief experience that will stand the tests of life." More is needed than simply cerebral doctrine or theological theories—mere matters of the mind. The Christian must have a religious experience of the heart, a living encounter with Jesus, for "doctrine and the experience of faith cannot be divorced from each other." Ellen White concurs, stating, "Those who *believe* present truth are to *practice* the truth, live the truth."[4] As Holmes notes: "Redemption, therefore, does not happen only on the cross, but *in* the believer in whom Christ dwells by faith."

Although Holmes does not dwell on the dangers of questionable aspects of "spiritual formation" as practiced by some, he clearly does confront key controversial concerns. He correctly complains that some of these mystical mentors of "spiritual formation" are "*stealing our language.*" For, in and of itself, "spiritual formation" is *not* innately evil. Holmes aptly indicates that our interest in genuine "spiritual formation" (that is, character development) should not instill fear, "*provided* that our search is based on Scripture." Very directly he warns against the anti-biblical practices of concentrating on breathing in and breathing out, or repeating mantras, or staring at a blank wall in order to empty one's mind.

Put plainly, Holmes declares: "Adventist spirituality does not seek accommodation with non-Christian faiths nor with Christian traditions that are in the process of abandoning *sola scriptura*. What Adventist Christians desire more than anything else is a spirituality in harmony with Scripture, confirmed and affirmed by the Spirit of Prophecy, which fortifies them for the demands of mission in the time of the end."

The author shares much more in this meaningful memoir—including scriptural foundations for spiritual friendships, the necessity for nurturing pastors-in-training to become sound spiritual shepherds and not just textual technicians, and the importance of having the Word of God transform the life before it can become effective in communication.

Let's return once more to Ellen White's "something better" motif, this time directly in the context of true "spiritual formation," or character development. She says, "The Lord shows that there is something better for His people than mere outward worship. He demands of them a pure and undefiled religion. The gold He bids them buy of Him is the gold of character."[5]

Yes, there are some today promoting pagan practices under the guise of "spiritual formation." However, do not let the misuse and misapplication of a basic biblical belief deprive you of developing a dynamic relationship with God.

"The way to dispel darkness is to admit light. The best way to deal with error is to present truth."[6] Here is a book that seeks to do just that—to build on the Bible, to practically apply the plain truths of Scripture. Read it, ruminate on it, and "grow in the grace and knowledge of our Lord and Savior Jesus Christ. To Him be the glory both now and forever. Amen" (2 Peter 3:18, NKJV).

Ron du Preez, Th.D., D.Min.

---

[1] Ellen G. White, *Testimonies for the Church* (Mountain View, Calif.: Pacific Press Pub. Assn., 1948), vol. 6, p. 64.

[2] Ellen G. White, *Education* (Mountain View, Calif.: Pacific Press Pub. Assn., 1903), p. 296.

[3] E. G. White, *Testimonies,* vol. 4, p. 535. (Italics supplied.)

[4] Ellen G. White, *Christ Triumphant* (Hagerstown, Md.: Review and Herald Pub. Assn., 1999), p. 247. (Italics supplied.)

[5] Ellen G White, in *General Conference Bulletin*, June 6, 1909.

[6] Ellen G. White, *The Desire of Ages* (Mountain View, Calif.: Pacific Press Pub. Assn., 1898), p. 498.

INTRODUCTION

*"Let's not be afraid to use good words. Let's not allow others
to steal good words from us. If we allow that to happen, we will be the losers,
because our understanding will be truncated, incomplete, and impoverished.
Consequently, our experience will be incomplete, limited, distorted—
even perverted and depraved. But at the same time, let's be careful to give
these words meaning that is based on the Bible and from within
the Seventh-day Adventist understanding of biblical faith."*

Those familiar with the emerging church and the popular concepts of
spiritual formation and spiritual disciplines may readily identify the
various buzzwords and key ideas to which the author alludes within these
pages. However, it may not be entirely clear to those new to this ideology
why the author addresses issues such as spiritual friendship, the reality of
Christ's presence, obedience, or training spiritual leaders. These topics may
seem unrelated, even random, in their treatment. There is, though, a common theme.

At the heart of the emerging church movement is a deep dissatisfaction with the status quo in Christianity, with a mere assent to doctrine
without the accompanying transformation of the life. This dissatisfaction
has led to the adoption of a variety of well-intentioned yet flawed beliefs—
truth mixed with error, if you will. Rather than simply identifying the
dangers inherent in these beliefs, the author has chosen instead to highlight
their *truths* and weave them into the fabric of genuine biblical spirituality.
His overarching purpose is not to debunk myths, but to uphold biblical
truth and guide a specifically Adventist discussion on genuine spirituality
and the subsequent expression of faith in the Christian's life.

Interspersed among chapters relevant to the emerging church are those related to spiritual formation and spiritual disciplines—practices intended to cultivate spirituality. The chapters are not identified as relating to one or the other, but a basic knowledge of the popular views of each will assist the reader in identifying the particular error the author desires to conquer with God's Word. Admirably, the author refrains from attacking falsehood, but concentrates on defending truth and challenging the body of Christ to live as He did.

"Though our outer self is wasting away,
our inner self is being renewed day by day.
For this light momentary affliction is preparing
for us an eternal weight of glory beyond all comparison,
as we look not to the things that are seen
but to the things that are unseen. For the things
that are seen are transient, but the things that
are unseen are eternal."
—2 Corinthians 4:16-18

"Understand by experience what it means
to have fellowship with Christ."
—Ellen G. White, *Testimonies for the Church,* vol. 9, p. 285

Chapter 1

HE'S THERE,
AND HE SPEAKS

It's hard to communicate when using certain words becomes the equivalent of waving a red flag in front of a bull. The flag itself is not a weapon and cannot harm the bull, but waving the flag frightens him and makes him mad. He perceives it as a threat, and his immediate response is defensive, then offensive. Words such as *discipline, silence, contemplation, meditation, direction, consciousness, inner dimension, formation, spiritual friend,* and *spirituality* are red flags that make some folks apprehensive or threatened or confused—especially in the contexts in which they are so often used today. The most contemporary example is the phrase *emerging church*. (More on that later.) So what do we need in order to communicate effectively? Accurate definitions and clarifications of the meaning of these words in our own context—the context of the Seventh-day Adventist understanding *and experience* of the Christian faith.

Let me give you an example. For a long time after I became a Seventh-day Adventist, I was hesitant to use the word *sacrament* until my happy discovery that Ellen White used it. *That ought to settle it!* The most delightful example is her statement: "The light shining from that Communion service in the upper chamber [on the eve of Christ's passion] makes sacred the provisions for our daily life. The family board becomes as the table of the Lord, and every meal a sacrament."[1] That brings it down to earth. She called that Communion "the sacramental service"[2] and "the sacramental supper."[3] She talked about "the administration of the Sacrament."[4] Notice she capitalized the word in that last use. To be sure, she used the word synonymously with "communion" and "Lord's supper" and "ordinance" in the same pages. But she did use it. She wasn't afraid to use it. It's a good word. But when you read everything she said about the Lord's Supper, it becomes clear that she did not mean what Catholics, Anglicans, and Lutherans mean when they use the word *sacrament*. In the course of her discussion she gave the word its proper meaning. She emptied it of its traditional meaning and filled it with biblical meaning.

My point? Let's not be afraid to use good words. Let's not allow others to steal good words from us. If we allow that to happen, we will be the losers, because our understanding will be truncated, incomplete, and impoverished. Consequently, our experience will be incomplete, limited, distorted—even perverted and depraved. But at the same time, let's be careful to give these words meaning that is based on the Bible and from within the Seventh-day Adventist understanding of biblical faith. We do not need to go outside our own Christian tradition or to non-Christian sources for that understanding. Of necessity, that understanding must include what we unashamedly call "the Spirit of Prophecy"—the collective writings of Ellen G. White—that includes this plaintive cry: "My soul is burdened as I see the great want of *spirituality* among us."[5]

Spirituality is one of the words we use to describe the Christian believer's story of faith, also referred to at times as the "spiritual journey," the "spiritual pilgrimage," the "journey of faith," the "spiritual life," the "Christian pilgrimage," or the "walk with God." Can you think of some other examples? *The Seventh-day Adventist Hymnal* has collections of hymns under the headings "Spiritual Gifts," "Christian Life," and "Pilgrimage." Check them out.

God Who Is There Speaks

It is possible to recall evidence of God's presence and guidance and, by so doing, to trace His footprints in our faith life. To become aware of just how He has worked to shape us. To remember, in particular, how His Word has been spoken to us by others. I don't mean through quoting the Bible or preaching, although these are not excluded. I mean recollecting sensitive responses from Spirit-led people whom God used as His "voice" and that we recognize, sometimes instantaneously, as such. This "voice" moves us at critical moments in the direction He wants us to go, sometimes in a direction we may not have chosen otherwise. Seventh-day Adventists, as well as other Christians, experience this phenomenon, but when we talk about it we tend to use the word *impression* instead of *voice*. "I felt impressed," we say when we want to indicate that we have heard God speak to us inwardly. Both expressions convey the same idea, just in different words. It's curious, isn't it, that we also use the word *felt,* which puts the emphasis on the affective level of experience, rather than on the purely cognitive level. (More about that later.) Perhaps a few stories from my own experience may help illustrate what I mean.

I had never learned to study in high school, so I faced a major challenge when the Lord entered my life. I sensed an inner "call" to the ministry and enrolled in Suomi College,[6] a small Christian institution in

Hancock, Michigan, way up in the Keweenaw Peninsula of the state's beautiful Upper Peninsula. Suomi was not only a liberal arts junior college but the training school for pastors of the Finnish Evangelical Lutheran Church.

I did extremely poorly with the first midsemester exams. I believe I actually flunked some of them. Lonely, confused, and depressed, I was making secret plans to pack my things and sneak away during the night. I went to the chapel to think and pray. After all, I was in the early stages of learning what the Christian life is all about and how to deal with personal crisis and challenge. The sky was as dark and forbidding as it can be in January in the Upper Peninsula, and I felt the same way inside. Then I heard a voice—a real human voice, not a figment of my imagination. The voice said, "Isn't it wonderful to know that above those clouds the sun is shining?" It was the local Lutheran pastor, who had come to conduct the chapel service that morning. I hadn't spoken to him about my dilemma or my mood. I hardly knew him. He knew absolutely nothing about what was going on in my head and heart. *Or did he?* Perhaps he somehow sensed that he was in the presence of a troubled young man. Was his pastoral heart in gear that morning?

That's all he said. I said nothing. We can argue until we are blue in the face about whether his words penetrated my head or touched my heart. But I know what those words did inwardly. I know the effect they had on my mood. I know the long-term consequences of those words. They snapped me right out of my fear and depression. They took away my doubts about whether God was actually leading in my life. My questions about why had He called me to ministry and brought me into an academic environment with its demands on a brain I had never learned to use evaporated. That was the first instance in which God spoke to me through another. It turned out to be one of the first steps on the spiritual road I travel. It also affirmed His active presence.

So what happened? I stayed in school. But that's not all that happened. By the end of that year I was on the dean's list. Who knows where or what I would be today if I had not heard God speak to me through that pastor. I would not have graduated from Suomi College (1956), Northern Michigan University (B.A., 1958), the Lutheran School of Theology (M.Div., 1961), Andrews University (M.Th., 1972, and D.Min., 1975), ending up as a professor in the Seventh-day Adventist Theological Seminary. Whether the event is referred to as a "voice" or an "impression," something always happens when God speaks, no matter the means He uses.

A few days later I was sitting in the college library, reading a history textbook, when a hand reached over my shoulder and propped a 3" x 5" card against the book. On the card were these words, handwritten in blue ink: "I can do all things through Christ who strengthens me, Philippians 4:13."[7] The hand belonged to my history professor, a layman. I had not talked with him about my dilemma, but somehow he knew. Those words on that card, right from God's Word, together with my teacher's sensitivity, confirmed what had happened a few days earlier in the chapel. God had spoken to me again. I still have that card. It is one of my most precious possessions and a lifelong reminder of God's grace, of His presence and guidance in my life. It is one of His footprints. That was an instance in which God spoke to me through His Word as it was called to my attention by another. Both of these instances prove that (1) "the Bible is God's voice speaking to us just as surely as though we could hear Him with our ears" and that (2) "the word of the living God is not merely written, but spoken."[8]

Years later, after completing college and seminary, and after almost 10 years of ministry as a Lutheran pastor, I was faced with an agonizingly difficult spiritual crisis when my wife decided to join the Seventh-day Adventist Church. You can read that story in my book *Stranger in My Home* and in her book *No Turning Back*. Suffice it to say that my father's wise counsel to me as a kid has proved invaluable many times over. He said, "You'll never get so old that you can't learn something new every day." He wasn't speaking theologically or spiritually, but his words have proved true in those areas of my life.

Let me tell you a part of the story that I did not include in *Stranger in My Home*, a part that further illustrates how God has given me guidance directly from His written Word and also through the words of others. The event occurred in the midst of my spiritual crisis. At the height of my dilemma, I desperately needed to share, with someone I could trust, what had been happening. When I briefly explained the situation to my former teacher, Walter Kukkonen, a Lutheran seminary professor, he invited me to his home in Homewood, Illinois. We spent two intense days together as I unloaded the burden on my heart, sharing my anguish, my struggle, my search for direction. He listened intently, with no interruption. His eyes never left my face. There was no indication that he was bored, disinterested, or unconcerned. Finally I had said it all; there was nothing more to say. I waited. Then he spoke—not as a theologian on a doctrinal level, but as a sensitive, spiritual friend on the level that my need was most acute. He said, "Ray, you need to ask God what He's trying to say to you." It was a totally unexpected response from a theologian who dealt primarily with the cognitive, but it was powerful in its effect.

My gratitude for the way Professor Kukkonen allowed himself to be used by the Christ we both knew is beyond words. What he said had the power to change my attitude and thus to change my life. His brief words gave me the courage to take the next step in following Christ, who leads the way because He is the way. Professor Kukkonen was my Elihu, who said to Job, "Surely you have spoken in my ears, and I have heard the sound of your words" (Job 33:8). He helped me hear God. In order for him to do that, he had to listen to my story and be sensitive to what God might be doing. Then he had to speak out of that kind of listening. What happened was the result of what he would call "transformative interaction." Coming from a Lutheran theologian who was my spiritual friend, his words gave me permission and the freedom to take the next step of faith. Where did that step take me? To the seminary at Andrews University, to baptism by immersion at Pioneer Memorial church, and to ordination into the ministry of the Seventh-day Adventist Church.[9] How wonderfully right was Elihu in the easily over-looked words, embedded in his long monologue to Job, "The ear tests words as the palate tastes food" (Job 34:3).

The fact that I did not include the above story in *Stranger in My Home* mystified me for many years until the spiritual significance of that event finally dawned on me. Strange as it may seem, that understanding did not happen until the 1980s while I was teaching a course titled Spirituality for Ministry for doctoral students at Andrews University.

In the earlier experience, confirmation from the Word of God came after I had heard the word spoken to me by others. In this last instance the word spoken to me by my professor in 1969 confirmed the Word of God that I had heard a year earlier, when I had opened my Bible at random one day, and my eyes fell upon these words from the Revised Standard Version: "I know the plans I have for you, declares the Lord, plans for welfare and not for evil, to give you a future and a hope" (Jer. 29:11). It took a whole year before I began to get a glimmer of what His "plans" might be for my future, but I knew that whatever it would be, it would be good, not "evil." I clung to that promise. For a year I lived on hope, meanwhile doing my best to "let the work of the Spirit of God reach deeper than the external . . . down to the deep springs of every action."[10]

Why am I telling these stories? Because they represent my first experiences with the conflict between the kingdom of light and the kingdom of darkness, the inner dimension of what Adventists refer to as the great controversy. But primarily I am telling them because they helped me learn that in a certain sense the Bible serves as a commentary on the Christian experience and that similarly Christian experience serves as a commentary on the Bible. One illuminates the other. All of this is part of what we call *spirituality*. It needs to be said here that Christian experience is tested and validated by the Bible. Christian experience does not test and validate the Bible. I tell these stories because the events they describe helped me discover that Someone is in charge of my life, that I am not alone on the road I travel. I tell these stories because the Spirit of Prophecy affirms that "God speaks through human lips. The heart is reached. Humanity is brought into touch with divinity."[11] I also tell these stories, and others that will follow in these pages, because I dread the spiritual stagnation that is described in the following statement:

"Many who have an intelligent knowledge of the truth, and are able to defend it by arguments, are doing nothing for the upbuilding of Christ's kingdom. We meet them from time to time, but they bear no fresh testimonies of personal *experience in the Christian life*; they relate no new victories gained in the holy warfare. Instead of this you notice the same old routine, the same expressions in prayer and exhortation. Their prayers have no new note; they express no greater intelligence in the things of God, no more earnest, living faith. Such persons are not living plants in the garden of the Lord, sending forth fresh shoots and new foliage, and the grateful fragrance of a holy life. They are not growing Christians. They have limited views and plans, and there is no expansion of mind, no valuable additions to the treasures of Christian knowledge. Their powers have not been taxed in this direction. They have not learned to view men and things as God views them, and in many cases unsanctified sympathy has injured souls and greatly crippled the cause of God. The spiritual stagnation that prevails is terrible. Many lead a formal Christian life and claim that their sins have been forgiven, when they are as destitute of any real knowledge of Christ as is the sinner."[12]

Someone Is in Charge

My discovery in 1954 and 1968-1969 that Someone was in charge of my life continued in 1970. If you read *Stranger in My Home*, you will find that the story I tell now is not included in that book. I debated for some time before I decided not to mention it, even though it was a vital part of the journey of faith that took me from the Lutheran to the Seventh-day Adventist Church. I left it out because I was afraid readers might think I had gone over the edge. Many thought so anyway. One Lutheran layman slammed his fist on my desk, yelling in my face that it would have been more acceptable had my wife and I become Catholics. But if I was writing *Stranger in My Home* today, I would include this story—perhaps because I am braver now than then, but also perhaps because I am better equipped, as a result of my own developing spirituality, to deal with the negative reactions the story may produce. At any rate, the event is a reminder for me of just how serious my spiritual crisis was.

Having enrolled as a Master of Theology student in the Seventh-day Adventist Theological Seminary at Andrews University, and still a Lutheran, I immersed myself in intense study and research regarding the seventh-day Sabbath. One afternoon, alone in our student apartment, I was reading a passage about the Sabbath in my Bible. Suddenly I heard a "voice" calling me by name: "Ray!" It was a very pleasant, appealing voice—not angry or strident. You might imagine my initial reaction. *Is the whole situation causing hallucinations?* I ignored the "voice," but then I heard it call out again. I put down my Bible and sat up. Then I heard, "Ray, if you love me, stop reading!" Fortunately, I had enough spiritual sense to realize immediately that God would never ask one of His own to stop reading His Word. Instantly I knew the "voice" was not from God. You know, don't you, whose "voice" it was! Never before, or since, have I heard the "voice" of Satan. I knew, then, that Satan did not want me to study the Sabbath question seriously. I remembered the apocryphal story of Martin Luther throwing an inkwell at Satan when he was translating the Bible in the ancient Wartburg Castle. I also remembered that Luther once remarked that even "the devil is God's devil." Luther meant that because He is sovereign, God can use even Satan to fulfill His own purpose. Was that event that day one of God's footprints on the path of my spiritual journey? I think it was. This is, after all, *my* story. I didn't throw an inkwell at Satan, but I did throw the Word of God at him, just as Jesus did (see Matt. 4:4-7, 10). "Resist the devil, and he will flee from you" is the Lord's promise (James 4:7).

I learned something else that day. God allowed the encounter with Satan to take place so that I could perceive the reality of what Adventists call the great controversy. The conflict between God and Satan, between good and evil, right and wrong, righteousness and unrighteousness, is not a figment of imagination. It is real, and it is waged in the inner being—not just out there in the cosmos somewhere.

But I needed to perceive something else. When I arrived at Andrews University in the fall of 1970, my initial goal was to discover if Jesus Christ was present at that institution in the lives of the faculty and students. I found that He was. I took a course, The Doctrine of the Atonement, from Wilber Alexander. His lectures during the first half of the course were no problem; they were orthodox Christian teaching from the Old Testament prophecies concerning the Messiah through the life, teachings, and ministry of Christ in the Gospels, including His passion, crucifixion, resurrection, and ascension. Then he began to lecture about Christ's ministry in heaven as high priest. Whoa! That was new to me! In spite of the fact that the book of Hebrews is part of the New Testament and I had preached from it a number of times, this aspect of Christ's mission had not registered with me. I felt like bolting from the classroom, because I thought it was a theological invention of Adventists. But there it was in the Bible. I could not deny it. Troubled, after class I asked Alexander if I could speak with him privately, and he invited me to his office for the next hour. He sat behind his desk while I paced back and forth and spoke about my dilemma. Finally I broke down in tears. At that point I heard someone sobbing. Turning to face him, I saw my professor crying, with tears running down his cheeks. He said, "I'm not crying *for* you; I'm crying *with* you." That was not the time for a theological, doctrinal lecture, and he knew it. Like my Lutheran professor, my Adventist professor responded not on the cerebral level but on the level that my need was greatest. He responded as a brother in Christ and became a true spiritual friend. What happened? I perceived the presence of Christ— the same Christ who had been there all the time. With that assurance, I was again enabled to take the next step of faith on the road I travel.

Then there was the time God spoke to me through Luther. No, I did not hear Luther's audible voice, but God did speak to me through Luther's words. God knew that I admired Luther and would ponder his words— words that I had read before but that took on new meaning and significance as I read them from within a new and critical context. It happened this way. Continuing my study of the Sabbath question with renewed determination after the incident described above, I was rereading Luther's *Large Catechism*, published in 1529, which was designed to be a book of religious instruction for clergy and adults. I was astounded as I read what Luther wrote in the preface: "Every morning, and whenever else I have time, I read and recite word for word the Lord's prayer, *the Ten Commandments*, the Creed, the Psalms, etc. . . . You will never offer up any incense or other savor more potent against the devil than to occupy yourself with *God's commandments* and words and to speak, sing, and meditate on them. This is indeed the true holy water, the sign which routs the devil and puts him to flight. . . . This much is certain: anyone who knows the *Ten Commandments* perfectly knows the entire Scriptures. In all affairs and circumstances he can counsel, help, comfort, judge, and make decisions in both spiritual and temporal matters. He is qualified to sit in judgment upon all doctrines, estates, persons, laws, and everything else in the world."[13]

Wow! That didn't sound like someone who believed that God's moral law, the Ten Commandments, was no longer binding on the Christian, no longer relevant for Christian theology, morality, and spirituality. If Luther had thought so, surely he would not have included an entire section on the

Ten Commandments in the *Large Catechism*. My astonishment was even greater when I took a close look at the section under the Sabbath commandment. Although Luther followed the Catholic numbering of the commandments rather than the biblical numbering,[14] what he said about the Sabbath commandment was extremely important to me. It hit me like an exploding bomb when I discovered a major discrepancy between his translation of the Sabbath commandment in his German Old Testament and his translation in his *Large Catechism*. In his German Old Testament, Luther rendered the commandment accurately (Ex. 20:8-10). He had such reverence for the Word of God that he dared not tamper with it. His translation: *Gedenke des Sabbattages dass du ihn heiligest. Sechs Tage sollst du arbeiten und alle deine Werke tun. Aber am siebenten Tage ist der Sabbat des Herrn, deines Gottes.* ("Remember the Sabbath day that you keep it holy. Six days shall you do all your work. But the seventh day is the Sabbath of the Lord your God.") So far, so good.

But then, to my astonishment, I saw that in his *Large Catechism* Luther took liberties with the Word of God and altered the commandment, making it read: *Du solst den Feiertag heiligen* ("You shall sanctify the holy day"). The context that follows makes it obvious he was referring to the first day, Sunday. What a moment of disillusion—and revelation—that was for me. Because with a stroke of his pen, Luther made the commandment mandate what God does not in fact command, Sunday sacredness.

Luther was correct when he said, "When you are asked what 'You shall sanctify the holy day' means, answer: 'It means to keep it holy.' What is meant by 'keeping it holy'? Nothing else than to devote it to holy words, holy works, holy life. In itself the day needs no sanctification, for it was created holy. But God wants it to be holy to you. So it becomes holy or unholy on your account, according as you spend the day in doing holy or unholy things." Astoundingly I saw that this statement, while true and accurate in itself, was not in reference to the seventh-day Sabbath that God Himself sanctified at Creation, but to Sunday, which He had not sanctified. Which simply reveals Luther's inconsistency!

Luther spoke to me loud and clear, and by so doing made it possible for me to hear God and to become a Sabbathkeeper and a Seventh-day Adventist Christian. In fact, he made it "necessary." The issue that hit me right between the eyes was whether I would follow the Word of God or Luther. Luther's own principle of *sola scriptura* prevailed. When I saw the truth about the seventh-day Sabbath, which Luther helped me to see, there was no other alternative. But that's not all.

Luther also said that the Sabbath commandment "was given to the Jews alone."[15] Wrong. Jesus said, "The Sabbath was made for man [humanity]" (Mark 2:27). It was not for Jews alone, but for the whole of humanity without distinction. Furthermore, the Sabbath dates to Creation, before there ever was a Jew, and God Himself made it holy (see Gen. 2:1-3). Luther said the observance of the Sabbath was only an external matter, from which Christians are "set free through Christ."[16] Wrong again. Because if that is so, Christians are also set free from the observance of baptism and the Lord's Supper, which would also be external matters. Because there are no scriptural passages that support Luther's argument for Sunday, he couldn't use any. Instead, he appealed to "good order." On this issue he trashed *sola scriptura*. There's still more. To cap it off, he made the following astonishing statement: "Since so much depends on God's Word that no holy day is sanctified without it, we must realize that God insists upon a strict observance of this commandment and will punish all who despise his Word and refuse to hear and learn it, especially at the times appointed."[17]

The times appointed by whom, Martin? You? The pope? The church? Or God Himself? Luther was right when he said that no holy day is sanctified without the Word of God. He was right when he said that God insists on a strict observance of this commandment, as well as of all the others. He was right when he said that God takes obedience to His moral law so seriously that He will punish all who despise it. But he was mightily and tragically wrong when he said that God will punish those who do not observe a day that He has not commanded. By this statement, Luther, the Reformation's great advocate of God's grace, turned Sunday observance into legalism.

Yes, Luther was right when he said, "Remember, then, that you must be concerned not only about hearing the Word but also about learning and retaining it."[18] One who, in faith and obedience to the truth of the Word, keeps the seventh-day Sabbath has learned and retained that Word. Conclusion? Seventh-day Adventist Christians are more faithful to the Word of God than those who keep a day that God has not sanctified. Were these insights that came to me from the pages of Luther's *Large Catechism*, from his own words, some of God's footprints? I know that they were. Did God speak to me through Luther's words? You bet He did!

If you were asked whether you wanted to experience an authentic and meaningful spiritual life, you would say yes! You would say that you want and need the kind of personal relationship with Christ that meets your deepest inner needs—whatever that may mean. If you were asked whether you were completely satisfied with your present spiritual experience, what would your answer be? Most of those to whom I have put these questions have said yes to the first question and no to the second.

The words "spiritual" and "spirituality" are used quite freely by religious people. We hear them all the time. But they often mean different things to different people because of the varied and contradictory backgrounds of individuals. These words are used by Christian, non-Christian, and even nonreligious people. For example, I recently saw a health program on TV that referred to the benefits of swimming as "spiritually refreshing." Such use leads to a lot of confusion and suspicion, especially if elements of contradictory religious traditions get mixed up together. If elements of Catholic or Asian mysticism, of Eastern religions, or of New Age or secular psychology are added to the mix, the consequence is mixed-up heads that lead to mixed-up experience and to mixed-up ministry.

I was once seated next to a woman at an interdenominational fellowship gathering at which the subject under discussion was fasting. With a marvelous smile on her face this woman said confidently and affirmatively, "The Holy Spirit told me that I can drink coffee when I fast."

"That's very interesting," I responded, "because the Holy Spirit has indicated to me that it is best if God's people do not use caffeine products at all."[19] She looked startled, but said nothing. I then asked, "Which message from the Holy Spirit can we depend on? Which message is right and not misleading? Which is true and which false?"

She stared at me for a moment and then turned away. End of conversation. What gets into the head affects the way we experience faith. That is why spirituality cannot be understood or experienced apart from the revealed truth in the written Word of God. We can't ever get away from this fact.

But having said that, we must also be sensitive to the fact that it is not authentically possible to talk about life in the Spirit, or spirituality, without being open to the Holy Spirit—to what He might say to us and the ways He might lead us. The Spirit sometimes has a disturbing way of upsetting our presumptions. When it comes to spiritual growth, we may first have to suffer pain before we can know healing and the joy that such healing brings. Remember, we are in the process of becoming. We are on the way. We are pilgrims on the journey of faith. Just as God's grace is new every day and just as there is always more grace (see James 4:6), so also the experience of receiving His grace and living in it is new every day. And it brings daily surprises, sometimes, to the one who is in the Spirit.

Faith That Believes or Believing Faith?

What kind of faith do you have? Is it a faith that believes? That is to say, is your faith oriented solely toward doctrines, theological propositions, systems of belief—as true and as vital as they might be? Is your faith only cerebral, analytical, rational? Or is it a believing faith?[20] I have known many people, and so have you, who had a faith that believes, but when crises came they questioned the reality of God in their lives, and the doctrines gave them no hope.

In one of my Seventh-day Adventist congregations I discovered an entire family in such a crucible of doubt. I had recently arrived as pastor when members called my attention to the fact that this family was no longer attending Sabbath school and the worship service. When I called on them, they were all gathered in the living room—father, mother, college-age kids—and they told a sad tale. The father had recently been laid off from his job just months before retirement. Because he had been faithful to his convictions and was not a member of the local labor union, he lost his retirement pension. Their lament went like this: "We have been faithful to the Lord most of our lives. We have tithed faithfully. We have attended church regularly. We have served as deacon, deaconess, local elder, Sabbath school superintendent and teacher, and Pathfinder leaders. We have put our children through church school at great financial sacrifice. Now see what God has done! It's not fair! Doesn't He care anymore? Does He even exist?"

No matter what I said, I was unable to help them. They left the church and the faith they had believed and confessed for so long. Pondering their story, I realized that theirs was a vivid example of the difference between a faith that believes and a believing faith. Ellen White referred to this difference when she wrote: "The greatest deception of the human mind in Christ's day was that a mere assent to the truth constitutes righteousness. In all human experience a theoretical knowledge of the truth has been proved to be insufficient for the saving of the soul. It does not bring forth the fruits of righteousness."[21] Theological ideas are a matter of the mind, whereas religious experience is a matter of the heart.

You see, believing faith emerges in times of testing. It is then that faithfulness is formed and becomes a component of one's spirituality. As my wife has written: "The place of greatest testing is the place of greatest blessing. . . . Even from nightmares, visions are born."[22] This is the kind of faith experienced and exhibited by Job, who said, "The Lord gave, and the Lord has taken away; blessed be the name of the Lord" (Job 1:21). "Shall we receive good from God, and shall we not receive evil?" (Job 2:10). "Though he slay me, I will hope in Him" (Job 13:15). "I know that my Redeemer lives, and at the last he will stand upon the earth" (Job 19:25). This kind of faith is not just cerebral. It is not second-hand language. It comes from deep within.

Meditation

Before you read further, may I suggest that you spend some time thinking about your own spiritual journey until you are able to identify God's footprints in your life? Then ask yourself if your faith is a faith that believes or a believing faith.

---

[1] E. G. White, *The Desire of Ages*, p. 660.

[2] *Ibid.*, p. 653.

[3] *Ibid.*, p. 655.

[4] *Ibid.*, p. 659.

[5] E. G. White, *Testimonies*, vol. 5, p. 10. (Italics supplied.) Ellen White never uses the word *soul* in the dualistic sense, referring to something that has an existence of its own apart from the body and that lives on after death. At times she uses it in the sense of a living being or person. In this instance she uses the term in reference to what the apostle Paul calls the "inner being." The same is true of her use of *mind* and *heart,* though at times *mind* is used in reference to "the intellect" and *heart* to "emotions" or "feelings."

[6] Now Finlandia University.

[7] New King James Version.

[8] Ellen G. White, *In Heavenly Places* (Washington, D.C.: Review and Herald Pub. Assn., 1967), p. 134.

[9] My baptism was performed by Thomas Blincoe, of the seminary faculty, and my ordination by Robert Pierson, president of the General Conference.

[10] Ellen G. White, *Counsels on Diet and Foods* (Washington, D.C.: Review and Herald Pub. Assn., 1938), p. 63.

[11] Ellen G. White, *Gospel Workers* (Washington, D.C.: Review and Herald Pub. Assn., 1915), p. 214. In context, this statement is a reference, not to biblical writers, but to any believer who "speaks helpful, appropriate words" (p. 214), which Jesus then applies to the situation.

[12] E. G. White, *Testimonies,* vol. 5, pp. 264, 265. (Italics supplied.)

[13] Martin Luther, *Large Catechism,* in *The Book of Concord,* edited and translated by Theodore G. Tappert (Philadelphia: Muhlenberg Press, 1959), pp. 359-361. (Italics supplied.)

[14] In the Catholic catechism the Sabbath commandment is listed as the third, whereas in Exodus 20 it is clearly the fourth. The biblical second commandment (Ex. 20:4-6), dealing with the veneration of images, is omitted.

[15] *Ibid.*, p. 375.

[16] *Ibid.*, p. 376.

[17] *Ibid.*, p. 378.

[18] *Ibid.*

[19] I was referring to the counsel of the Spirit of Prophecy.

[20] I first heard this distinction from my former Lutheran seminary professor. In academic theology *fides qua* is the faith by which one believes, meaning the relationship, and *fides quae*, the faith which is believed, meaning the content of that faith. Many theological disputes have revolved around which one is dominant. A primary example, even within the Adventist tradition, is pietism versus orthodoxy. Another way of putting it is objective truth versus subjective experience. It is very revealing that both perspectives quote Ellen White to support their point of view, just as Lutherans do with Luther. Why not learn to appreciate the value of both the objective and subjective dimensions of faith and so find balance theologically and spiritually?

[21] E. G. White, *The Desire of Ages*, p. 309.

[22] Shirley S. Holmes, *No Turning Back* (Berrien Springs, Mich.: Pointer Publications, 1988), pp. 155, 156.

Chapter 2

TRAINING
SPIRITUAL LEADERS

When I taught a course on spirituality at Andrews University, I always began by talking about the use of language and the fact that God always speaks a creative word. When He speaks, something happens—as when He says, "'Let there be light,' and there *was* light" (Gen. 1:3). As when Jesus says, "'Lazarus, come out' [and] the man who had died *came out*" (John 11:43, 44). Part of what it means to be created in the image of God is the gift of speech, using language to communicate with one another. There is power in speech. Just as God spoke and things happened, so likewise, things happen when we, who have been created in His image, speak. We can make someone mad, sad, or glad by the words we choose and the way we say them—or even by the look on our faces when we speak. Try it with kids sometime; the power is awesome. Besides, as Ellen White says: "If you are abiding in Christ, and Christ in you, you cannot speak angry words."[1] That's an important "if." Christ "in you" is essential to not speaking in anger.

In my course on spirituality, I talked about how language and its use is a way of life. How we cannot be human apart from our use of language. The struggle we all face is the struggle to find the reality that lies behind our words, and there may be times that that can be done only in silence. Responsible use of language demands a way of life that is in harmony with our words. Otherwise, our Christianity is incredible, which is why budding pastors and spiritual leaders must learn that ministerial authority is related to personal authenticity, rather than to merely academic training and/or ordination.

Back in the 1960s I heard my former professor explain to a group of children the role and function of a seminary. He told them that a seminary prepares ministers the way that a potter makes pots out of lumps of clay. The potter uses both hands as the clay turns round and round on a wheel. With one hand he shapes the outside, and with the other he shapes the inside. Years later, as a seminary professor myself, I took that explanation

36

very seriously. A seminary trains spiritual leaders not only by focusing on outward skills—preaching, administration, counseling, evangelism, organizing, community relations, etc. It trains also by focusing on developing, shaping, and forming *the person* of the spiritual leader—the inner things, such as faith, obedience, the practice of prayer, sensitivity to the spiritual needs of others, how to be nonjudgmental, how to set aside personal agendas and listen, how to exercise pastoral care, how to learn to love the members of one's congregations, how to learn to hear the "voice" of God, how to recognize His footprints, etc. This training is what is called pastoral formation and "spiritual formation." We Adventists call the latter "character development." So when we talk about spiritual growth, let's use our own language and call it "character development." That's exactly what it is. What I say about spirituality in this book arises from a Seventh-day Adventist perspective that recognizes the validity of the *concepts* of spiritual formation and spiritual discipline, but not the *methods* espoused by some other religious traditions. That Adventist perspective also gives those concepts the special meanings that are essential for us.

Ministerial Training

As long as I am talking about training spiritual leaders and the role of the seminary in that training, let me digress for a bit. We will get back to the discussion about speech and the use of language shortly.

When I arrived to take my place on the faculty of the seminary at Andrews University in the early 1980s, I not only taught courses in preaching and worship but was appointed to the position of director of student life. In that capacity I served, together with the dean and associate dean, as part of the seminary administration. By the time I arrived, some changes had already been made in the approach to ministerial training. The concept of "pastoral formation" was already in place. During the previous two decades many denominations had added the phrase "spiritual formation" to the process of ministerial training. The Association of Theological Schools, to which the Seventh-day Adventist Theological Seminary belongs for the purpose of academic accreditation, had sponsored workshops on "spiritual formation" and encouraged discussions of the topic at its conventions. That development alerted many seminaries and schools of theology to an aspect of ministerial training either that had been ignored or taken for granted or for which there was no identifiable label. Obviously, such a revived interest in the spiritual dimension of ministerial training would take different forms in the different schools.

In schools in which religious exercises were common (such as our own), one would expect an increase or expansion of religious activities and the establishment of chaplaincies, pastors-in-residence, directorships of student life, individual spiritual-guidance programs, and courses on spirituality added to the curriculum. Some seminaries with strong liturgical traditions would shift from more corporate events to small-group events and to individual spiritual growth. (My former professor became very much involved in such small groups at the Lutheran School of Theology at Chicago—not without some opposition and suspicion, I might add.)

Seminary activities, thought to implement "spiritual formation," included such things as Bible study groups, prayer groups, prayer vigils, spiritual retreats (on or off campus), meditation (on Scripture), journaling, dedication services (climaxing in campus revivals), more frequent chapel services, and workshops on wellness. Because the Seventh-day Adventist Church has a long and successful tradition of revivals, camp meetings, retreats, Weeks of Prayer, Weeks of Spiritual Emphasis, prayer meetings, Bible study groups, etc., such activities certainly did not sound strange. After all, theologically they fall under the umbrella of sanctification and growth in Christlikeness in which attention is given to the nurture of the believer's inner-faith life. The emphasis is placed not just on getting people into the church, but on keeping them in the faith and in the church.

The question that our seminary began to ask was: Does spiritual character formation take place in the context of an academic study of theology, or does the study of theology take place in the context of such spiritual development? It was recognized instinctively that the whole idea of "spiritual formation" or "character development," *as then perceived*, was basically compatible with Adventist theology, experience, and church life. Asking this question focused attention on the very philosophy of ministerial training and its goals—goals that were viewed in relation to the demands and needs of the contemporary congregations that our graduates would serve.

At that time Fuller Theological Seminary in Pasadena, California, stood out among evangelical seminaries as a major center of ministerial training in which "spiritual formation" was a vital component. This was largely on account of Professor Roberta Hestenes, who went there originally to teach communications and noticed what she considered to be a major void in the program—a predominant emphasis on skills rather than on developing spiritual character, on theological disciplines rather than on the persons who were preparing to minister to others. Of course, change did not happen overnight. It never does.

The 1980s and early 1990s saw a major shift in focus at our Adventist seminary, largely because of the demands of the field, and we began to speak not only of academic theological training but also of "pastoral formation," which involves a sensitivity to personal spiritual needs in addition to skill development. As a result, pastoral formation groups were introduced for Master of Divinity students. At the time "spiritual formation" was not part of our vocabulary. It was not the umbrella under which we were engaged in preparing persons for ministry. None of us had any inkling, then, of the direction this concept of "spiritual formation" would take in subsequent decades in spiritual traditions other than our own. However, it needs to be said that because of more than 150 years of Adventist experience, the terms and the basic concept did not, in themselves, alarm us or raise red flags at the time. Because of that experience, or tradition, the concept was taken for granted. In other words, we had the feeling that we were already practicing it. It seemed to us that the seminary, by its very nature, had an obligation to think about the reality that pastoral education and spirituality are complementary aspects of ministerial training and that their relationship and implementation should be intentional. Simply adding more religious activities, without any adjustment in rationale that would integrate these components, would not prove satisfactory. We felt that spirituality must not be seen as simply one component among many but as the overall context in which all else occurred in the seminary and in our churches.

Congregations want spiritual leaders who are experts not only in theology and doctrine but also in spiritual life—who, in their counseling, know how to help people in their relationship with God. In short, they want spiritual guides. This used to be called "soul care." This concern is reflected in the prayer of the apostle Paul, who was "made a minister," whose call was "to bring to light for everyone what is the plan of the mystery hidden for ages in God who created all things" (Eph. 3:7, 9):

"For this reason I bow my knees before the Father . . . that according to the riches of his glory he may grant you to be strengthened with power through his Spirit *in your inner being*, so that Christ may dwell in your *hearts* through faith—that you, being rooted and grounded in love, may have strength to comprehend with all the saints [believers] what is the breadth and length and height and depth, and to know the love of Christ that *surpasses knowledge*, that you may be filled with all the fullness of God. Now to him who is able to do far more abundantly than all that we ask or think, according to the power *at work within us*, to him be glory in the church and in Christ Jesus throughout all generations, forever and ever. Amen" (verses 14-21).

We are good at training future ministers how to be problem solvers, forgetting that every human problem is a spiritual problem, a sin problem. That reality is the dilemma that pastoral care ought to deal with. The "Readiness for Ministry" team of the Association of Theological Schools reported in 1976 that "a closer scrutiny reveals the continuing request of the community of faith that their leaders be more than persons who have learned facts and mastered techniques. First the community demands that they be persons who have experienced the reality of being freed by the Gospel. . . . The language of the Bible reflects the distinction between 'knowing about' and 'knowing experientially.'"

If we take seriously what has been said so far in our approach to ministerial training, we must resist any trend toward thinking of the seminary as simply a graduate school of higher education, a place where we train scholars of religion. For this reason, the Ministerial Department of the General Conference—rather than the Department of Education—should have major involvement in the selection of faculty for our seminary and in its programs and administration. Furthermore, questions such as the following need to be asked:

- What is the relationship between our doctrines and Adventist spirituality?
- How can we help our students to internalize and personally demonstrate the great Bible truths we hold?
- Are there ways of teaching our theological disciplines while at the same time having professors take a pastoral approach in the classroom?
- Does a dialogical teaching methodology lend itself better to this approach than a monological methodology? (Today we would call this monological approach "data-downloading"—i.e., lectures by professors, with students just listening.)
- Have we developed intentional, mutually explored assumptions and rationales of our own of the kind of "spiritual formation" that we prefer to call "character development"?
- Is it adequate to assume that pastoral formation assignments in local churches are the appropriate venue for such spiritual character development?
- How can we achieve a balance between passing on information (doctrinal/theological/practical) and the seminary student's experiential spiritual growth?

No doubt there are other similar questions that could be asked.

Someone has remarked, "It is not instruction that educates; it is the teacher who educates." In the context of ministerial training we would say, "It is not instruction that trains; it is the teacher who trains." That assertion makes sense and requires a follow-up question. Should not those who train future ministers be experts not only in the theological disciplines but in spirituality as well? To put it another way, Should they not be, for their students, models of both deep Adventist theological thinking *and* of perceptive and demonstrable Adventist spirituality?

What does it mean to go "from faith to faith" (Rom. 1:17, NKJV), to strain "forward to what lies ahead" (Phil. 3:13), to be transformed "from one degree of glory to another" (2 Cor. 3:18)? What does Paul mean when he says that Christ's servants, by their constant humiliation in the world, "have become, and are still, like the scum of the world, the refuse of all things" (1 Cor. 4:13)? Is growth in spirituality measured by something acquired, such as an education, the accumulation of academic degrees, etc.? What does it mean to live in the insecurities of faith, in the "conviction of things not seen" (Heb. 11:1)? Does discipleship mean power over others, or the imitation of Christ's humility?

The academic study of theology, pastoral formation, and "spiritual formation," *as we understand them*, are the three basic components of a ministerial training program. The academic study of Adventist theology has to do with the knowledge of the faith we confess. Pastoral formation has to do with the development of pastoral skills and the ability to teach, in order to communicate to others, the faith we confess. Spiritual character development has to do with the personal practice of the faith we confess in the presence of others, both within and without the community of faith. Spiritual character development, *as we understand it,* should be the foundational component and not simply parallel to the other two, because Adventist spirituality makes theology and ministry meaningful, justifiable, and credible both in the world and in the church.

This kind of thinking undergirded my time of service as director of the Doctor of Ministry program at our seminary. I was pleased that a few candidates elected to implement and write project dissertations in the area of spirituality. The November 2008 brochure advertising the Doctor of Ministry program clearly states: "Inspired by the promise of Christ's soon return, the Doctor of Ministry program at Andrews University is designed to develop spiritually mature and accomplished professionals in ministry for worldwide church leadership." Heading the list of program competencies is "deeper spirituality."

The Ministerial Association of the General Conference of Seventh-day Adventists recognizes this need. The second chapter of the revised edition (2009) of the *Seventh-day Adventist Ministerial Handbook* is titled "Spiritual Formation" and speaks of the importance of "spiritual discipline" in the life of the pastoral disciples of Christ. It encourages a "spirituality resulting from a personal encounter with Christ" that results in a ministry of preaching that "derives its power from *personal experience* with the Lord."[2] The *Handbook* quotes the Spirit of Prophecy: "All who are under the training of God need the quiet hour [of meditation in the Word of God] for communion with *their own hearts*, with *nature*, and with *God*. . . . We must individually hear Him speaking to the *heart*. When every other voice is hushed, and in quietness we wait before Him, the silence of the soul makes more distinct the voice of God."[3] The *Handbook* also suggests that besides private study of the Bible, "a spiritual support group may provide additional opportunity to share with others in the spiritual journey."[4] It then quotes from the Spirit of Prophecy: "It would be well for us to spend a thoughtful hour each day in *contemplation* of the life of Christ. We should take it point by point, and let the *imagination* grasp each scene, especially the closing ones. As we thus dwell upon His great sacrifice for us, our confidence in Him will be more constant, our love will be quickened, and we shall be more *deeply* imbued with His spirit."[5] If we are going to adopt the terms and the concept of "spiritual formation," then we need to be careful that they accurately express the Seventh-day Adventist understanding and meaning. It is my hope and prayer that this book will assist in that endeavor.

This digression fits in with what I was saying about speech and the use of language, so let's get back to that discussion.

Telling the Story

I began my course, Spirituality for Ministry, by encouraging the students to use firsthand rather than secondhand language in the class sessions. A major problem for preachers, and for church members as well, is the all-too-frequent use of secondhand language. Today religious assent is not given to religious language, because people are bored with words. Yet this boredom with words does not mean people no longer yearn for the true Word. How can they find it, hear it, if most of our God-talk is secondhand language—if it is someone else's language, not our own? We can do that with Scripture, with the writings of theologians, even with the writings of Ellen White. Christian language must never be allowed to take on an existence of its own, isolated from a basis in experience, which is why theology is often defined as faith seeking understanding, not the other way around.[6] Giving birth to authentic Christian language "cannot be done without pain anymore than giving birth to a child."[7] It is for this reason that writing and sermonizing always should be difficult. What is said always falls short of what should be said or could be said.

Obviously words can be spoken only by a person. It is always "I" who speaks. But I must always be certain that it is truly "I" who speaks; that is, to use words that arise out of my own experience, using primary language. Thus, "the relationship of language to the situation in which it is uttered means that in and through language, the speaker is irreplaceably present and answerable."[8] The model for this, of course, is the Lord Himself.

Secondhand language, especially in the pulpit, is usually technical, analytical, cold, and impersonal, whereas primary language is warm, personal, and basically descriptive in nature. It speaks of a believing faith, rather than a faith that believes, and is rooted in experience. Without this kind of faith, it is impossible to please God (see Heb. 11:6). What is at stake is not belief in doctrines correctly stated and repeated, but *believing*, which is a process more like a story, a narration. While genuine Christian faith rests on objective truth, believing arises out of experience born of that truth. Those who have walked with God for many years know that He carries the heavy end of the load, and they are able to tell the story of their walk in warm, personal terms. But we need to be aware, as painful as it may be, that what were significant, insightful words for one generation often become a tired body of dead clichés for the next—not because they have lost truth content, but because they have become secondhand. While I do not hold with much of her theology, I agree with the following statement by Sallie McFague:

"The language of a people is their sense of reality; we can live only within the confines of our language. If that language is one-dimensional . . . if it is jargon, the jargon of technocracy, of Madison Avenue, of politics—or of theology—then we lead one-dimensional lives, meaningless lives, lives within language that has ceased to express our depths for it is not capable of expressing anything but the limits of what we *already* know and feel. It is no longer open to or suggestive of any reality beyond itself, and hence we have no means of renewing ordinary life and language, of seeing it in new contexts. Our ability to express the deeper dimensions of human existence is determined by the metaphorical aliveness of our language, and that language in turn is controlled by the vision of reality we hold."[9]

Let me connect the two emphases in this chapter—the use of primary language and seminary training for ministry—in the following way. Spirituality is not learned in a seminary classroom or in any other classroom. It is not taught as much as caught. For that we need role models more than professors. Ideally, a professor can be, should be, a role model, and a seminary classroom should be a place in which spirituality is caught. But the process is more by absorption than by data transfer from the mind of the teacher to the mind of the student. In this process the fellowship of the church is a vital factor. That is to say, how the members of the body of Christ relate, associate, rub shoulders with one another. I am talking about qualitative, rather than quantitative, church growth—not the witness of the church to the world, but witness within the church. If God's people are to be a "city set on a hill," they first have to *be* such a city. If the members of the church are to be "the light of the world," they must first shine for one another. This is the kind of church life that keeps members in. Furthermore, we have to give folks a reason for choosing the Seventh-day Adventist Church as their spiritual home. Sound Bible doctrine and truth? Yes! By all means. But it has to be more than that. It has to be personal. It has to be the demonstration of a believing faith within the fellowship of believers, a faith whose core values determine and shape spirituality. A faith that helps the newly baptized member feel safe. This has certainly been my experience over the past four decades, serving as pastor, missionary, and professor in my beloved spiritual home, the Seventh-day Adventist Church.

In order to faithfully train spiritual leaders, we need to know and understand what spirituality is. Can it be defined? The next chapter will attempt to do just that.

Meditation

Pause here before you go on to the next chapter and ask yourself whether there is a significant relationship between "character development" and the use of firsthand language as you communicate to others the faith you confess. Is that something you need to pray about?

---

[1] E. G. White, *In Heavenly Places,* p. 99.

[2] *Seventh-day Adventist Minister's Handbook* (Silver Spring, Md.: Ministerial Association, General Conference of Seventh-day Adventists, 2009), p. 18. (Italics supplied.)

[3] E. G. White, *The Ministry of Healing,* p. 58. (Italics supplied.)

[4] *Seventh-day Adventist Minister's Handbook,* p. 20.

[5] E. G. White, *The Desire of Ages,* p. 83. (Italics supplied.)

[6] This does not mean that theology is not a necessary component of Christian experience. However, if faith is a gift from God, He does not wait to give it until there is full understanding. I had faith long before I understood what the Bible taught about the seventh-day Sabbath.

[7] Gerhard Ebeling, *Introduction to a Theological Theory of Language* (Philadelphia: Fortress Press, 1971), p. 77.

[8] *Ibid.,* p. 95.

[9] Sallie McFague, *Speaking in Parables* (Philadelphia: Fortress Press, 1975), pp. 22, 23.

Chapter 3

SPIRITUALITY IN PERSPECTIVE

I always began the first day of my seminary course on spirituality by asking the students to indicate what, in their thinking, was evidence of spirituality. In other words, how they would identify "spiritual" Seventh-day Adventist Christians. I wrote their responses on the board.

The Evidence

Here is the "evidence of spirituality" they often came up with. "Spiritual" Adventists read the Bible every day. They read the Spirit of Prophecy every day. They read other devotional literature every day. They pray. They diligently observe the Sabbath. They pass out literature. They tithe. They support outreach ministries. They support Week of Sacrifice offerings. They support church schools. They call on people door-to-door. They visit shut-ins and the sick. They visit people in prison. They give Bible studies. They attend Sabbath school and worship services regularly. They attend midweek prayer meetings. They faithfully attend church business meetings. They serve on local and conference committees. They attend camp meetings and retreats. They consistently support and attend evangelistic meetings. They readily accept leadership positions.

All good things . . . as long as they are not seen as the conditions, or the basis, of a genuine believing faith As long as—because they are all externals—they do not lead to a Christless formal profession. "None are further from the kingdom of heaven," wrote Ellen White, "than self-righteous formalists, filled with pride at their own attainments, while they are wholly destitute of the spirit of Christ."[1] Paul, she said, had to learn the difference "between a living faith and a dead formalism."[2] As do we all. "The cold formalism that is now prevailing among us must give place to the *living energy* of experimental [experiential] godliness."[3] Godliness has to be inward before it can be anywhere else. It is a life that is "radiant with the light of an *indwelling* Savior."[4] Note this perceptive insight: "The sanctification of the soul [inner being] by the working of the

45

Holy Spirit is the *implanting* of Christ's nature in humanity. Gospel religion is Christ *in the life*—a living, active principle."[5] Or this one: "The great change that the truth makes is *inward*. It begins in the heart, and works outwardly. With the heart, man believeth unto righteousness, and with the mouth confession is made unto salvation. . . . God is not pleased with pharisaical pretense."[6]

When we were finished, I asked my students if they would consider their list as representing outer or inner manifestations of spirituality. It was always immediately obvious that the items were outer (observable) manifestations. The conclusion was that our perception of Adventist spirituality tends to be activistic rather than meditative. We even think of personal devotions as something to be done early, sometimes very early, before the "real" business of the day begins. *Well, I got that out of the way.* Out of the way? Out of the way for what? Why would we consider devotional time to be "in the way" of our "real" life? Of course, we know that the outer is motivated by the inner, good or bad. But that's the whole point.

I recall that when I was a full-time pastor some members of my congregations (both Lutheran and Adventist) felt that I was not really doing anything during the hours I spent in my study with the Bible and the Holy Spirit. Unfortunately, pastors themselves often feel that way. I wonder if the members realized that while I had to prepare and preach a sermon every week, the Holy Spirit had to prepare me to preach. Much was going on in me during those quiet hours. Dare I say it? Don't interrupt your pastor during those hours unless it's an emergency. Pastor, take the phone off the hook. Turn off your cell phone, if you have to!

Spirituality Defined

What is spirituality? It's not easy to define. The words *spirit, spiritual,* and *spiritually* are found in the Bible, but not the word *spirituality*. That makes it that much more difficult to define *spirituality,* but we cannot simply ignore a word that is used so abundantly today. Instead we should explore the meaning of that word in the hope of arriving at an understanding and definition that satisfies both intellectually and experientially—especially in light of the fact that the Spirit of Prophecy uses the word. We may disagree on a definition of spirituality, but I don't think we would disagree that serious attention needs to be given to the spiritual life. That it needs to be nurtured, cared for, developed. After all, that is the way of character development, and character is what one *is*.

How is it possible for us to "[pray] at all times in the Spirit" (Eph. 6:18) without being "filled with the Spirit" (Eph. 5:18)? How can we "walk by the Spirit" (Gal. 5:16) without the "fruit of the Spirit," which is "love, joy, peace, patience, kindness, goodness, faithfulness, gentleness, self-control" (Gal. 5:22, 23)? Have you noticed that these fruits are all *inner* qualities? They first have to be inner before they can be outer. The fruit of the Spirit is the essence of Christian character. One first has to be a loving person before one can love as Christ loved. In these texts the Greek word for *love* is *agape,* which means divine, sacrificial love—the kind demonstrated by Christ. Not one of us is that way by nature.

The fruit of the Spirit is just that—the Spirit's fruit, not ours. We can never claim credit for it. We cannot produce it. We can only receive it. It is the gift of grace for those whose inner being the Holy Spirit has access to, for those who have surrendered to Christ and to the Holy Spirit who works from the inside. The word *commitment* is used a lot these days in Christian circles, but it is a weak word. Why? Because one can be partially committed. *Surrender* is a stronger word and therefore a better word. Why? Because one cannot be partially surrendered. To surrender means to give up, to lay down the weapons with which one has fought against the Lord, to yield to His authority, to become His captive. When one has surrendered to Christ, then the Holy Spirit has access to the inner being and produces His fruit within.

These fruit of the Spirit are in stark contrast to what Paul refers to as "works of the flesh." There is a big difference between the fruit of the Spirit and the works of the flesh. The first is produced in us by the Holy Spirit; the latter are our own works, our own doing. Like weeds in a garden, we don't plant them; they are just there, because that's the way we are by nature. What are the works of the flesh? The Word of God does not pull any punches; it does not hesitate to tell us what they are and what they produce. "Now the works of the flesh are evident [unmistakable; we can observe them everywhere]: sexual immorality, impurity, sensuality, idolatry, sorcery [evil spirits, occultism], enmity, strife, jealousy, fits of anger, rivalries, dissensions, divisions, envy, drunkenness, orgies, and things like these" (Gal. 5:19-21). How serious is this? How badly do we need the fruit of the Spirit? Clearly, unequivocally, God's Word tells us: "I warn you, as I warned you before [pause here and let that sink in], that those who do such things *will not* inherit the kingdom of God" (Gal. 5:21). To do such things closes the door to the kingdom of God—whether or not we like it, whether or not we believe it. We need to be set free from such works of the flesh that control us.

In the past few decades there has appeared on the Protestant religious scene a concern for, and an interest in, spirituality. Like so many other things, this may be only a passing fad. The church is as plagued with fadism as is the garment industry. But concern for spirituality is not something that

should be allowed to wax and wane if what we have observed so far has
validity. No matter what direction theological debates may take, at the
center of the church's life there should always be concern for its spiritual
nature.

There are those who are fearful of any interest in the spiritual, who are
afraid that such an interest will lead us to become exclusivistic, other-
worldly, charismatic, mystical, or, heaven forbid, too pietistic. Even among
those Lutherans who prefer to keep things on the level of sacramentalism
and ritualism, I have heard such interest referred to as "navel-gazing" and
"sentimental slush." All of this, no doubt, reflects uncertainty and bewilderment as to the nature of spirituality. But Seventh-day Adventist
Christians have nothing to fear *provided* that our search is based on
Scripture and affirmed in the Spirit of Prophecy, as opposed to other
sources.

The Bible has a lot to say about spirituality. So does the Spirit of
Prophecy. Here is a representative example: "The ministry is corrupted by
unsanctified ministers. Unless there shall be altogether a higher and more
spiritual standard for the ministry, the truth of the gospel will become more
and more powerless."[7] Here Ellen White associates the gospel's power
with the spirituality of those who preach it.

Paul's letters are full of spirituality. He expresses his longing to "impart
to you some spiritual gift to strengthen you" (Rom. 1:11). He says "the
law is spiritual, but I am of the flesh [unspiritual], sold under sin" (Rom.
7:14). He speaks of the Gentiles sharing the Jew's "spiritual blessings"
(Rom. 15:27). He says that he interprets "spiritual truths to those who are
spiritual" (1 Corinthians 2:13). He says that things that come from the
Spirit of God are "spiritually discerned" (1 Cor. 2:14). He does not speak
to the Corinthians "as spiritual people, but as people of the flesh [worldly]"
(1 Cor. 3:1). He speaks of sowing "spiritual things among" them (1 Cor.
9:11). He talks about "spiritual food" and "spiritual drink" and the "spiritual Rock . . . and the Rock was Christ" (1 Cor. 10:3, 4). He urges believers to "desire the spiritual gifts" (1 Cor. 14:1). Those who are spiritual
are responsible for the restoration of one who sins (see Gal. 6:1). God's
people "wrestle against . . . the spiritual forces of evil in the heavenly
places" (Eph. 6:12). Paul prays that believers be "filled with the knowledge
of his will in all spiritual wisdom and understanding, so as to walk in a
manner worthy of the Lord, fully pleasing to him, bearing fruit in every
good work and increasing in the knowledge of God" (Col. 1:9, 10).
Believers sing "spiritual songs" (Col. 3:16). The apostle Peter urges believers to "long for the pure spiritual milk" and refers to the fellowship of believers as a "spiritual house" that offers "spiritual sacrifices acceptable to

God through Jesus Christ" (1 Peter 2:2-5). These are but a few references. Surely that which has been given such a prominent place in Scripture, as well as in the Spirit of Prophecy, warrants our disciplined attention. It would seem that the need to understand and define spirituality is obvious.

But that is not so easy to do, because spirituality is not so much a subject to be discussed as it is a reality to be experienced. Still, there are things that can and must be said about it. After all, it is possible to have a religious experience that is out of touch with God's revelation. Spirituality is not easy to define, because it means many things to different people, influenced by the religious context in which they have been nurtured. Catholic spirituality involves adoration of Mary, confession to a priest, the veneration of the crucifix, the saying of the rosary and the Hail Mary, etc. Perhaps it is good that spirituality is not easily defined, because we are dealing with that which, although rational, is beyond rationality, and, although knowledgeable, is beyond knowledge. It is not taught or learned by human wisdom. Spiritual truths are "spiritually discerned," and the "spiritual person judges all things" (1 Cor. 2:14, 15).

Various authors have attempted to define spirituality. Others, although discussing it, have not even tried. Here are a few attempts. Urban Holmes (no relation) defines it primarily as relationship, saying that it is "(1) a human capacity for relationship (2) with that which transcends sense phenomenon; this relationship (3) is perceived by the subject as an expanded or heightened consciousness independent of the subject's efforts, (4) is given substance in the historical setting, and (5) exhibits itself in creative action in the world."[8] Complicated? It takes considerable thought to try to unravel that definition.

Rowan Williams defines spirituality as a task, "each believer making his or her own that engagement with the questioning at the heart of faith which is so evident in the classical documents of Christian belief." Then he adds a caveat: "The questioning involved here is not our interrogation of the data, but its interrogation of us." This data challenges "the fixed assumptions of religiosity." He goes on to say that the goal of Christian life is "not enlightenment but wholeness."[9] By "classical documents" Williams, who is an Anglican, means the Scriptures, particularly the New Testament, the Gospels of Jesus Christ, and the writings of the Church Fathers, such as Ignatius, Irenaeus, Tertullian, Polycarp, Origen, Athanasius, Gregory of Nyssa, together with the Cappadocian Fathers, Augustine, and Aquinas. These latter we would not include in such a list, although we would certainly include Luther and many of the other Reformers whose writings have contributed to the development of Adventist doctrinal beliefs and spirituality.[10]

Francis Schaeffer sees spirituality as something inward, primarily a matter of thinking. "The inward area is the first place of loss of true Christian life, of true spirituality, and the outward sinful act is the result." "Basically," Schaeffer says, spirituality is "a matter of our *thoughts*. The external is the expression, the result. Moral battles are not won in the external world first. They are always a result flowing naturally from a cause, and the cause is in the internal world of one's thoughts."[11] However, while certainly involving thought, spirituality is more than cerebral.

Robert Roberts sees the centrality of spirituality as primarily involving the emotions, "a passion we might call the heart's seeking for the kingdom of God,"[12] which is how he refers to Paul's fruit of the Spirit. For Roberts, Christian spirituality, as an experience, is made up of both beliefs and emotions. He says, "Beliefs are dispositions, whereas emotions are occurrences in consciousness." Belief alone "is not enough for spirituality. Christians must not only believe, but also must learn to *attend* to the things of God. For only in doing so will they begin to bear the fruits of God's Spirit."[13] In other words, spirituality is not only believing revealed truths but also "moral striving," which "is both an essential part of spiritual growth (that is, spiritual growth *is* moral growth) and a ground of self-despair which sensitizes the individual to the grace of Jesus Christ. The more serious you have become about attaining moral goodness, the more serious you have become about God's kingdom."[14]

Lewis Sperry Chafer defines spirituality as "that quality of life in the child of God which satisfies and glorifies the Father." A "triumph of grace." He asks, "What, then, is true spirituality?" Then he answers:

"It is the unhindered manifestations of the indwelling Spirit. There are in all, seven of these manifestations. These blessed realities are all provided for in the presence and power of the Spirit and will be normally produced by the Spirit in the Christian who is not grieving the Spirit, but has confessed every *known* sin; who is not quenching the Spirit, but is yielded to God; and who is walking in the Spirit by an attitude of dependence upon His power alone. Such an one is spiritual because he is Spirit-filled. The Spirit is free to fulfill in him all the purpose and desire of God for him. There is nothing in daily life and service to be desired beyond this."[15]

Some writers see spirituality primarily in terms of inner transformation. Others, fearful that inner transformation is too subjective, see it primarily as the outward manifestation of faith. Even Bill O'Reilly uses the word *spirituality*, which, he says, "is a very positive thing." By *spirituality* he means the "Catholic way of life" he practices.[16] He talks about priests, nuns, the catechism, Mary, Mass, obeying the rules, etc. But he never mentions the Bible, and although he mentions Jesus three times, all three are in a kind of detached, nonpersonal way. His book is fascinating and insightful when it comes to the man himself, but the spirituality he describes leaves one cold.

Webster's definition of the word—"sensitivity or attachment to religious values"—doesn't help much, either.

All these attempts to define spirituality represent a search, which is really what spirituality is. It is a process as opposed to a state of being, as is sanctification. Spirituality is active rather than passive, dynamic rather than static. It contains both the elements of dissatisfaction and satisfaction, death and life. It is not a settled issue, as though one had "arrived." It is a constant reaching out, a struggle to be believing. It goes beyond the facts of faith, the truths, the doctrines believed, to the act and experience of faith—to believing! The facts of faith, internalized, produce the acts of faith, which is exactly why James said, "So also faith by itself, if it does not have works, is dead" (James 2:17). For this reason Ellen White also says: "The principles of true spiritual life are not understood by those who know the truth, but fail to practice it. The Lord calls for reforms, marked, distinct reforms. Those in whose *hearts* Christ *dwells* will reveal His presence in their dealing with their fellow men. But the principles of some have been so long perverted that they have lost their discernment, and the arrow seldom reaches its mark. How can this be cured? Only by heeding Christ's prayer, "Sanctify them through thy truth: thy word is truth . . . (John 17:17-19)."[17]

There has to be more tangible evidence of faith than simply knowing the truth and an "I believe." I'm so glad that the seventeenth verse from the second chapter of James is there in the Word of God. Aren't you? No thanks to Luther, who called the letter of James an "epistle of straw." If Luther had had his way, James—and Revelation, too—would have been expunged from the Bible. Luther was right about much, but he was wrong about that—as wrong as he was about the biblical seventh-day Sabbath.

Both Robert Roberts and Francis Schaeffer recognize the significance of death in Christian spirituality, underlined by the good news that baptized believers have first been baptized into the death of Christ, and that then, and only then, can they claim to be baptized into His resurrection. Perhaps one reason we see so little genuine spirituality is that we tend to avoid the consideration of death, spiritual death as the Bible speaks of it, though we think about it all the time, without wanting to admit it. Roberts describes this in his chapter (pp. 44-47) about Tolstoy's fictional story concerning the death of Ivan Ilyich. Schaeffer's discussion is more traditional and orthodox, while saying essentially the same thing. Instead of quoting Tolstoy, Schaeffer quotes Scripture: "We were buried therefore with him by baptism into death" (Rom. 6:4). "We know that our old self was crucified with him in order that the body of sin might be brought to nothing, so that we would no longer be enslaved to sin" (Rom. 6:6).

Before one can be born again to the new life in Christ, that person must die to sin, the flesh, the world. He or she must first face the cross, the way of renunciation, which is not a list of taboos. It is more profound and transformational than that. It is daily saying no to the dominance of self and things. Today, as perhaps in no other period of human history, we live in a yes culture. People say no to very little—except to righteousness. Anything goes. Anything is acceptable. The slogan is, "If it feels good, do it"—no matter what happens to you or to others. That's why we find it so hard to listen to Scripture verses such as those quoted above. No one wants to deny self. Yet Jesus said to His disciples, "If anyone would come after me, let him deny himself and take up his cross and follow me. For whoever would save his life will lose it, but whoever loses his life for my sake will find it" (Matt. 16:24, 25).

A contemporary example is the explosive, and emotional, issue of abortion. Pro-abortionists are concerned primarily about the rights of the mother and of society in general. Anti-abortionists are primarily concerned about the rights of the unborn fetus. Both are saying yes. But who is talking about the problem of human depravity and lust that is behind the issue? Who is saying that there are times to say no? There was a time in America that one didn't need laws in order to be pro-life. A sense of morality regarding this issue was self-imposed. Although abortion was accepted in special circumstances, the moral consensus was that it was appalling to take the life of an unborn child. Abortion was generally considered a desperate measure, reluctantly performed. Now it has become virtually routine. The sense of horror has largely disappeared, because we have lost our moral moorings. Actually, we have not just "lost our moral moorings," as though that were something over which we have no control; instead, we are deliberately and consciously abandoning them. We have become a nation that kills its unborn children. We have made it legal. Let's call abortion what it is—prenatal murder.

The marriage union between one man and one woman, an institution established in the beginning by the Creator God, was designed for the most intimate form of human relationships, as well as for the propagation of the human race. Pregnancy was welcomed as proof of the legitimacy and success of the union. It was accepted as a blessing and gift from God, as husband and wife became father and mother, lovingly caring for and nurturing their offspring. Today pregnancy is often viewed as a curse, the unwanted consequence of a fleeting moment of pleasure. Or, especially among celebrities who are seen as role models, being unmarried and pregnant is viewed as desirable and praiseworthy. Sad to say, we are faced with the spectacle of churches that once claimed unmovable loyalty to *sola scriptura* now actively supporting and even promoting the abandonment of moral consensus.[18] A great burden of responsibility for this radical change in morality rests with the churches that have taught that the moral law of God in His Ten Commandments was done away with on Calvary.

Humans have resisted death to self ever since Satan said to Eve, "You will not surely die" but "you will be like God" (Gen. 3:3-5). To be like God, oddly enough, *is* the goal of the Christian life. The problem is that we see everything from the perspective of the fallen world, as though there were no other, instead of from the perspective of the kingdom of God. We need to be reminded over and over that the very center of the Christian message is the death of Christ. In Isaiah's prophecy concerning Him we read words such as *wounded, bruised,* and a "lamb . . . to the slaughter" (Isa. 53:7). Hebrews 5:8 says of Jesus, "Although he was a son, he learned obedience from what he suffered." What was that experience, that discipline, all about? It was basic training for the job the Father sent Him to do. Did Jesus struggle with that? Of course He did. Jesus knew and understood His Calvary destiny when He went with His disciples to Gethsemane. Faced with the realization of that destiny, He went there to pray, and was "sorrowful and troubled . . . even to death" (Matt. 26:37, 38). What did He say to His Father, whose plan was unfolding? "My Father, if it be possible, let this cup pass from me; nevertheless, not as I will, but as you will"(verse 39). He repeated that petition again: "My Father, if this cannot pass unless I drink it, your will be done" (verse 42). It was not possible; it had to come to pass. The Father's plan was afoot. The Son knew that too. He was willing, no matter the consequences. Though He was the Son of God, He had to learn the discipline of obedience. Obedience is learned behavior. If Jesus had not learned to obey, the Father's plan would have ended right then and there! That's how critical it was. That is the kind of spiritual discipline that really matters.

When Moses and Elijah met with Jesus on the Mount of Transfiguration, what was the topic of conversation? His redemptive death on the cross! "I have been crucified with Christ," said Paul. "It is no longer I who live, but Christ who lives in me" (Gal. 2:19, 20). First comes crucifixion, death to self, and then life—but life with a big difference. Christ living *in* me, *in* you. Life that is radically new.

Spiritual life begins with our death by choice. "As Christ's rejection and death are the first steps in the order of redemption, so our rejection and death to things and self are the first steps in the order of true and growing spirituality."[19] Yet everything we say and do is designed to be rid of this perceived negative idea, often at any cost. The Ten Commandments, the moral law of God, direct our attention in specific ways to this negative. That's why we don't like them. That's why we resist them. That's why even some Christian theologians stand on their heads to interpret them in a way that they think makes them disappear in spite of the fact that Jesus Himself made the opposite absolutely clear: "*Do not think* that I have come to abolish the Law or the Prophets; I have *not* come to abolish them but to fulfill them. For truly, I say to you, until heaven and earth pass away [until the end], not an iota, not a dot, will pass from the Law until all is accomplished" (Matt. 5:17, 18). This unambiguous statement by Jesus established the principle for interpreting everything said about the moral law of God in the New Testament.[20] Put "fulfill" and "accomplished" together, and add them up. The sum? Jesus was sent by the Father for a twofold purpose. First, to pay the price on Calvary for the sin that causes our disobedience. "Behold, the Lamb of God, who takes away the sin of the world!" (John 1:29). Second, by the power exhibited in His resurrection, to put God's moral law of the Ten Commandments, together with the prophets, which includes Daniel, into effect. He takes away sin so that we can learn to obey. "If you keep my commandments, you will abide in my love" said Jesus, "just as I have kept my Father's commandments and abide in his love" (John 15:10).

So the commandments do not disappear. Paul said, "When the commandment came, sin came alive and I died. The very commandment that promised life proved to be death to me." If that was all he said, we would have a problem, but hear the rest of his thought. "For sin, seizing an opportunity through the commandment, deceived me and through it killed me" (Rom. 7:9-11). What did Paul say deceived and killed him? *Sin did it, not the law!* That commandment, that law, Paul says, "is spiritual" (Rom. 7:14). It has a spiritual function, to provide the opportunity for sin to cause death so that we will listen to the gospel and open ourselves to the positive message of the resurrection, the new birth, and the new life in Christ. To walk this way by faith is to take up our cross and follow Him. The upshot of it is that because the law of God fulfills its spiritual function and does the job for which it was intended, it proves to be "holy and righteous and good" (Rom. 7:12). Not unholy, but holy. Not unrighteous, but righteous. Not bad, but good. Ellen White hit the proverbial nail on the head when she said, "As disease is the result of the violation of natural laws, so is spiritual declension the result of a continued transgression of the law of God. And yet the very transgressors may profess to keep all of God's commandments."[21] Now, before we get all bent out of shape by her statement and scream "legalism!" let it be understood that she was speaking of Christian believers. But believers who were "ever ready to see and hear some new and strange thing," who drifted "on the surface of excitement and [moved] from impulse," and who were "spiritual dyspeptics in the church." she called them "self-made invalids."[22]

Paul devoted all of chapter 8 of his letter to the Romans to describing the new life in which "the righteous requirement of the law might be fulfilled *in us*, who walk not according to the flesh but according to the Spirit" (verse 4). Walking according to the Spirit is living in accordance with the Spirit, with a mind controlled by the Spirit, putting to death the misdeeds of the body by the Spirit, being led by the Spirit who testifies that we are God's children. To share in Christ's sufferings is to share in His glory.

There is a definite relationship between the ministry of the Holy Spirit and the life to be lived by the born-again, transformed Christian. Why was the Holy Spirit, the "Counselor" (as Jesus refers to Him), given to God's church and to the world? Paul says that it is by the Spirit that we have access to the Father (see Eph. 2:18). John says that the Spirit acknowledges that Jesus Christ has come in the flesh (see 1 John 4:2) and that the Spirit testifies of Jesus (see 1 John 5:6). He quotes Jesus as saying, "When the Spirit of truth comes, he will guide you into all the truth, for he will not speak on his own authority, but whatever he hears he will speak. . . . He will glorify me, for he will take what is mine and declare it to you" (John 16:13, 14). In His great prayer Jesus prayed, "Father, I desire that they also, whom you have given me, may be with me where I am, to see my glory" (John 17:24). The point is that the Holy Spirit glorifies Jesus Christ, not Himself. The sin against the Holy Spirit, therefore, is to deny and reject Jesus and the forgiveness and transformation He offers. Adventist spirituality is permeated by the inner desire to be guided by the Holy Spirit into all the truth. It is God's truth embedded within, then, that determines the outer manner of life.

What is the goal of the Christian life? It is that "we should be holy and blameless before him . . . having been predestined according to the purpose of him who works all things according to the counsel of his will, so that we who were the first to hope in Christ might be to the praise of his glory. In him you also, when you heard the word of truth, the gospel of your salvation, and believed in him, were sealed with the promised Holy Spirit, who is the guarantee of our inheritance until we acquire possession of it, to the praise of his glory" (Eph. 1:4-14). How is Christ glorified in us? He is glorified as we become like Him and reflect His character. That is spiritual *trans*formation for Seventh-day Adventist Christians! The personal goal of ministry, as it was with Paul, is that "Christ is formed in you!" (Gal. 4:19). For this reason, in our little church in Bessemer, Michigan, we sing on our knees at the close of the general prayer:

> Change my heart, O God, make it ever true;
> Change my heart, O God, may I be like You. . . .
> You are the potter, I am the clay,
> Mold me and make me, this is what I pray.
> Change my heart, O God, make it ever true;
> Change my heart, O God, may I be like You.

So a spiritual Seventh-day Adventist Christian is Spirit-conscious, Spirit-dependent, Spirit-led, Spirit-filled, and Spirit-fruited. The result is a life that glorifies the Lord Jesus Christ. As interior criteria of spirituality, the fruit of the Spirit are descriptive of Christlike attitudes. As exterior criteria, they are descriptive of Christlike responses and behavior. This spirituality does not destroy selfhood, though self-will must die. One actually discovers the true self, which is now free, no longer in bondage to the flesh and the power of sin, free to receive the Spirit's work and fruit and to glorify Jesus. Each person is a unique individual under the influence of the Holy Spirit and has a unique spiritual experience, an experience that is based on, and informed by, eternal truth.

Spirituality and the Spirit of Prophecy

The writings of Ellen White, like Luther's, do not present a "systematic" theology. One has to look for it in bits and pieces. For example, she used the term "spirituality" approximately 873 times throughout her works. I have looked in vain for a specific definition. However, from selected statements it is possible to discover clues to her meaning. Looking at the Seventh-day Adventist Church of her day, Ellen White asked, "Why was there such a destitution of spirituality, so few who had a living experience in religious things?" Spirituality is a living experience, involving "holiness of heart and purity of life." These were "the great subjects of the teachings of Christ." The absence of spirituality is the danger that "leads to unrighteous acts, to envy, hatred, jealousy, evil surmisings, and every hateful and abominable sin." "Not all professed Christians are Christians *at heart*." Hence, they are "unready to stand pure from evil and lust amid the perils and corruptions of this degenerate age."[23] Spirituality includes being "heavenly-minded,"[24] thinking God's thoughts. Growth in spirituality means to "come out from the world and be separate."[25] "Spirituality is dying," she lamented. "Self-esteem and self-sufficiency are killing spiritual life."[26]

In one reference she connected "spirituality" with the "religion of the Bible" and "true principles of Christianity," concluding that such religion "is a continual well-spring, from which the Christian can drink at will, and never exhaust the fountain."[27] Few, she wrote, "hunger and thirst for divine knowledge revealed in the Bible, and the result is inefficiency and weakness as far as spirituality is concerned. God will not work by miracles to solve the mysteries of His Word to the lazy, careless, inattentive student. If you . . . want to be a strong [person] in the understanding of the Word, search the Scriptures with a humble, prayerful *heart*."[28] Hunger and thirst for an authentic Adventist spirituality can be satisfied only by a heart-searching of the Scriptures, not by searching within oneself. The fourth and fifth verses of an old Swedish hymn say it well:[29]

I look not inward; that would make me wretched;
For I have naught on which to stay my trust.
Nothing I see save failures and shortcomings,
And weak endeavors, crumbling into dust.

But I look up—into the face of Jesus,
For there my heart can rest, my fears are stilled;
And there is joy, and love, and light for darkness,
And perfect peace, and every hope fulfilled.

In another reference Ellen White reiterated that spiritual life is killed by self-esteem and self-sufficiency:

"When this proud, boasting *self-sufficiency* and this complacent *self-righteousness* permeate the soul [the inner being], there is no room for Jesus. He is given an inferior place, while *self swells* into importance and fills the whole temple of the soul. This is the reason why the Lord can do so little for us [because there is no room for Him]. Should He work with our efforts, the instrument would appropriate all the glory to his own smartness, his wisdom, his ability, and he would congratulate himself, as did the Pharisee: 'I fast twice in the week, I give tithes of all that I possess.' When *self shall be hidden in Christ*, it will not be brought to the surface so frequently."[30]

In another passage she connected the Bread of heaven and Christlikeness with spirituality:

"If we eat of the bread which came from heaven we shall be Christlike in spirit and character. We are living in an age when there is to be no spiritual idleness. Every soul [being/person] is to be charged [empowered] with the heavenly current of life. The question is often asked: 'What is the cause of the dearth of spiritual power in the church?' The answer comes: 'The members allow their minds to be drawn away from the word of God.' We are built up physically from that which we eat, and in like manner the character of our spirituality is determined by the food given to the mind. We are to give the mind *and heart* proper nourishment by eating the flesh and drinking the blood of the Son of God."[31]

"We must abide in Christ, and Christ must abide in us," she says. "It is [the Christian's] privilege to live in Christ by eating the bread of life. Those who do this will have a healthy, growing *experience*, and the righteousness of God will go before them as they do the work specified [true fasting] in the fifty-eighth chapter of Isaiah."[32] "Each one is to awake to the necessity of having personal holiness and a personal, living faith [a believing faith]. Then will God's work be done. Then will reformations take place. Souls will be rescued from the grasp of selfishness, and in love, patience, and Christian forbearance, will help one another to work for those perishing out of Christ."[33]

In another passage she connected a dying spirituality with backsliding, selfishness, pride, and conformity to fashion, indicating the effect of the outer on the inner person:

"Not a few of our people are backsliding. They are imitating the fashions of the world. Their spirituality is dying. Step by step they are approaching world-loving. Selfishness and pride are taking possession of them, and the love of God finds little room in their *hearts*. Some who were once zealous reformers are now indifferent. Sisters who were once plain in dress are now conforming to fashion. God expects his commandment-keeping people to be distinct from worldlings, but in many instances the line of demarcation is hardly discernible."[34]

This dynamic works both ways. The inner person affects the outer person too, revealing a lack of spirituality:

"This needless display reveals a love for those things which are supposed to place a value upon the person. It gives evidence to the world of a heart destitute of the *inward* adornment. Expensive dress and adornments of jewelry give an incorrect representation of the truth that should always be represented as of the highest value. An overdressed, outwardly adorned person bears the sign of *inward poverty*. A lack of spirituality is revealed."[35]

It is obvious that the spirituality Ellen White talked about is heart religion before it is anything else. It is heavenly-minded and does not willfully participate in degenerate evil and lust. It cannot grow and develop if the confessed believer remains attached to the world in which self-esteem is a primary value. There certainly is an "inner being," but it is not the source of spirituality. The source of spirituality is the Word of God and the indwelling Christ. The inner being receives and responds to both the living Word (Christ) and the written Word (the Bible), which produce a living, believing faith.

In the light of all the above from Scripture and the Spirit of Prophecy, let's see if we can come up with a definition of spirituality that can readily be recognized as a "Seventh-day Adventist" definition. How about this? *For the Seventh-day Adventist Christian, spirituality is the shape or form that believing faith and active obedience take in the heart, the inner being, and the life of the individual believer, and that glorifies the Lord Jesus Christ in its outward and ethical manifestation.* Does that make sense? Is this definition clear or ambiguous? Is it true to the Word of God and the Spirit of Prophecy? Is it true to our doctrines and to our theology?

Pause

At this point in writing this chapter I had to pause and take a break. So I left it alone for some time, sensing that the chapter was somehow incomplete, that something was still needed, that something more needed to be said. But I didn't know what it was. Early in the morning of December 12, 2008, I was awakened at 1:00 a.m., conscious of the thought *Spirituality cannot be defined; it can only be described.* I spent the next hour mulling that over and finally realized it was so. Webster explains the word *define* as "marking the limits of " and "to determine and identify the essential qualities or meaning of." Webster identifies *description* as a word picture "intended to give a mental image of something experienced." Spirituality cannot be defined because, as has already been pointed out, it is primarily experiential.

Going over what I had written so far, I realized that defining was what I had been doing without being conscious of it. Though Adventist spirituality has common components that shape believing faith and obedience and that must be present in every Adventist believer's life, the experience of spirituality is intensely personal. Add to those common components others that are unique to each person—circumstances, events, people, words spoken, insights gained, and directions taken. There is *my* spirituality, and there is *yours*. Does that mean that everything in this chapter prior to this paragraph is irrelevant? Of course not. But this concept has helped me, and I trust it has helped you, to arrive at a more complete and satisfying perspective. Now this chapter is finished, and we can proceed to discuss doing theology and spirituality as life in the Spirit.

Meditation

Before you go to the next chapter, spend some time in contemplation.

Have you been baptized into the death and the resurrection of Jesus Christ? If so, how is that death and resurrection demonstrated in your spiritual life?

---

[1] E. G. White, *Testimonies,* vol. 5, p. 226.

[2] Ellen G. White, *The Acts of the Apostles* (Mountain View, Calif.: Pacific Press Pub. Assn., 1911), p. 190.

[3] E. G. White, *Testimonies,* vol. 4, p. 445. (Italics supplied.)

[4] *Ibid.,* vol. 5, p. 50. (Italics supplied.)

[5] Ellen G. White, *Christ's Object Lessons* (Washington, D.C.: Review and Herald Pub. Assn., 1941), p. 384. (Italics supplied.)

[6] Ellen G. White, *The Upward Look* (Washington, D.C.: Review and Herald Pub. Assn., 1982), p. 30. (Italics supplied.)

[7] E. G. White, *Testimonies,* vol. 4, p. 442. (Italics supplied.)

[8] Urban T. Holmes, *Spirituality for Ministry* (San Francisco: Harper and Row, 1982), p. 12.

[9] Rowan Williams, *Christian Spirituality* (Atlanta: John Knox Press, 1979), pp. 1, 2.

[10] See W. L. Emmerson, *The Reformation and the Advent Movement* (Ukiah, Calif.: Orion Publishing, 2001).

[11] Francis Schaeffer, *True Spirituality* (Wheaton, Ill.: Tyndale House, 1971), pp. 14, 18-45, 110.

[12] Robert C. Roberts, *Spirituality and Human Emotion* (Grand Rapids: William B. Eerdmans, 1982), p. 55.

[13] *Ibid.,* pp. 23, 24.

[14] *Ibid.,* p. 56.

[15] Lewis Sperry Chafer, *He That Is Spiritual* (Grand Rapids: Zondervan, 1918), preface and p. 133. He identifies seven manifestations of the Spirit as: restraining, reproving, regenerating, indwelling, baptizing, sealing, and filling (pp. 29-39).

[16] Bill O'Reilly, *A Bold Fresh Piece of Humanity* (New York: Broadway Books, 2008), p. 76.

[17] Ellen G. White manuscript 16, Feb. 25, 1901. (Italics supplied.) See also E. G. White, *The Upward Look,* p. 7.

[18] See Marvin Olasky, "The 'Blessing' of Abortion," *World,* May 9, 2009, p. 88. Olasky reports the zealously pro-abortion Episcopalian, the Rev. Katherine Hancock Ragsdale, who was slated to become the president of Episcopal Divinity School on July 1, 2009, as saying that abortionists are doing "holy work" and that abortion "is a blessing." Her radical position as an ecclesiastical figure is determined by her view of Scripture. Olasky reports that in an Easter sermon she said that the Resurrection may never have happened. She said that the suffering and death of Jesus for our sin and salvation is "an interesting theory, but not one that I find compelling." Olasky concludes his article with "the tragedy of abortion is bad enough, but the origin of the tragedy, and so many others of our time, emerges from worship not of Christ but of 'me, me, me.' Katherine Ragsdale may show this tendency in a heightened form, but all of us display it to some degree." See also George Conger, "Second Thoughts on Syncretism," *Christianity Today,* May 2009, p. 18.

[19] Schaeffer, p. 26.

[20] The reference to "the Law or the Prophets" encompasses the first five books of the Old Testament, which include the Ten Commandments of Exodus 20:1-17. The context of Matthew 5 indicates that Jesus was referring both to the moral law and the civil law in the Torah. He certainly was not affirming, as some suggest, that by fulfilling the moral law He was abrogating, destroying, or doing away with it. The best commentary on Matthew 5:17 is: "Christ Himself had given both the moral and the ceremonial law. He did not come to destroy confidence in His own instruction. It was because of His great reverence for the

law and the prophets that He sought to break through the wall of traditional requirements which hemmed in the Jews. While He set aside their false interpretations of the law, He carefully guarded His disciples against yielding up the vital truths committed to the Hebrews. . . . His mission to the world is to vindicate the sacred claims of that law which they [the Pharisees] charge Him with breaking. If the law of God could have been changed or abrogated, then Christ need not have suffered the consequences of our transgression. . . . The law is still an agent in bringing us to Christ, that we may be justified by faith. . . . The system of types [in the ceremonial law] that pointed to Jesus as the Lamb of God was to be abolished at His death; but the precepts of the Decalogue [the moral law] are as immutable as the throne of God" (*The Desire of Ages*, pp. 307, 308). See also *Handbook of Seventh-day Adventist Theology* (Hagerstown, Md.: Review and Herald Pub. Assn., 2000), p. 469.

[21]E. G. White, *Testimonies*, vol. 4, p. 75.

[22]*Ibid.,* pp. 73, 74.

[23]*Ibid.,* vol. 2, pp. 444-446. (Italics supplied.)

[24]*Ibid.,* vol. 5, p. 520.

[25]Ellen G. White, *Life Sketches of Ellen G. White* (Mountain View, Calif.: Pacific Press Pub. Assn., 1915), p. 351.

[26]E. G. White, *Testimonies,* vol. 5, p. 538.

[27]James and Ellen G. White, *Christian Temperance and Bible Hygiene* (Battle Creek, Mich.: Good Health Pub. Co., 1890), p. 13.

[28]Ellen G. White letter 23, 1879. (Italics supplied.) See also Ellen G. White, *Manuscript Releases* (Silver Spring, Md.: Ellen G. White Estate, 1990), vol. 4, p. 212.

[29]*The Hymnal* (Rock Island, Ill.: Augustana Book Concern, 1925), no. 431.

[30]E. G. White, *Lift Him Up*, p. 310. (Italics supplied.)

[31]*Testimonies*, vol. 8, p. 169. (Italics supplied.)

[32]*Ibid.,* p. 170. (Italics supplied.)

[33]*Review and Herald*, Sept. 10, 1903. (Italics supplied.)

[34]*Review and Herald*, Nov. 17, 1904. (Italics supplied.)

[35]Ellen G. White manuscript 56, 1900. (Italics supplied.) See also E. G. White, *Manuscript Releases,* vol. 6, p. 159.

Chapter 4

LIFE IN THE SPIRIT

Ministers of the gospel are not only pastors, counselors, administrators, evangelists, and preachers, but also theologians—those who think. They are individuals who must think thoughts about God and His revelation; therefore, they must think right thoughts. Thinking is hard work, which is why we tend to be mentally lazy. As astounding and awesome as it sounds, ministers must know the mind of God—not that their words become God's words, but that God's words become theirs. They must "know" their subject, which is God and the gospel, or what we Seventh-day Adventists call "the message." And they must know in the experiential sense, not just intellectually, cerebrally.

Sacred or Diabolical Theologians

The prophet Ezekiel wrote, "Thus says the Lord God, Woe to the foolish prophets who follow their own spirit, and have *seen* nothing! . . . They have seen false visions and lying divinations. They say 'Declares the Lord,' when the Lord has not sent them, and yet they expect him to fulfill their word" (Eze. 13:3-6). This is serious business. If ministers/theologians are not thinking God's thoughts, they are false prophets, speaking false words and lying visions. Theologians are not machines, but persons—not pieces of wood upon which God whittles. So the best way to do theology is not to reflect on the thought and experience of others, but to reflect on the Word of God and on their own experiences of faith in the light of Scripture. Helmut Thielicke was right when he wrote, "Theological thinking can and ought to grip a man like a passion. But passionate devotion means a way of thinking and speaking which all too consistently is borrowed from the circles in which a person has just been moving."[1] Remember our discussion on secondhand language. Furthermore:

"Speaking figuratively, the study of theology often produces overgrown youths whose internal organs have not correspondingly developed.

This is a characteristic of adolescence. There is actually something like theological puberty. Every teacher knows that this is a matter of signs of natural growth over which there is no need to become excited. Churches
must also understand it and have it explained to them in every possible
way.

"It is a mistake for anyone who is just in this stage to appear before a
church as a teacher. He has outgrown the naïveté with which in young
people's work he might by all means have taken this part. He has not yet
come to that maturity which would permit him to absorb into his own life
and reproduce out of the freshness of his own personal faith the things
which he imagines intellectually and which are accessible to him through
reflection. We must have patience here and be able to wait. For the reasons I have mentioned I do not tolerate sermons by first-semester young
theological students swaddled in their gowns. One ought to be able to
keep still. During the period when the voice is changing we do not sing,
and during this formative period in the life of the theological student he
does not preach."[2]

No doubt Thielicke's wisdom is not appreciated in our time when the
young are idolized and pampered and are not inclined to listen to older
folks. I can understand some of that reluctance. After all, we have not be-
queathed to them the best possible world. Most of my life has been lived
during what contemporary sociologists and historians call the "century of
warfare." I was born 10 years after World War I ended and lived through
World War II, the Korean War, Vietnam, and Desert Storm, plus smaller
skirmishes in between. Then came September 11, 2001, and the strange
sense of foreboding that this event brought to my heart. Now it's Iraq,
Afghanistan, and the war against terrorism, as well as poverty, genocide,
and epidemics such as AIDS—you name it. No, I am not being gloomy.
That's just the way things are, in spite of the head-in-the-sand ideas of so-
called progressives. Substance abuse and addiction, child abuse and mo-
lestation, the sex-crazed culture, abortion on demand, same-sex marriage,
are not—repeat, *not*—progressive. They are regressive. A blind man can
see that the world isn't any better. Humanity, as a whole, is not any better. Mean people were everywhere when I was a kid, and they are
everywhere in my old-age world today. I was born at the start of the Great
Depression, and now that I am in my 80s the politicians and pundits alarm
me with forecasts of another, even worse, depression. Economic crises and
possible catastrophes are predicted. Even the "solutions" of economic
bailouts and stimulus packages will, some are saying, eventually produce
out-of-sight inflation. Nobody wins, especially the average individual
whose major goal is simply to earn a decent living and support a family. So

I can understand young people's loss of confidence in the older generation. Still, when it comes to ministers and ministry, I have to agree with Thielicke. In my book he's right on.

A professor of theology devoted to his students, Thielicke quotes the words of a young medical student who dared to pose questions during a Bible study group session and was pounced on by equally young erstwhile theologians. The medical student recalled: "Although my fate and my life were at stake, those others came at me with their routine. I found in them no trace of life or truths learned by experience. I smelled only corpses of lifeless ideas. I would rather go back to the less rigid young heathen. Granted that they haven't much to say to me, and that that little is probably wrong, at least it is genuine. I was looking for a Christian in whom I could detect a flame. I found only burnt-out slag. Maybe there was a glow underneath, but I am just so unused to it that I wouldn't see such hidden fire."

Professor Thielicke comments: "I know, dear students, that it hurts when I speak in such harsh and perhaps exaggerated terms. But I had to show you rather dramatically how seriously I regard my advice that you above all restrain yourselves with your theological concepts."[3]

In a provocative passage in which he associates doing theology with the spiritual life, Thielicke says: "Whoever ceases to be a man of the spirit automatically furthers a false theology, even if in thought it is pure, orthodox and basically Lutheran [or Seventh-day Adventist]. But in that case death lurks in the kettle. . . .

"Sacred theology therefore is not a word to be lightly taken upon our lips. Theology is a very human business, a craft, and sometimes an art. In the last analysis it is always ambivalent. It can be sacred theology or diabolical theology. *That depends on the hands and hearts which further it.* . . .

"How all-important it is that a vigorous spiritual life, in close association with the Holy Scriptures and in the midst of the Christian community, be maintained as a background to theological work, and that the unformed shadows of thought always derive their life-blood from that source. All this becomes impressively clear to me particularly by the way in which historical-critical study of the Bible affects young theologians. Why is it that it often inflicts upon the young believers severe and sometimes deadly wounds, while we theological teachers are unable to spare anyone these attacks?"[4]

Although Thielicke says it much better than I do, I have been trying to express these very sentiments so far in this book and will try to express them in the rest of it—that the "lecture room in dogmatics is filled with a congregation of Christian students."[5] Persons, not just brains. Thielicke closes his marvelous little book of only 41 pages with these words: "The connection between the theologian and the spiritual man has come home to me with quite new strength."[6] Sacred theology is born out of personal dialogue with God, not out of dialogue with theology and theologians.

Whatever we may think about Richard Foster's ideas, we surely would agree with the opening statement of his popular yet controversial book: "Superficiality is the curse of our age. The doctrine of instant satisfaction is a primary spiritual problem. The desperate need today is not for a greater number of intelligent people, or gifted people, but for *deep people*."[7]

If we are going to be sacred theologians rather than diabolical theologians, if we are going to know the mind of God and think His thoughts, the most profound transformation of life is required. The apostle Paul put it this way: "For no one is a Jew [Christian] who is merely one outwardly, nor is circumcision outward and physical. But a Jew [Christian] is one inwardly, and circumcision is a matter of the heart, by the Spirit, not by the letter" (Rom. 2:28, 29). Inner righteousness is required, and only God the Holy Spirit can work from the inside. It bears repeating: the fruit of the Spirit are the Spirit's fruit, not ours, and are first manifested inwardly before they can be manifested outwardly. One must first have a Christlike heart of love before one can love as Christ loved. Do you believe that? Of course you do. Nothing else makes sense. Read this perceptive observation:

"As our numbers are increasing, broader plans must be laid to meet the increasing demands of the times; but we see no special increase of fervent piety, of Christian simplicity, and earnest devotion. The church seems content to take only the first steps in conversion. They are more ready for active labor than for humble devotion, more ready to engage in outward religious service than in the *inner work* of the heart. Meditation and prayer are neglected for bustle and show. Religion must *begin* with *emptying* and *purifying* the heart, and must be nurtured by daily prayer.

"The steady progress of our work, and our increased facilities, are filling the hearts and minds of many of our people with satisfaction and pride, which we fear will take the place of the love of God *in the soul*. Busy activity in the mechanical part of even the work of God may so occupy the mind that prayer shall be neglected, and self-importance and self-sufficiency, so ready to urge their way, shall take the place of true goodness, meekness, and lowliness of *heart*."[8]

Here Ellen White condemns the activistic life with its focus on doing and tells us to concentrate our major efforts on the inner life, on *being*. If we take her words literally, she tells us that religion begins with emptying and purifying the heart, that is to say, the inner being. She also says that this is accomplished by means of meditation and prayer, which are so often neglected. If that was true in 1875-1881, what about today? During 2006, 1,107,425 people joined the Seventh-day Adventist Church by baptism or confession of faith. That's 92,285 baptisms per month, 21,297 per week, 3,034 per day, 126 per hour, and two every minute! If there ever was a time for us to pay attention to fervent piety, earnest devotion, meditation and prayer, emptying and purifying the heart, love of God in the soul, goodness, meekness, and lowliness of heart—all of which involve the inner work of the heart—it is now. Why? Because the phenomenal worldwide growth we have been experiencing puts us in extreme danger of promoting the acceptance into membership of folks who have taken only the first steps in conversion. It places us in danger of being satisfied with mere outward religious service and busy activity, resulting in satisfaction and pride, self-importance and self-sufficiency. I recall one of my Lutheran seminary professors commenting back in the early 1960s that "the wheels of this church [the Lutheran Church in America] are so well greased, it is so well organized, that if the Holy Spirit were withdrawn it would continue operating as if nothing had happened." He was referring to the kind of "busy activity" that Ellen White described in the above passage. Another way of saying it is becoming more interested in preserving and promoting tradition than in the kind of spirituality that we Adventists call "present truth," which in reality is believing faith *today*.

Hunger and Thirst

Jesus graphically tells us that evil comes from the inside, not from the outside. The Pharisees and the teachers of the law raised the issue of clean and unclean regarding the nature of human beings. The disciples heard the discussion, but didn't fully understand Jesus' reply, and questioned Him about it. In answer He said to them and to the crowd that had gathered, "Hear me, all of you, and understand: There is nothing outside a person that by going into him can defile him, but the things that come out of a person are what defile him" (Mark 7:14, 15). Later He said to the disciples, "What comes out of a person is what defiles him. For from *within*, out of the heart of man, come evil thoughts, sexual immorality, theft, murder, adultery, coveting, wickedness, deceit, sensuality, envy, slander, pride, foolishness. All these evil things come from *within*, and they defile a person" (verses 20-23).

What is needed today is not more theology, but more *hunger and thirst*. Jesus put it this way: "Blessed are those who hunger and thirst for righteousness, for they shall be satisfied" (Matt. 5:6). Just as those who read the Bible once and think that they don't need to read it any more but spend the rest of their lives talking about it, are we in danger of thinking that because we feel that we have all the right answers, there is nothing more to seek? Theological knowledge is indispensable, but it is not sufficient. It has the same relationship to my spiritual life as does a well to my physical life. It's the water that sustains life—not the well. Theological knowledge alone does not quench the hunger and thirst of the inner being for God. *Truth leads to God.*

Ellen White once wrote, "The new birth is a rare experience in this age of the world. This is the reason why there are so many perplexities in the churches. Many, so many, who assume the name of Christ are unsanctified and unholy. They have been baptized, but they were buried alive. Self did not die, and therefore they did not rise to newness of life in Christ."[9] Baptism itself, she said, is not rare. Many people participate in the ritual. What *is* rare is the death of self and the new birth. I think we know what "new birth" means. We know what Jesus meant when He said, "You must be born again." We can discuss it intelligently. We can explain it. We can articulate it theologically. Even that is not rare. What is rare is the "experience" of the new birth, an experience that can be attested to by evidence. Ellen White was right, because if self does not die in baptism, the Christlike life is not only improbable but impossible! If we only assume the name of Christ, then we have only assumed the Christian life. It lacks foundation, power, and reality. It is a fake. Such a life will fail in moments of crisis or spiritual need. Adventists call this "the shaking" of the church.

The Seventh-day Adventist Church believes and teaches that those who are baptized "received the imprint of God by baptism."[10] The baptized receive something, and they receive it by baptism. What do they receive by baptism? "Upon them [the baptized] the Lord has placed His signature, declaring them to be His sons and daughters."[11] The Lord acts. How? By putting His stamp of ownership on the baptized and declaring, announcing, to them and to the whole world that they now belong to Him. They are His. Therefore, God has the right, and His church has the right, to expect the baptized person to be spiritually transformed and to give moral, ethical, spiritual evidence of such transformation—not by virtue of the candidate's decision to be baptized, but by virtue of the grace fact that "as many of you as were baptized into Christ have put on Christ" (Gal. 3:27). Being clothed with Christ ought to make a difference. Do you agree? The power for a transformed life resides not in the human decision to be baptized, but in the fact that the Lord has made the baptized individual His own possession. That's what the Bible, supported by the Spirit of Prophecy, says.

Baptism is the outward sign that the one baptized is under the authority of the Father, Son, and Holy Spirit, in whose name the ritual, whether it is called "sacrament" or "ordinance," is being performed. The ritual of burial and resurrection is meant to demonstrate that worldliness is being renounced and that all has been surrendered to the lordship of Christ. God makes all things new. He makes things right. He heals wounds, whether self-inflicted, inflicted by others, or by sin. He grants new beginnings. He gives a new direction for life. Baptism signifies that one can start over again. In Paul's words, we "walk in newness of life" (Rom. 6:4), and "the life he lives he lives to God" (verse 10). Those who have been "brought from death [burial, down into water] to life [resurrection, up out of water]" now offer themselves "to God as instruments of righteousness" (verse 13).

In Christ's Great Commission we have the formula for the process of inclusion in the church, the body of Christ (*ekklesia*, the called-out ones): "Go therefore and make disciples of all nations, baptizing them in the name of the Father and of the Son and of the Holy Spirit, teaching them to observe all that I have commanded you" (Matt. 28:19, 20). Notice the sequence: 1. Make disciples (followers of Christ who accept the truths of His Word and willingly share them with others as "instruments of righteousness"). That requires a significant decision. 2. Baptize. God puts His stamp of ownership on them and declares them His, sealing the surrender of the life to the One who called them to discipleship. 3. Teach them to obey everything the Lord has commanded in His Word. Why this sequence? Because it is only the disciple who *is,* not *was,* baptized that is teachable and who can be empowered to obey. Bring them in, disciple them, baptize them, teaching them to obey God's Word and keeping them in through spiritual nurture.

Paul summarizes the goal of all of this: "For sin will have no dominion over you, since you are not under law but under grace" (Rom. 6:14). It is on the authority of texts such as this and those quoted above, as well as the perceptive counsel of Ellen White, that we can best avoid baptizing persons who would be "buried alive," who are "unsanctified and unholy," and "who did not rise to newness of life in Christ." That is to say, we can do so if we are determined and single-minded enough to do what the Lord tells us to do.

If we are "under grace," something more must be said. Although baptism, as we have seen, signifies that the one baptized has received the imprint of God, the power to live a transformed life comes from being united with Christ. The baptized person has heard the gospel, repented of sin and rebellion, believes in Jesus as Savior and Lord, and is surrendered fully to His lordship. Now, it is possible for the Holy Spirit to undertake a sanctifying ministry in the heart. The Spirit begins the interior work of sanctification, because it is inside where change, spiritual transformation, takes place. You and I can usually take care of the outside and put on a good front. It is not difficult to give the appearance of the Christian life. But the change that is necessary in order to see and be part of God's kingdom takes place inwardly. Only the Holy Spirit works from the inside. Such transformation does not depend on resolutions or promises. It requires death, the crucifixion of the old person, symbolized by immersion in baptism.

When Jesus told His disciples, "You will drink the cup I drink and be baptized with the baptism I am baptized with," He was speaking about His crucifixion and death. His water baptism was the first step on His way to Calvary. To follow Jesus means to go the way of the cross, the way of renunciation. The old life of willful sin comes to an end. While the unconverted lives *for* sin and *to* sin and *in* sin, the born-again believer's desire and passion is to live so as *not to sin*. While the unconverted loves sin, the baptized believer hates it. Yes, God accepts us just as we are. But He expects the baptized person to be a transformed person, determined to live in harmony with His will. Why can He expect this? Because He has made it possible. It is possible as long as we abide in Christ. He said: "I am the vine; you are the branches. Whoever abides in me and I in him, he it is that bears much fruit, for apart from me [abiding in you] you can do nothing" (John 15:5). You see, it's not a matter of having once been saved. It's a matter of abiding in Christ. Now. Today. "Those who receive Christ by faith become one with Him in principle and action. They are united to Him, and the life they live is the life of the Son of God. They derive their life from Him."[12] It is possible, indeed He wills it, that our entire lives can consist of unbroken communion with Christ. Jesus said, "Blessed are those who hunger and thirst for righteousness, for they shall be satisfied" (Matt. 5:6).

Only the hungry can hunger, and only the thirsty can thirst. If you wish it, God will make you so hungry and so thirsty for His righteousness that you will ask Him for it. It is only the hungry and thirsty who can be satisfied. What we all need today is not more knowledge, new views, new ideas, new excitement, etc. Our greatest need is for more hunger and more thirst for God's righteousness. Those who receive it and are satisfied are renewed. They look at life from God's perspective, rather than from the narrow, limited human perspective. They become people of hope, people of principle. Of such the Lord says, "I will fasten him like a peg in a secure place, and he will become a throne of honor to his father's house. And they will hang on him the whole honor of his father's house" (Isa. 22:23, 24).

Dietrich Bonhoeffer wrote, "When Christ calls a man, He bids him come and die."[13] Some folks want a little bit of the Lord, but not enough to disturb their conscience. Anyone who wants to be partly devout and partly worldly will always be unhappy and discontented. A little bit of God is dangerous. It leads to religious restlessness and boredom. The roots of depression are in a divided heart. If you have just a little bit of God, you will see Him only as a brake, an impediment, a pain. A divided heart is one that usually limps along the edges of sadness and depression, anger and hostility. A little bit of God and a little bit of the world do not mix; it produces only bitterness and bad temper. We get mad at God, at ourselves, and at everyone else. We cannot truly love the Lord if we won't let go of the devil. A half Christian envies both the thoroughgoing worldling and the thoroughgoing believer, while feeling guilty about his envy. What the Lord has to offer we receive and experience only when we are willing to take a chance with Him—to fully surrender to Him.

Humans have no adequate means for measuring the cost of following Christ against the alternative. Why? Because the things that He gives us cannot be gotten without the cross. Many things have to be surrendered to death by those who would follow Jesus. Peace with God and with ourselves comes only by way of the cross. Where Christ is king, everything is changed. Whenever someone surrenders to Jesus, God always cleans up, renews, transforms, and empowers that person for victorious living.

The apostle Paul preached "in demonstration of the Spirit and of power, that your faith might not rest in the wisdom of men but in the power of God" (1 Cor. 2:4, 5). He preached the "secret and hidden wisdom of God" (verse 7) that was "revealed to us through the Spirit" (verse 10). He made it clear that "no one comprehends the thoughts of God except the Spirit of God" (verse 11). He continued his profound thought in verses 12-16: "Now we have received not the spirit of the world, but the Spirit who is from God, that we might understand the things freely given us by God. And we impart this in words not taught by human wisdom but taught by the Spirit, interpreting spiritual truths to those who are spiritual.

"The natural person does not accept the things of the Spirit of God, for they are folly to him, and he is not able to understand them because they are spiritually discerned. The spiritual person judges all things, but is himself to be judged by no one. 'For who has understood the mind of the Lord so as to instruct him?' But we have the mind of Christ."

This is the only explanation for Paul's great accomplishments as a missionary, evangelist, and preacher. And it is the only explanation for our success in preaching, teaching, and testifying to the power of the gospel. Such success is not the result of cleverness, charisma, or the ability to turn a fancy phrase. The message of the Bible that God has given to His church consists of spiritual truths that can be taught only by the Spirit of God. The meaning and application of those great truths can be interpreted and understood only by spiritual people. Christ is true wisdom. This alone ought to serve as a red flag, warning of the dangers of mysticism, the occult, psychic phenomena, Eastern religious thought, pantheism, panentheism, the New Age, etc. Those who do not accept the Bible and the Bible alone (*sola scriptura*) as the source of the wisdom revealed by the Spirit, who do not accept the centrality of the cross of Christ as the way of salvation revealed in the Bible, are not the "spiritual" persons the apostle spoke of here. The gospel is folly, foolishness, to them, and they are not able to understand it. That's why Paul said that he "could not address you as spiritual people, but as people of the flesh" (1 Cor. 3:1). Experiential knowledge of God and His Word is a matter of spiritual perception or insight. A fleshly, worldly life is a Christless life, and therefore a loveless life.

In the Spirit

If we are to be theologians who know the mind of God, if we are to see things that no one else can see and hear things that no one else can hear, then we must be *en pneumati*, "in the Spirit." Four times in the book of Revelation John spoke of being "in the Spirit."

1. "I was in the Spirit on the Lord's day [i.e., the seventh-day Sabbath], and I heard behind me a loud voice like a trumpet saying, 'Write what you see in a book and send it to the seven churches, to Ephesus and to Smyrna and to Pergamum and to Thyatira and to Sardis and to Philadelphia and to Laodicea'" (Rev. 1:10, 11). John was in the Spirit, and he "heard." What did he hear? The message of Christ to the seven churches. The Word of God. The truth that gives light and life. The mind of God. The thoughts of God.

2. "After this I looked, and behold, a door standing open in heaven! And the first voice, which I had heard speaking to me like a trumpet [referring to Rev. 1:10], said, 'Come up here, and I will show you what must take place after this.' At once I was in the Spirit, and behold, a throne stood in heaven, with one seated on the throne" (Rev. 4:1, 2). What did he hear? The same voice he had heard the first time. Who told John what he was to do ("'Come up here,'") and what the Speaker would do (show him something extraordinary)? What did he see? God seated on His throne in heaven. God's magnificence and glory. The activity taking place around the throne of God. John must have been struck with awe as he witnessed the magnificence of celestial worship.

3. One of the angels said to John, "'Come, I will show you the judgment of the great prostitute who is seated on many waters.' . . . And he

carried me away in the Spirit into a wilderness, and I saw a woman sitting on a scarlet beast" (Rev. 17:1, 3).

4. Finally, another of the seven angels said to John, "'Come, I will show you the Bride, the wife of the Lamb.' And he carried me away in the Spirit . . . and showed me the holy city Jerusalem coming down out of heaven from God" (Rev. 21:9, 10). "And its lamp is the Lamb" (verse 23). What did John see? All of world history from his day until the end of time. He communicated what he heard in simple terms, and what he saw in metaphorical terms and images. He described the indescribable and expressed the inexpressible![14]

In the Spirit, John could hear things and see things that others could not hear and see. Revelatory things. The mind of God. He was able to see with the mind's eye, to dream dreams, to imagine the glorified life and the very environment of heaven. He could hear the sound of trumpets, smell the smoke of the seven lamps, and sing a new song. "You must *learn* to see with your brain as well as your eyes," said Ellen White.[15]

Is such an experience reserved only for the likes of John? Should it be, in some sense at least, repeated for us? Should we not hear what others cannot hear, see what they cannot see? If we are in the Spirit, and the Spirit is in us, we can expect great things to happen in our lives. Then Jesus will not ask us as He did His disciples, "Why are you discussing the fact that you have no bread? Do you not yet *perceive* or *understand?* Are your hearts hardened? Having eyes do you not see, and having ears do you not hear?" (Mark 8:17, 18).

To be in the Spirit requires devotion to Scripture and that we walk not according to the flesh. "If by the Spirit you put to death the deeds of the body, you will live. For all who are led by the Spirit of God are sons of God" (Rom. 8:13, 14). To those in the Spirit, God bears witness that He leads them (verse 14), that they are His children (verse 16), that He gives them victory in suffering (verse 18), that He helps them in their weakness (verse 26), that He intercedes for them (verse 26), that He searches their hearts (verse 27), that He predestined them to be like Jesus (verse 29), and that He causes all things to work together for their good (verse 28). Amazing!

Having begun in the Spirit, let us not end in the flesh. That was the spiritual danger for the Galatians—not remaining yielded and dependent, and so ending in the flesh. Those who walk in the Spirit "*will not* gratify the desires of the flesh" (Gal. 5:16). Their will is to do His will when they know His mind. "For we are the real circumcision, who worship by the Spirit of God and glory in Christ Jesus and put no confidence in the flesh" (Phil. 3:3). True spirituality is the unhindered manifestation of the indwelling Spirit, not quenching the Spirit but yielding to the Spirit and depending on His power alone.

To be sure, life in the Spirit is life in this world, too. It is life lived with the tensions described in Romans 7—tensions between life and death, between present suffering and the glory to be revealed, between the groaning of the world, our own groaning, and the groaning of the Holy Spirit. It is life lived with that yearning, often silent, sometimes audible, keening of the human heart for ultimate freedom and release from bondage to decay, understood by the Spirit and shared by the Spirit. Our groans say what language cannot say and are forced to the surface of our consciousness by the reality of experience.

What has been said in this chapter is best summarized by this statement by Ellen White: "The followers of Christ are to become like Him—by the grace of God to form characters in harmony with the principles of His holy law. This is Bible sanctification. This work can be accomplished only through faith in Christ, by the power of the indwelling Spirit of God. Paul admonishes believers: 'Work out your own salvation with fear and trembling. For it is God which worketh in you both to will and to do of his good pleasure.' Philippians 2:12, 13, KJV."[16]

By the way, before we proceed any further I want to share with you, in the next chapter, a theological insight that has had a major impact on my own developing spirituality. Because it presents the theological foundation for this book, as well as for my own experience, I will be forced to lapse into some technical, theological language. I hope you don't mind, and I pray that the discipline of plowing through the next chapter will prove to be an informative blessing as you think about the sublimity of the Adventist message.

Meditation

Stop and think for a few moments. If you confess to having been born again, did that new birth involve the death of self? If so, what is the moral, ethical, spiritual, evidence that self has died and that Christ has taken its place?

---

[1] Helmut Thielicke, *A Little Exercise for Young Theologians* (Grand Rapids: William B. Eerdmans, 1962), p. 9.

[2] *Ibid.*, p. 12.

[3] *Ibid.*, pp. 14, 15. It is not just theological students who need to exercise theological restraint.

[4] *Ibid.*, pp. 36, 37. (Italics supplied.)

[5] *Ibid.*, p. 40.

[6] *Ibid.*, p. 41.

[7] Richard J. Foster, *Celebration of Discipline* (San Francisco: Harper and Row, 1978), p. 1. (Italics supplied.) As in many books, good statements with which we can agree are mixed with those with which we cannot agree. Though Foster's book is popular with those inclined to mix a biblical faith with Catholic mysticism and Eastern religions, his espousal of the New Age (p. 170) and his use of the historical-critical method of biblical interpretation make his path to spiritual growth highly questionable.

[8] E. G. White, *Testimonies,* vol. 4, p. 535. (Italics supplied.)

[9] *The Seventh-day Adventist Bible Commentary*, Ellen G. White Comments (Washington, D.C.: Review and Herald Pub. Assn., 1980), vol. 6, p. 1075.

[10] *Ibid.*

[11] *Ibid.*

[12] E. G. White, *In Heavenly Places*, p. 56.

[13] *The Cost of Discipleship* (New York: Macmillan Company, 1948), p. 73.

[14] There is absolutely no evidence in the text of Revelation that John practiced some unique esoteric method that enabled him to hear and see what he recorded. The experience of being "in the Spirit" is initiated by God alone, not by rituals or techniques we may employ.

[15] Ellen G. White, *Sons and Daughters of God* (Washington, D.C.: Review and Herald Pub. Assn., 1955), p. 283. (Italics supplied.)

[16] Ellen G. White, *The Great Controversy* (Mountain View, Calif.: Pacific Press Pub. Assn., 1911), p. 469.

Chapter 5

THE ONE
SUBLIME MESSAGE

While a professor at the Seventh-day Adventist Theological Seminary, I became aware of the commonality in the stories told by the students and the faculty about their spiritual journeys. All the stories shared three elements: events or circumstances, people and what they did or said, and literature—purchased, found, or given to them by others. This is true of my story, too.

When my wife, Shirley, became a Seventh-day Adventist and I was trying to make sense out of it all and was in the valley of decision myself, the office staff of the Michigan Conference of Seventh-day Adventists sent me a marvelous gift—a beautifully bound five-volume set of The Conflict of the Ages Series, by Ellen White. Each volume was inscribed in gold letters, "Rev. and Mrs. C. R. Holmes." They were so beautiful (and I really do love books) that I couldn't bring myself to burn them, as I had done with other Adventist literature, pitching it into the fire at the Bessemer city dump. These books have occupied a prominent place in my library ever since.

I have learned to appreciate and enjoy all five. But two of the volumes impressed me the most when I finally found the courage to read them—*The Desire of Ages*, which is a deeply moving biography of Jesus, and *The Great Controversy*. I was thrilled to discover in the latter an excellent treatment of the Protestant Reformation, with particular emphasis on the role of Martin Luther. In it Ellen White writes:

"Counterfeit holiness, spurious *sanctification*, is still doing its work of deception. Under various forms it exhibits the same spirit as in the days of Luther, diverting minds from the Scriptures and leading men to follow their *own* feelings and impressions rather than to yield obedience to the law of God. This is one of Satan's most successful devices to cast reproach upon purity and truth.

"Fearlessly did Luther defend the gospel from the attacks which came from every quarter. The Word of God proved itself a weapon mighty in every conflict. With that Word he warred against the usurped authority of

75

the pope, and the rationalistic philosophy of the schoolmen, while he stood firm as a rock against the fanaticism that sought to ally itself with the Reformation.

"Each of these opposing elements was in its own way setting aside the Holy Scriptures and exalting *human wisdom* as the source of religious truth and knowledge. Rationalism idolizes reason and makes this the criterion for religion. Romanism, claiming for her sovereign pontiff an inspiration descended in unbroken line from the apostles, and unchangeable through all time, gives ample opportunity for every species of extravagance and corruption to be concealed under the sanctity of the apostolic commission. The inspiration claimed by Münzer and his associates proceeded from no higher source than the vagaries of the imagination, and its influence was subversive of all authority, human or divine. *True Christianity receives the Word of God as the great treasure house of inspired truth and the test of all inspiration.*"[1]

"The study of the Scriptures was working a mighty change in the minds and *hearts* of the people. The papal rule had placed upon its subjects an iron yoke which held them in ignorance and degradation. A superstitious observance of forms had been scrupulously maintained; but in all their service the *heart* and intellect had had little part. The preaching of Luther, setting forth the plain truths of God's Word, and then the Word itself, placed in the hands of the common people, had aroused their dormant powers, not only purifying and ennobling the *spiritual nature*, but imparting new strength and vigor to the intellect."[2]

This passage helped me become aware that the Seventh-day Adventist Church is deep in the stream of the Reformation. Fast-forward to the year 2000, when I was given another book that made a major impact on me and further affirmed and confirmed Adventist theology and spirituality. The confirmation happened in the midst of a phone conversation with a Lutheran pastor friend, Antti Armas Isaakki Lepistö. (I love pronouncing his Finnish name!) He and I were ordained together in 1961 and have been friends ever since. He said, "I'm sending you a book!" A few days later I happily opened the package. No pastor ever turns down a free book. It was a copy of *Union With Christ: The New Finnish Interpretation of Luther.*[3] Of course, because the book had to do with a *Finnish* interpretation of Luther, who remains one of my spiritual heroes even though he was wrong on the Sabbath issue, I devoured it immediately.

Some years previously I had found another book in a used book store. A dog-eared and coverless copy of *Christ Our Righteousness,* by Arthur G. Daniells,[4] for which I paid the munificent sum of 25 cents! It was worth every penny and much more. Reading *Union With Christ,* I was reminded of Daniells' first sentence: "Christ our righteousness is the one sublime message set forth in the Sacred Scriptures."[5] Of immediate interest were the parallels between the Seventh-day Adventist understanding of Christ our righteousness and the new Finnish interpretation of Luther, which confirmed the roots of that understanding in the Reformation.

Context and Methodology

In the mid-1970s the Lutheran Church of Finland was involved in an ecumenical dialogue with the Russian Orthodox Church that had reached an impasse. Archbishop Martti Simojoki assigned the theological faculty at the University of Helsinki the task of finding a point of contact on which the dialogue might proceed. The results of more than 20 years of research were introduced to the English-speaking world during a seminar at St. Olaf College in Minnesota on June 1, 1996, and published in *Union With Christ*.

The Finnish scholars began by posing two questions: (1) How does modern Luther scholarship understand the presence of Christ? and (2) What were the philosophical assumptions used in defining the nature of Christ's presence? In seeking answers, they became aware of the influence of the German philosopher Hermann Lotze (1817-1881) and the German theologian Albrecht Ritschl (1822-1889) on the thinking of contemporary Luther scholars and theologians, especially with reference to understanding the nature of being (the essence of the living person). According to Lotze, as far as knowledge of things is concerned we can "know" them only by how they affect us, rather than by any sense of their entering into us. In other words, that which knowledge grasps is not real; only the effects are real.

With respect to the God/human relationship, the Finnish scholars discovered that Ritschl's theology followed Lotze's philosophical thinking, concluding that Christ's presence for the believer is the *effect* of God's will. God acts in terms of His will, which then causes human actions (effects). The union created between God and humanity is one not of being but of willing. God's will effects our wills, and we then act accordingly. That is to say, "Christ in us means therefore that we ourselves live a moral life for Him."[6] What this means is that union with Christ is not a reality in itself, but rather is a union of divine and human wills. The Finnish scholars referred to this as "transcendental effect orientation," which has determined the understanding of revelation, as well as the interpretation of Luther, for the past century and a half. Says Professor Tuomo Mannermaa: "On the basis of this tradition one can make hardly anything . . . of those passages in Luther that speak of real participation in God."[7] (Or those of the apostle Paul, we might add.)

Rejecting Lotze's philosophical presupposition and digging into the writings of Luther himself as the primary source, the Finnish scholars concluded that Luther followed the Hebrew way of thinking in that the thing that is known (Christ) is itself present in the one who knows (the believer). In Hebrew thought, the attributes of God—such as righteousness, wisdom, power, holiness, joy, peace, eternal life, and love—constitute His essence or being. Based on the Hebrew way of thinking, Luther understood that because God and His Son are one, these attributes are present in Christ and also, because of the indwelling Christ, that the believer is able to share these attributes. On this basis Luther was able to say, "Thus the righteousness of Christ becomes our righteousness through faith in Christ, and everything that is His, even He Himself, becomes ours . . . and he who believes in Christ clings to Christ and is one with Christ and has the same righteousness with Him."[8] In other words, believers have no righteousness of their own, but are made righteous because of Christ's righteousness. Hence, for Luther, oneness with Christ, or union with Christ, constitutes being. This being is never static, because God is always creating. It is a continuous reception of God's gifts in which Christ is present and in which Christ Himself is given. Believers in Christ are always being born, renewed, transformed. Luther understood this truth relationally. Christians are "in Christ," understood not only forensically (declared to be so) but in reality. In other words, the relationship is not with a Christ who remains outside of the believer. Rather, Christ is received internally as a new spiritual reality. "Therefore, if anyone is in Christ, he *is* a new creation. The old has passed away; behold, the new has come" (2 Cor. 5:17). The old person has *really* died, and the believer *really* is a new creation. Professor Sammeli Juntunen states that the medium (or means) of spiritual existence "is not the event of 'forensic justification' but the divine person of Christ" Himself.[9] Juntunen refers to this insight as "Luther before Lutheranism." If he and his colleagues are correct, Lutheran*ism* has been Luther's worst enemy! The Finnish scholars did not begin where much of contemporary Luther study begins, with the Formula of Concord, or with subsequent works on Luther, but with Luther himself, who began with Scripture. They went beyond the traditional idea that faith is an act of the will.

Luther died in 1547. The Formula of Concord was completed in 1577, becoming the final section of the *Book of Concord,* published in 1580.[10] The intent and purpose of the Formula of Concord was to settle the controversies over Reformation doctrine that had arisen following Luther's death and to secure a united front against Roman Catholic pressure. By then the formulation and propagation of doctrine and theology was in the hands of the second generation of Reformers, and consequently the style of the Formula of Concord was decidedly scholastic.

Justification

The Lutheran World Federation, meeting at Helsinki in 1963, was unable to produce a satisfactory statement on justification because of its inability to answer the modern question Does God exist? The so-called sixteenth-century question, assumed to be the underlying and central question for Luther—"How can a sinner find a gracious God?"—is not being asked today. The scholars had no answer for the modern question, because they were still looking at Luther through Formula of Concord glasses and missing his emphasis on the indwelling Christ. Professor Carl Braaten wonders if it makes any sense for Lutherans to continue holding justification as the chief doctrine of the Christian faith "if they are so unclear and in fact in wide disagreement about its material content."[11]

The Formula of Concord states that the righteousness of Christ is "reckoned to us," that it is "reckoned to faith," that therefore sinners are "accounted righteous and holy by God," that they are "regarded as holy and righteous through faith," and that the "righteousness of faith before God consists solely in the gracious reckoning of Christ's righteousness to us."[12] The words *reckoned, accounted,* and *regarded* mean "to consider" or "impute." However, in the same section the Formula of Concord states that "a person must *be* righteous before he can do good works."[13] This last is an ontological statement, having to do with being, not a forensic statement. It is, of course, true that a person must *be* righteous in order to produce good works. No question about it. Remember Luther's Hebrew way of thinking, in which oneness with Christ, or union with Christ, constitutes being.

The Bible says, "None is righteous, no, not one" (Rom. 3:10), using three negatives for emphasis. If none is righteous, then all are unrighteous, right? And this is proved by what they are and do: ungodly, suppressors of the truth, impure, committing shameful sexual acts, sensuous, evil, covetous, malicious, envious, murderous, full of strife, deceitful, gossips, slanderers, insolent, inventors of evil, faithless, heartless, ruthless, drunkenness, etc. (see Rom. 1 and Gal. 5). The evidence of unrighteousness is everywhere. But the Bible also says, "The prayer of a righteous person has great power" (James 5:16). So which New Testament statement is right and which is wrong—James or Romans? Or are they both right? What has to happen before the unrighteous becomes righteous? He or she has to be born again. "If you know that he [God] is righteous, you may be sure that everyone who practices righteousness has been born of him. . . . No one who abides in him keeps on sinning. . . . Whoever practices righteousness is righteous, as he is righteous. . . . No one born of God makes a practice of sinning, for God's seed abides in him, and he cannot keep on sinning because he has been born of God" (1 John 2:29-3:9). How does one become righteous? "For as by the one man's disobedience [Adam's] the many were made sinners, so by the one man's obedience [Christ's] the many will be made righteous" (Rom. 5:19). "By this we know that we abide in him and he in us, because he has given us of his Spirit" (1 John 4:13). "Christ in you, [is] the hope of glory" (Col. 1:27). We cannot achieve it. We can only receive it, by grace through faith. It is always an alien righteousness, not our own—a gift of God. But this righteousness is not just an idea, not just something declared or announced (imputed). It is *really real* righteousness, given to the believer as a gift (imparted).

The Formula of Concord includes only a brief reference regarding the "indwelling of God's essential righteousness," stating negatively that it is "not the righteousness of faith of which St. Paul speaks and which he calls the righteousness of God, on account of which we are declared just before God." It is obvious that the writers of the Formula of Concord were stuck on the forensic nature of imputed righteousness, which was all they could see in the Pauline letters, and were unable to articulate what the Finnish scholars refer to as Luther's understanding of "donated" righteousness (Finnish, *lahja vanhurskaus*—"gifted righteousness"), which is the righteousness of the indwelling Christ. That inability has plagued Lutheranism ever since, which is why there has been little appreciation for, and much opposition to, the kind of spiritual life fostered by Lutheran pietists and others. What the Finnish scholars refer to as "donated" righteousness, Seventh-day Adventists refer to as "imparted" righteousness. For Lutheran pietists, 2 Peter 1:3, 4 was most significant: "His divine power has granted to us all things that pertain to life and godliness, through the knowledge of him who called us to his own glory and excellence, by which he has granted to us his precious and very great promises, so that through them you may become partakers of the divine nature, having escaped from the corruption that is in the world because of sinful desire." For them, to become "partakers of the divine nature" was not understood forensically (by declaration) but in reality.

The Presence of Christ in Faith

The central idea in the Finnish insight into Luther is that "in faith itself Christ is really present." This represents a radical departure from the concept of forensic justification, largely based on the Formula of Concord, in which Christ *for us* was separated from Christ *in us*. As we shall see, this insight articulates Luther's belief that by faith the believer receives the righteousness of God. The believer is not just *declared* righteous because of Calvary, but receives Christ and His righteousness by faith and thereby be-

comes righteous. The language of this insight, says Carl Braaten, "falls like a thud on Lutheran ears accustomed to hearing from Luther chiefly what echoes their Lutheran tradition."[14] Luther wrote:

"Christ is God's grace, mercy, righteousness, truth, wisdom, power, comfort, and salvation, given to us by God without any merit on our part. Christ, I say, not as some express it in blind words, 'causally,' so that he grants righteousness and remains absent himself, for that would be dead. Yes, it is not given at all unless Christ himself is present, just as the radiance of the sun and the heat of fire are not present if there is no sun and no fire."[15]

All of the attributes of God are present in the person of Christ. The Finnish scholars have recognized that central to Luther's thought is the idea that Christ must become present in the believer through faith if the believer is to receive His gifts of life and salvation. Christ and His gifts are inseparable.

Faith results in union with Christ. He becomes present the moment He gives the gift of faith. He lives and works His will in us, not as an idea but as a present reality. On the basis of this understanding a believer can participate in God's essential goodness, which is love, and become loving. Redemption, therefore, happens not only on the cross but also *in* the believer in whom Christ dwells by faith. The Christ who is thus inwardly present transforms the believer into His own likeness. In this way the believer participates in the attributes of Christ. The presence of Christ in faith, therefore, is not only the result of justification but is also the basis of sanctification. The inward knowledge of Christ has a sanctifying effect. With some exceptions, this view has been generally denied by Lutherans, and the consequence has been an inability to understand that obedience is a fruit of faith. It is also the reason for the contemporary problem in the church, which is not legalism but licentiousness. Furthermore, on the basis of these recent insights into Luther, it cannot be claimed any longer that justification and sanctification are separate theological categories; they must be properly understood as equally significant aspects of the salvation process. The impact of this understanding of Luther on preaching and on the subsequent lifestyle of God's people would be dramatic.

Luther says that "to preach Christ means to feed the soul, make it righteous, set it free, and save it, provided it believes the preaching," and that faith "unites the soul with Christ as a bride is united with her bridegroom." He says further that "a man is abundantly and sufficiently justified *inwardly*, in his spirit, and so has all that he needs, except insofar as this faith and these riches must grow from day to day [sanctification] even to the future life [glorification]; yet he remains in this mortal life on earth." Luther proposes to "examine more profoundly that grace which our *inner man* has in Christ." In the section in which he speaks of the believer's good works, Luther says, "Surely we are named [Christians] after Christ, not because He is absent from us, but because he dwells in us."[16]

Luther's view is not the Roman Catholic view, in which the sanctifying grace of God is *infused* into the believer by means of sacraments, which then becomes meritorious and therefore the basis of justification. The error of Catholicism is not the idea that the sinner is renewed inwardly by grace, but that such inward renewal gives the sinner merit before God. In all fairness we must acknowledge that the emphasis in the Formula of Concord on the forensic aspect of justification was in reaction to the views of Andreas Osiander (1498-1552), who held that by virtue of Christ's divine nature the believer is justified by His sanctifying presence rather than by His saving merits. It is unfortunate that this rejection of Osiander's view, while perhaps necessary under the circumstances of sixteenth-century Germany, ultimately resulted in the one-sided position of the Formula of Concord and of much subsequent Lutheran theology. The Formula of Concord failed to address the significance of the emphasis of both Luther and the apostle Paul on the indwelling Christ and union with Christ.

Arthur G. Daniells writes that the heart of the gospel is "union with Christ. No man can overcome sin except by this union. . . . Union with Christ is a satisfying reality in all that pertains to the Christian life."[17] Ellen White writes: "The righteousness by which we are justified is imputed; the righteousness by which we are sanctified is imparted. The first is our title to heaven, the second is our fitness for heaven."[18]

Grace and Gift

Professor Simo Peura, one of the Finnish scholars, recognizes: "One of the most difficult problems to be solved in Lutheran theology concerns the relation between the forensic and the effective aspects of justification. . . . The two aspects of justification are expressed in Luther's theology in his conceptions of grace (*gratia, favor*) and gift (*donum*). One indicates that a sinner is forensically declared righteous, and the other that he is made effectively righteous."[19] In a footnote on the same page, Peura, commenting on contemporary ecumenical dialogue, observes, "We Lutherans will encounter great difficulties if we try to represent only the forensic aspect of justification."

Luther's understanding of the relationship between grace and gift is based on Romans 5:15-17, especially verse 17, which reads: "For if, because of one man's trespass, death reigned through that one man, much more will those who receive the abundance of grace and the free gift of righteousness reign in life through the one man Jesus Christ." In this text we see that the grace of God and the gift of righteousness are identical— righteousness given to believers through Christ. Righteousness replaces sin in the believers, and thus the believers are purified.

Following the Formula of Concord, traditional Lutheranism has insisted that justification involves primarily imputed righteousness, the declaration of the forgiveness of sin. What is not included in the traditional Lutheran doctrine, as understood by many contemporary theologians, is the renewal of the believers and the removal of sin. When the Formula of Concord speaks of "gift," it means correct knowledge of Christ and the assurance based on the knowledge that God considers believers righteous because of Christ's obedience. Excluded from "gift" is everything that Luther included in it—regeneration, renewal, and, above all, the presence in the believers of Christ who is our righteousness. This exclusion is based on the philosophical assumption that God's being is separated from His effects. Therefore, with reference to the doctrine of justification, much of post-Formula of Concord Lutheran theology has failed to consider the ontological, experiential dimension of faith. All that justified believers can claim by faith is that they understand they have a new (legal) position, or standing, before God. What happens to believers happens only cognitively, not in reality. In contrast to this view, Professor Peura's study of Luther's thought leads him to conclude: "Justification is not only a change of self-understanding, a new relation to God, or a new ethos of love. God changes the sinner ontologically in the sense that he or she participates in God and in his divine nature, being made righteous. . . . This interpretation is based on the thesis that both grace and gift are a righteousness given in Christ to a Christian. This donation presupposes that Christ is really present and that he indwells the Christian. Christ on the one hand is the grace that is given to the sinner that protects him against the wrath of God (the forensic aspect), and on the other hand he is the gift that renews and makes the sinner righteous (the effective aspect). All this is possible only if Christ is united with the sinner through the sinner's faith."[20]

If Luther is understood this way, it can no longer be said that his central teaching was justification by faith. Faith *in* Christ does not itself justify; rather it is Christ Himself, who gives faith and who is *present in faith*, who justifies the sinner. When the sinner is united with Christ in faith, he receives the forgiveness of sin and Christ's righteousness as a divine gift of grace (see Rom. 5:15-17). Furthermore, there is no justification outside of personal faith and union with Christ. For Luther, then, union with Christ is essential for salvation. As Peura says:

"Thus the basic starting point of Luther's interpretation of Romans

5:15 (*gratia Dei et donum in gratia*) is as follows: Christ himself is grace and gift. Christ himself is the grace that covers a sinner and hides him from God's wrath, and Christ himself is the gift that renews the sinner internally and makes him righteous. This occurs, then, when Christ unites himself with a sinner."[21]

Just as faith comes by hearing the Word of God, so also the preaching of the gospel of the indwelling Christ brings the promise to pass. The goal of such preaching is the restoration of the image of God in fallen humanity.

Reinhold Seeberg, in his *History of Doctrines,* considers it most important "to observe that he [Luther], at the very beginning of his career, makes practical application of his new idea of faith; for the leverage of Luther's reformatory principle lies, not in justification, nor in a new theory of grace, but in the conviction that faith is the *form* of true religion."[22]

Many Luther scholars have become bored with Luther, assuming that he has nothing more to say and that a continued poring over his works will produce nothing new. However, the Finnish scholars have brought excitement back into Luther research, and he is once again an open book. They have served to reveal that the old stuff, the classic literature, is the best stuff.

If we Seventh-day Adventists lean exclusively in the direction of the doctrine of forensic justification, we will find ourselves in the unfortunate position of being tempted to abandon the one sublime truth upon which all else depends—Christ our righteousness. Salvation by grace through faith involves both that which Christ has done for us on Calvary's cross and that which He does in us by virtue of His indwelling presence. Remember, the believer's "hope of glory" is "Christ in you" (Col. 1:27).

Justification by grace alone, received by faith alone, is a great blessing. However, as J. I. Packer says: "Justification does not of itself imply any intimate or deep relationship with God the judge."[23] But the greatest blessing of all is what justification received by faith results in—Christ in you. It is this union that provides the stability and security the believer can rely on in the last day and every day. It is the perception of this union that controls and guides our lives.

While post-Formula of Concord Lutheranism employed justification in opposition to the Catholic concept of grace, infused in the believer by means of sacraments and the ministry of priests, Luther himself focused on the indwelling Christ and union with Christ, identifying justification with the presence of Christ in faith. For Luther, the righteousness that Christ imparts to the believer by virtue of His indwelling presence is always an alien righteousness. The sinner can never claim righteousness on the basis of personal merits—only on the merits of Christ. It needs to be observed that while Luther held that union with Christ is effected in baptism, for Seventh-day Adventists that union is effected in faith. For Adventists, baptism signifies that which has already taken place in faith, illustrating and demonstrating that fact. It is only on the basis that the believer has by faith received Christ, and thereby His righteousness, that the church can expect the baptized person to exhibit evidence of the Christlike life. We also need to remind ourselves that the indwelling Christ will never lead His people in ways that contradict, ignore, or supersede the written Word of God.

The apostle Paul, in a marvelous Trinitarian statement, puts it this way: "You, however, are not in the flesh but in the Spirit, if in fact the Spirit of God dwells in you. Anyone who does not have the Spirit of Christ does not belong to him. But if Christ is in you, although the body is dead because of sin, the Spirit is life because of righteousness. If the Spirit of him who raised Jesus from the dead dwells in you, he who raised Christ Jesus from the dead will also give life to your mortal bodies through his Spirit who dwells in you" (Rom. 8:9-11). God is not aloof from humanity, making declarations from on high. Instead, by means of the ministry of the Holy Spirit and through His Son, Jesus Christ, He is personally involved in the believer's struggle for wholeness. He is present, and makes Himself known, through His gift of faith by which alone He can be known. Thus, Paul prays for the Ephesian church:

"For this reason I bow my knees before the Father, from whom every family in heaven and on earth is named, that according to the riches of his glory he may grant you to be strengthened with power through His Spirit in your inner being, so that Christ may dwell in your hearts through faith—that you, being rooted and grounded in love, may have strength to comprehend with all the saints what is the breadth and length and height and depth, and to know the love of Christ that surpasses knowledge, that you may be filled with all the fullness of God" (Eph. 3:14-19).

Nothing that has not been cleansed and purified by the gracious righteousness of Christ is acceptable to God. We have been saved not only from the penalty, or guilt, of sin, but from the power of sin. We are saved not just from sin but from sinning. The loss of this dynamic truth, central to Paul and to Luther, has served to leech biblical spirituality out of the church and has brought about the major problem of contemporary Protestant Christianity: licentiousness. This truth needs to be recovered. I, for one, am immensely grateful for the recent developments in Finnish research on Luther that have begun the task of recovery. It indicates, as Seventh-day Adventists have insisted, that the Reformation is *not* over and that there is still work to do. The Reformation was never meant to be over. It is a living tradition, not dead history. Ecclesiastical history reveals that apostasy frequently comes from above (i.e., godless leaders) but that awakening comes from below, from the rank and file who yearn for genuine faith and Christlikeness. Ellen White reminds us: "The same arguments are still urged against all who dare to present, in opposition to established errors, the plain and direct teachings of God's Word. 'Who are these preachers of new doctrines?' exclaim those who desire a popular religion. . . . 'How greatly superior in numbers and influence is our church! . . . How much more power is on our side!' These are the arguments that have a telling influence upon the world; but they are no more conclusive now than in the days of [Luther]."[24]

The disciplined, reverent study of the Bible alone can give to the world people of deep spirituality, strong intellect, and nobler principles than has ever been the result of training in human philosophy. We must be willing, as were the blessed Reformers, to accept the light at any cost to ourselves. Therefore, I make no apology for exhorting Adventists to stay true to the fundamental Reformation principle of *sola scriptura*. We must not participate in the scuttling of the Reformation. If we do, Christianity will sink into apostasy and civilization into barbarism. Luther discovered that it is not possible to reform an apostate church. Why? Because there is no basis for reform if the Bible is no longer accepted as the only authority for faith and life.

Why is this message of the righteousness of Christ so sublime, so grand, so lofty? Because of what it does *for* and *in* the born-again believer. "Righteousness within is testified to by righteousness without. He who is righteous within is not hard-hearted and unsympathetic, but day by day he grows into the image of Christ, going on from strength to strength. He who is being sanctified by the truth will be self-controlled, and will follow in the footsteps of Christ until grace is lost in glory."[25]

This sublime message constitutes the center of Adventist theology and spirituality. It profoundly affects the way we think about, and experience, the faith.

Meditation

Before you read further, ponder these questions: If you identify justification with the presence of Christ in faith, why are rituals unnecessary in order to experience it? Why is the faith Christ has given to you, as the means by which to experience justification, enough?

---

[1] E. G. White, *The Great Controversy*, p. 193. (Italics supplied.)

[2] *Ibid.*, p. 195. (Italics supplied.)

[3] Carl E. Braaten and Robert W. Jenson, eds, *Union With Christ: The New Finnish Interpretation of Luther* (Grand Rapids: Eerdmans, 1998).

[4] Washington, D.C.: Ministerial Association of Seventh-day Adventists, 1926.

[5] *Ibid.*, p. 15.

[6] Tuomo Mannermaa, in *Union With Christ*, p. 8.

[7] *Ibid.*, p. 9.

[8] Quoted in *Union With Christ*, p. 6.

[9] *Ibid.*, p. 153.

[10] The *Book of Concord* is the collection of Lutheran confessional documents that includes: the Preface (1580), the Three Chief Symbols (Apostles' Creed, Nicene Creed, Athanasian Creed), Augsburg Confession (1530), Apology of the Augsburg Confession (1531), the Smalcald Articles (1536), Treatise on the Power and Primacy of the Pope (1537), Luther's Small Catechism (1529), Luther's Large Catechism (1529), and the Formula of Concord (1577).

[11] *Union With Christ*, p. 71.

[12] Solid Declaration, Article III.

[13] *Ibid.* (Italics supplied.)

[14] *Union With Christ*, p. viii.

[15] Quoted by Mannermaa in *Union With Christ*, pp. 15, 16.

[16] *Three Treatises* (Philadelphia: Muhlenberg Press, 1960), pp. 280, 286, 294, 288, 305. (Italics supplied.) Adventists understand *soul* as referring to the "inner being" and/or person.

[17] A. G. Daniells, *Christ Our Righteousness*, p. 48.

[18] In *Review and Herald*, June 4, 1895.

[19] *Union With Christ*, p. 42.

[20] *Ibid.*, p. 48.

[21] *Ibid.*, p. 53.

[22] Reinhold Seeberg, *History of Doctrine* (Grand Rapids: Baker), p. 223.

[23] *Knowing God* (Downers Grove, Ill.: InterVarsity Press, 1973), p. 207.

[24] *The Great Controversy*, p. 148.

[25] Ellen G. White, in *Review and Herald*, June 4, 1895.

Chapter 6

THE WAY WE THINK

What I am going to discuss in this chapter has had a profound effect on my own spiritual life and on my professional life as a preacher and professor of preaching. It is a vital part of my own story; nevertheless, it is applicable for any student of the Bible who is interested in the meaning and application of Bible texts.

The day and the occasion are still vivid in my memory. One of my students came to my office to speak with me about the sermon he was preparing. It was obvious by his long face that he was troubled. The text he had chosen was Luke 1:26-55, with special emphasis on the song of Mary, in response to the message of the angel concerning her pregnancy. He had a folder of notes an inch thick. He had done a thorough job of research and uncovering what he felt to be the meaning of the text. But he was intensely disturbed because he sensed his work was somehow incomplete. He said, "I've done all this work and have all these notes, but I don't know what to say!"

I asked him if anything significant had happened to him while he was working with the text and as the text worked with him. His face and eyes lit up, and he responded with a very enthusiastic "Yes!" What had happened was that he felt like praising God. Then the light in his eyes dimmed as he suppressed his response to the text as being too subjective. He was conditioned to think that the Christian experience consists primarily of assent to a body of truth, agreement with a system of theological thought, and that God is not personally and actively involved in the believer's life. For him, the Word of God had become God, and he had difficulty relating to the reality behind the Word. All of this made him suspicious and caused him to deny his response to the text. His momentary experience of joy was real, but part of his brain suppressed it as unworthy and not to be trusted. What he really wanted to share in the sermon was what the Word of God had created in his own immediate experience. *Remember that when God speaks, something happens, because He always speaks a creative word.*

I was able to help this student see that as long as he suppressed that response, he had no living story to tell—only the cold facts his study brought to his attention, as sound as they might be. I suggested that he tell the story, in his sermon, of how the text had exercised its creative power for him—what it had done for and in him, not just what it said.

"Can I really do that?" he asked.

I assured him that indeed he could. When he preached his sermon, it was powerful. Do you know what happened? *It moved the listeners as it had moved him.* Instead of critiquing the sermon, which is always part of the discipline of learning how to preach, the whole class wanted to praise God. So we did! We sang a hymn a capella and knelt down to pray. The same thing happened to the class that had happened to him—when it was allowed to happen, when we did not suppress and hinder the Spirit. It is very unlikely that this student has forgotten what happened that day. I certainly have not.

The Problem

What was this student's problem? It was the same problem that afflicts so many of us. His response to the Word of God was incomplete, because he was a mental cripple. Why? Because of the centuries-old epistemological (way of knowing) split between rational and experiential knowledge, between the intellectual and the affective, intuitive approach to religious knowledge, which ends up with something less than human knowing and human experience. We have brains inside our skulls, but that's not all we are. Human knowledge is not just conceptual; it is also perceptual. This is the basic difference between a faith that believes and a believing faith. What is really at stake is not belief (in truths or doctrines), but believing. My student's sermon was able to move the class to praise, because the text moved him to praise when he was able to permit a total response to it himself.

I was able to help him because of something that had happened to me while I was teaching preaching at the Seventh-day Adventist Theological Seminary, Far East (1979-1981), near Manila, in the republic of the Philippines. It was a pedagogical awakening experience and more. It became a major turning point in my own development as a professor of preaching. I was teaching in eastern Asia, but my approach was typically Western, very technical and didactic. A sermon is made up of three points and a poem. First you tell the congregation what you are going to tell them (introduction); then you tell them (main body); and then you tell them what you told them (conclusion). In the process you transfer cognitive information from your mind to theirs.

Then a student from Africa preached a sermon in class, the major portion of which was a story about a duck indigenous to his homeland. I critiqued him rather severely, I'm ashamed to say. The next day he appeared at my office door, standing there very politely until I noticed him and invited him in. He proceeded to inquire about my wife, my children, our trip to the Philippines, etc. Did we like it here? And so on, consuming precious minutes. My Western mind was chomping at the bit to get down to business. Finally, at my insistence, he got to the point and tried to explain how communication takes place among his African people. But I wouldn't listen and told him that he would have to learn to preach the way I taught it. He suffered through my class, did his best to satisfy me, and graduated.[1]

Then something spiritually significant happened when some time later I preached at the Philippine Union Mission church in Manila. Architecturally the church was a typical basilica type of structure, with a number of pillars in the sanctuary. It was crowded that Sabbath; so many worshippers sat behind the pillars and could not see the preacher. About halfway through the sermon I was startled as heads suddenly appeared from behind every one of the pillars and people craned their necks to see me. I paused for a moment, then continued my sermon. Soon, as suddenly as they had appeared, all the heads disappeared behind the pillars again—which was equally startling.

On my way back to the campus I reconstructed the event in my mind, trying to understand what had happened. At last I realized that at that point in my sermon I had extemporaneously switched preaching methods to talk about how the Bible text affected me personally. That's what pulled all those heads from behind the pillars. They were as interested in my story as they were in the informational content of the sermon. The next day I looked for every book on Eastern anthropology that was available in the seminary library. I wanted to find out, if I could, how communication took place in other cultures, particularly among Filipinos. I discovered what I needed to learn not only from books but also by paying attention to experience, to what was happening around me. What I discovered transformed my own preaching and the way I taught it.

I learned that in that part of the world people are as interested in, and concerned about, the person to whom one speaks as they are in the informational content of the communication. In fact, it seems the person is more important than the information. For example, the woman we employed to help around our home would respond positively to my wife's request that she come on a specific day. She would readily agree, but the day would often come, and she would not appear, coming another day instead. Our Western interpretation was that she was not telling the truth, that she was being deceptive. But she did not see it that way at all. She did not want to disappoint my wife by saying that she could not come on the day requested. The issue was not the factual "No," but my wife's feelings. It is obvious the difficulties this issue can cause in a clash of cultures. But it was important for us to learn to understand how things worked if we were going to live and work in that culture.

In the midst of that learning and adjustment, what should have been obvious became vivid. The Bible is a product, not of the West, but of the Middle East. It is not just propositional truth. It is full of stories, narratives, parables, and symbolic language. What was God's motive for causing and inspiring the writing of the Bible? Love. Love, which is His own essence. The essential and central characteristic of His own person, His own being. "God is love" (1 John 4:16). Yes, love is a principle, but not a cold principle. Love is also an emotion, a feeling. God's brain works the way ours do. He did create us in His image, after all.

Love prompts action—action that is consistent with love's nature. Really and truly. Many times Jesus says, "Truly, I say to you" (Matthew 5:18). He speaks to a *you*, to a person or persons. God's Word is informational, yes, but for *persons*. The goal is not just the transfer of information, but the transformation of the person who reads it or hears it and who understands it. Who eats this bread (1 Cor. 11:26) internalizes it. He or she receives the Word by faith. "God so loved the world, that he gave," not words, but "his only Son" (John 3:16)—a Person given for persons. Are words unimportant then? Of course not. They are the vehicles that inform us of His love. But we are the ones loved. The preacher's task is to retell the old, old story without altering its fundamental truth, as revealed by God, its author, but to retell it in ways that engage the listener on the level where change takes place—the inner being.

How do we overcome the ancient split between rational and experiential knowledge? How can we fulfill Paul's counsel that we "be transformed by the renewal of your mind" (Rom. 12:2)? We need not be enslaved to a crippling mode of processing biblical information, to a total objectivity that is actually a myth. Experiencing this renewal of the mind, learning to respond to God and His revelation with all our faculties, will result in being better able to "discern what is the will of God, what is good and acceptable and perfect" (verse 2).

Cognitive Shift

Could it be that the quality of a person's spiritual life is linked to his or her ability to shift from one way of processing information to another, from logical to visual thinking and knowing? Could it be that it is linked to learning to utilize the power of the whole brain? This utilization involves an expansion of mental powers, a genuine renewal of the mind, leading to increased confidence with respect to an affective response to God and His Word. Perhaps we have not yet tapped the tremendous force and power of the total human brain. Perhaps we have not undertaken the task of overcoming barriers to creativity, barriers to the full impact of the Word on our human consciousness. In this computer age we are in grave danger of becoming data-dominated people, virtually detached from the human and the real. There are truths to be known and experienced from God that are beyond the reach of reason alone, truths that are a part of what Paul calls the "mystery" in Ephesians 3. Ellen White puts it this way:

"Many things are above finite comprehension. Truths are to be received not within the reach of our reason. and not for us to explain. Revelation presents them to us to be implicitly received as the words of an infinite God. While every ingenious inquirer is to search out the truth as it is in Jesus, there are things not yet simplified, statements that human minds cannot grasp and reason out, without being liable to make human calculation and explanations, which will not prove a savor of life unto life."[2]

That statement ought to put to rest, for Seventh-day Adventists, the temptation to toy with the idea that human thought and reason are the only source of religious knowledge. She is not saying that religious experience is the criteria for interpreting Scripture. She is warning us not to put either human reason or experience above God's revelation, which is to be "implicitly received," even though it cannot be fully grasped and explained. At the same time, she does not subordinate reason to that which is above finite comprehension, but says that reason alone inhibits, or blocks, the transmission of truth that is beyond reason. Her understanding is wholistic.

Truths that are beyond the reach of reason are to be received. Though they defy rational explanation, they are to be received as revelation from God. How does that happen? Remember: "You must learn to see with your brain as well as your eyes." The result is what we call insight. The function of the brain must be stretched beyond its traditionally understood mode if it is to be renewed. The brain is not just to think with analytically, but to "see" with by utilizing its imaging ability, the kind of imaging that produced Ezekiel 1, wherein the prophet describes what he "saw"—"visions of God" (verse 1) and "the appearance of the likeness of the glory of the Lord. And when I saw it, I fell on my face, and I heard the voice of one speaking" (verse 28). This method of seeing, of knowing, can be—indeed, must be—learned.

"The *faculties* of the mind need cultivation, that they may be exercised to the glory of God. Careful attention should be given to the culture of the intellect, that the *various organs* of the mind may have *equal* strength by being brought into exercise, each in its *distinctive office.* . . . If one faculty is suffered to remain dormant, or is turned out of its proper course, the purpose of God is not carried out. All the faculties should be *well developed.* Care should be given to each, for each has a bearing upon the others, and all *must be exercised* in order that the mind be properly *balanced.* If one or two organs are cultivated and kept in continual use because it is the choice of your children to put the strength of the mind in one direction to the neglect of other mental powers, they will come to maturity with *unbalanced* minds and inharmonious characters. They will be apt and strong in one direction, but greatly deficient in other directions *just as important.* They will not be competent men and women. Their deficiencies will be marked, and will mar the entire character."[3]

The practical application of Ellen White's insight is found in the statement of methodology with which she begins her study of Jesus' sermon on the mount: "Let us *in imagination* go back to that scene, and, as we sit with the disciples on the mountainside, *enter into the thoughts and feelings* that filled their *hearts.* Understanding what the words of Jesus meant to those who heard them, we may discern in them a new *vividness and beauty,* and may also gather for ourselves their *deeper* lessons."[4]

Why is this so vitally important? Because, as Ellen White so perceptively articulates, "the brain nerves which communicate with the entire system are the *only* medium through which Heaven can communicate to man and affect his *inmost* life."[5] Obviously this exclusive medium of communication between God and human beings involves both the left and right hemispheres of the brain. Writing about preachers, she says, "God wants all their brain power to be used in proclaiming the gospel as it is in Christ Jesus."[6] These are all-inclusive, comprehensive statements packed with wisdom and insight, written many decades before the exciting brain research of the 1960s and beyond.

Problem of Epistemology

The problem of epistemology, how human beings know, has intrigued humankind for centuries. Both philosophy and science have been interested in the question. It is a primary question today for a nuclear humanity who has not only lost faith in technology but is terrified by it. Fragmented people are those for whom the distinctions between good and bad, ugly and beautiful, attractive and repulsive, have lost their meaning. They are eager for any experience, eager to try anything, without questioning its value or morality.

Philosophically, we have been trapped by the popular notion that there is a division between thinking and perceiving, and that thinking (rational/analytical) is the higher cognitive function of the mind. The rationalists of the seventeenth and eighteenth centuries were of the opinion that the messages of the senses are confused and unreliable and that only reason can clarify them. Technicians would probably agree, while artists certainly would not. Early in the educational process the senses begin to lose educational status. Art, for example, becomes supplementary, and fewer hours of the week can be spared from studying things that "really matter" in a technological age. If Ellen White is right, this shift leads inexorably to underdevelopment, imbalance, deficiency, and incompetence, and the purpose of God for human life is thwarted. That is a serious charge and a serious situation indeed.

This loss of status for the senses in relationship to reason was certainly my experience as a kid starting out in the educational process. I still remember vividly my kindergarten class and my very lovable teacher, Miss Alice Kleffman. There were no desks in her classroom. The furniture consisted of small tables and chairs, moved about randomly to meet differing learning situations. There were big jars of colorful paints and large easels on which hung huge sheets of paper. With big brushes we enthusiastically dabbed away and created "works of art" that made Miss Kleffman and our parents exclaim with pleasure as our eyes beamed. Then they were displayed for everyone in the school to see. There was also a large, deep table filled with sand in which we constructed a Dutch village, complete with windmills and a "real" canal, filled with water and boats. There was also a large, comfortable rug on which we gathered to hear Miss Kleffman tell exciting stories. It was such a happy time. I loved it! I loved her, too. I wish I could have stayed in kindergarten forever. But that was not to be.

All of us kids were "promoted" to first grade. With such a wonderful experience behind me, I was eager for the next step. How disappointed I was when I walked into the first-grade classroom. Desks were lined up in neat rows, with a big teacher's desk up front. I don't remember the teacher's name. There was a huge blackboard on two long walls, and above them I saw numbers and letters—1234567890 and ABCDEFGHIJKLMNOPQRSTUVWXYZ. No more easels, paint, brushes, sand table, or rug. Everyone had to sit up straight and pay attention to what the teacher said. There was no moving around and very little interaction. I remember the day we kids were all excited about the bird that was building a nest in a tree just outside the window. The teacher rapped her ruler vigorously on her desk, saying sharply, "Children! Look at me and pay attention, or you won't learn anything today!" *Really?* What might have happened had she gathered us around the window instead and asked us questions about what we thought the bird was doing and why? She could have talked to us about birds and animals and nature and building a home for one's family and raising children. Maybe we would have learned something important that day. Don't you think that with understanding and sensitivity we can begin to heal the unwholesome split that actually cripples the whole process of human knowing?

Much more may have been involved when the ancient Hebrews destroyed a piece of sculpture—the golden calf that Moses burned, ground to powder, and scattered on the water that the Israelites were made to drink. That may have been the beginning, but it was the Greek philosophers who conceived of the dichotomy between reasoning and perceiving, even though they were not as rigid as we have become in Western thought. We call this dichotomy progress. Indeed it is, technically. But whether it has been progress, humanly speaking, is highly debatable. At least it has made psychiatry and psychoanalysis very lucrative professions in an entirely unbalanced civilization.

People noticed early on that what the eyes reported was not always true. A stick dipped in water appeared bent or broken. A distant object looked small. One suffering from jaundice saw everything yellow. The sun appeared to rise (pre-Galileo). Sensory perception is an illusion, some concluded. The criteria for evaluating perception was supposed to come from reasoning. Sensory perception and reasoning became enemies, though they were in need of each other.

Plato's views were ambiguous. He believed in the operation of logic, the study of which is no longer required for a B.A. degree, as it was when I was in college. But he also believed in direct vision. Reality can be grasped by direct vision, that is to say, all learning is by recollection or remembrance (*anamnesis* in Greek). In the Christian tradition there is no more vivid experience of this than in the Eucharist, the celebration of the Lord's Supper, during which the Last Supper of Christ is ritually acted out and experienced. "*Do* this in remembrance [*anamnesis*] of me" (Luke 22:19) is saying something far different than "*Think* this in remembrance of me." Plato warned of the danger of trusting the senses, yet speaks of "gazing upon truth." While he recognized the reality of sense perception, he mistrusted it profoundly. For him, sensory images were actually outside the realm of reality.

Aristotle introduced the idea of induction—knowledge based on an accumulation of similar and verifiable data. He is often referred to as the father of empirical research. Yet at the same time he said that the essence of matter was not material, but that which matters. So the Greeks learned to distrust the senses, while insisting that direct vision is the first and final source of wisdom and knowledge. Aristotle said, "The soul never thinks without an image."

The ancient Greeks also observed that loss of speech often followed injury to the brain in combat. By the beginning of the nineteenth century, medical science was aware that this phenomenon was associated with the particular side of the brain damaged. Injury to the left side usually resulted in loss of speech or serious speech difficulty. Gradually attention was given to the idea that particular functions could be assigned to specific regions of the brain. By 1870 the left hemisphere of the brain was considered to be dominant, or higher, because both producing and understanding speech, as well as the ability to read and write, were attributed to it. This was called cerebral dominance, based on the assumption that analytical powers are superior to intuitive and affective powers. By the 1930s enough data had accumulated, pointing to right-brain specialization, to cause a reconsideration of this view. Why is it that the ability to sing is frequently unaffected in people suffering from severe speech disturbances? Musical ability is often lost following damage to the right hemisphere, while speech ability remains intact.

Since the early 1960s it has been known that when the corpus callosum, a nerve cord that connects the two hemispheres of the brain, is severed in operations designed to relieve epileptic seizures, one side of the brain cannot communicate with the other. This has made it possible to gather more precise information on the specialization of the two hemispheres. Each side processes information in its own way.

Physiologically, the left side of the brain controls movement on the right side of the body, and the right side controls movement on the left. As far as the inner being is concerned, the left is the logical side of the brain, and the right is the intuitive. The left side is the verbal side that understands and chooses words with respect to speech, reading, and writing, while the right side is the nonverbal side, with the ability to understand and communicate via images. The left side is analytical, remembering facts, recalling names and dates, evaluating facts rationally, while the right side is wholistic, making leaps of insight, evaluating whole problems at once, and recognizing faces. The left side is literal and lineal in interpreting data (one-step-at-a-time thinking), while the right side is spatial, seeing persons, things, and places, in relationship. The left side is mathematical, while the right side is artistic, musical, and imaginative, dealing more comfortably with fantasy, dreams, visions, and speculation. That hemisphere must have been the side of the brain that Ezekiel used when in vision he described the glory of God as whirling "wheels" like the "gleaming of beryl" and "as it were a wheel within a wheel" (Eze. 1:16). How about John's descriptive visionary account in the book of Revelation, as well as Ellen White's experience with visions? The right brain is the emotional side. It is also the spiritual side that participates in, and enjoys, worship, prayer, and meditation, and appreciates religious symbols. While the left side is conceptual, the right is perceptual. The left side is cognitive, the right affective.

Perhaps this can help us understand why men, who tend to be left-brain dominant creatures, often don't understand their wives, who tend to be right-brain dominant and make intuitive leaps. We men find it difficult to comprehend how women can often arrive at correct conclusions so quickly, without going through the analytical, step-by-step process of logical thought. We find it difficult to understand why we cannot get a simple yes or no answer to a question. It drives us crazy! Maybe it also explains why some people cannot stand a digital watch, preferring to see the relationship between the numbers.

Modes of Consciousness

The human mind has two modes of consciousness: (1) rational/analytical, and (2) intuitional/wholistic. The first mode is concerned with the external world, objects, and events. The other mode is concerned with the world within, with feelings and imagination. The right brain readily employs figures, symbols, and images to mediate meaning. It makes judgments based on an internalized set of values. Spiritually speaking, this capacity to assess is why it is so essential to internalize the truth, to allow the truth as it is in Jesus to affect the right brain. In order to understand religious experience adequately, we must be ready to cultivate this faculty of our minds, as Ellen White suggests, accepting and trusting the intuitive/wholistic mode of consciousness, together with the rational/analytical. Combining the two is not only possible but desirable. If we did, we might have more appreciation for the liturgical drama involved in worship (see Revelation 4 and 5), in particular the symbolism of baptism and the Lord's Supper.

In order to experience a balanced spirituality fully, both hemispheres of our brains need to be engaged. The Bible says, "Do not despise prophecies" (1 Thess. 5:20), but it also says, "Do not quench the Spirit" (verse 19). We are to test them both, and "hold fast what is good. Abstain from every form of evil" (verses 21, 22). Left-brain consciousness is satisfied with a faith that believes, whereas right-brain consciousness wants a believing faith, an experiential knowledge of God in Christ. Not dead orthodoxy, but a living faith, which is "*present* truth."

Many people become acutely aware at midlife of this intuitive/wholistic consciousness that suddenly appears because of a crisis or aging, initiating a new awareness. The ego (self) ceases to demand exclusive control over the activities of life, recognizes its own limitations, and begins to allow new directions. The individual finds personal feelings, opinions, philosophies, attitudes, etc., undergoing sometimes radical and mysterious —even baffling—change. Religiously speaking, this change can be experienced as conversion that awakens and deepens spiritual growth, sanctification, and character building.

It is obvious that we need to accept the validity of the right-brain response spiritually and to recognize it as a special channel for receiving truths not accessible to the analytical left brain alone. We need to cultivate this faculty of the mind for God's glory and for a balanced and wholistic spiritual experience. Ellen White says:

"God takes men as they are, and educates them for His service, if they will yield themselves to Him. The Spirit of God, received *into the soul*, quickens *all its faculties*. Under the guidance of the Holy Spirit, the mind that is devoted unreservedly to God develops *harmoniously*, and is strengthened to comprehend and fulfill the requirements of God. The weak, vacillating character becomes changed to one of strength and steadfastness. Continual devotion establishes so close a relation between Jesus and His disciples that the Christian becomes like his Master in character. He has clearer, broader views. His discernment is more penetrative, his judgment better *balanced*. So quickened is he by the life-giving power of the Sun of Righteousness that he is enabled to bear much fruit to the glory of God."[7]

How do we maintain balance in the spiritual use of mental powers? "Christ came to this world and lived the law of God, that man might have perfect mastery over the natural inclinations which corrupt the soul. The Physician of soul and body, He gives victory over warring lusts. He has provided every facility, that man may possess completeness of character."[8] The whole mind must be brought under the control of the Holy Spirit. What is it that blocks full spiritual use of perception? Sin. "Pride, self-love, selfishness, hatred, envy, and jealousy have beclouded the *perceptive* powers."[9]

Putting together an understanding of the different ways that the two hemispheres of the human brain process information, along with Spirit of Prophecy counsel regarding the need to strengthen all the faculties of the brain, I learned to "see" insightfully with the brain and to recognize that there are things to know and understand that are above reason. Thus, I was prepared for a new approach to how to teach preaching.

New Approach

The opportunity for a new approach to teaching ministerial students how to preach came at Andrews University when I was scheduled to teach a course entitled Preaching From the New Testament.

I had discovered on that one momentous Sabbath in the Philippines that there is power in telling the story of how the biblical text affected my own faith experience—power that pulled heads from behind pillars. I have even noticed that when I am asked a direct question, I often begin my answer with "I'm going to tell you a story." So I determined to teach the students in that course how to preach, not didactic sermons, but narrative ones—to tell the story of the Bible text, their own story, and by doing so, to tell the listener's story. Preachers need to be careful that their stories and the listener's stories are analogous to the story in the text so that the listener can identify with, and become engaged in, the preaching and in imagination sit before the biblical scene. Have you noticed that adults in a congregation are often as interested in the children's story as the kids are, or even more?

Narrative preaching means preachers cannot confine themselves to a strictly historical/grammatical method of interpretation. They may skillfully ascertain the original meaning of a Bible text but fail to discover and articulate its meaning for contemporary life, because they never go beyond asking what the text says and what it means in its original historical context. And because they never ask (because they have never been encouraged to do so or learned to do so) what the text is doing in them and with them or how the Word of God is exercising its creative power. In their study, preachers may have discovered the meaning of the text *then*, whereas their listeners are interested in its meaning *now*. A strictly technical approach to textual interpretation usually does not ask experiential questions related to the meaning of existence. What the listeners need and want are new perceptions, new perspectives on life in the contemporary world that will contribute toward transformation. A strictly historical/grammatical method of interpretation, as necessary and valid as it is as a part of the preparation process, reduces interpreters to technicians, mere instruments for transmitting information. What preachers have to do is to help modern hearers apply the original, historical meaning of the text to contemporary life in order to discover meaning for their present existence. To do that effectively, preachers must permit the text to grip them, interpret them, so that they become participants in the biblical story, not just technicians who transmit the informational content of the text. Ultimately, the meaning of a text can be understood only in the context of contemporary life. The text is far more than an object of knowledge. It has an intentionality of its own that interprets us, illumines our lives, rather than being simply the object of our investigation.

This approach is based on a descriptive biblical theology, which makes possible a more direct translation of biblical meaning to contemporary life and thought. The intervening years between the time the text was written and the present, with their accumulation of theologians and theologies, are not a barrier to understanding. Interpreters' problems are not so much philosophical, traditional, or historical as they are linguistic. They ask: In what kind of language do I best describe what happened then so that the historical meaning of a biblical text can be related to contemporary life? So that it can *happen* again? After all, the Word came originally in the form of language, and it comes again in the same way— or it does not come at all.

To preach narratively, preachers have to gnaw on their text as a dog gnaws on a bone. A dog will gnaw on a bone all day because it's after the marrow that's inside. It won't stop until it gets to the marrow. One gnaws on a Bible text for preaching, as well as for general study, by asking questions that have to do with (1) what the text says, (2) what it means, and (3) what it does. Questions such as: What is the information from God in the text that is universally and eternally valid? What is the text saying when it speaks for itself? What is the intentionality of the text, the purpose for which it was written? To what human need does the text address itself? What are the explicit and/or implicit elements in the text that will make possible a narrative approach? Which elements have major referential value? Which have minor referential value? What makes the elements significant, and how do they relate to life? What are the factors that tie the elements together in a meaningful whole and provide the clue to contemporary meaning? What is the text's major emphasis, or underlying purpose, which will determine the direction of the sermon or the study? What are the students' own personal needs, fears, hopes, etc., that the text calls to their attention? What are the students' own reactions and attitudes toward life and the world in which they live and work that the text forces to the surface of their minds? What are the elements in the text that are models or examples of typical human life in the world? What is the connecting system, the arrangement of words, that gives unity and progression to the story? This list is certainly not exhaustive. Using both sides of your brain, you will learn to ask other questions as you gnaw on a Bible text for preaching or teaching or sharing.

Having discovered the goal of the text by this process of gnawing, preachers will focus sermons on a similar goal. The narrators must know what they are doing. They are not telling a story for the sake of the story, or to entertain, but for the sake of the persons who are listening for the creative Word of God and hearing it. Their concern must become apparent as the narration unfolds (see John 10:1-21). In order for them to do this, the narration must use concrete, commonplace imagery.

In order to help my preaching students learn how to engage the right side of their brains, I sometimes asked them to draw a picture of their response to the sermon text and bring it to class the next day for "show and tell." I recall one big guy, who was never shy about expressing an opinion, saying, "You've got to be kidding, Dr. Holmes! Are you serious?" I assured him that I was. Reluctantly, very reluctantly, he brought his work to class the next day. When it was his turn, he unrolled a large sheet of paper on which he had drawn a very large circle. Inside the circle was a scene including buildings, landscape, and people. Of course, some of it was upside down or sideways. After his explanation, I asked if the exercise had helped him get insight into the meaning of the text that he might not have had otherwise. Sheepishly he said, "Well, I hate to admit it, but it did. It gave me a new perspective that turned my assumptions upside down and inside out."

In preparation for narrative preaching, interpreters allow themselves to be drawn into the biblical story. They approach sermon preparation at the most personal level, which makes it an act of prayerful devotion. Interpreters do not stand aloof as mere technicians. Instead, they are participants, accomplices, collaborators. Without such involvement *the* Word cannot do its work; it cannot become *a* Word for them. Interpreters are not merely reacting to the data in the text; they become part of the biblical story because it has become part of their own faith story. They are there in the midst of their own thoughts and experiences. The issues Paul dealt with in Romans, for example, were personal experiential issues that he worked through and then communicated to the church. His reflections on God's revelation were inward-thinking, because the search for personal answers is always done inwardly. The kind of thinking that is done in biblical interpretation cannot be separated from the person (*being*) doing the thinking. Students must first listen to God, as He speaks through the text, before they can be communicators of that speech to others. Something happens to them in their personal Bible study. The Word does something to them, with them, in them. Change takes place as the Word draws preachers in, interprets their lives, executes its creative power, and shapes their own spirituality. Then they are compelled to share it with others, because they have been given a message. Much more is happening than the preparation of a sermon; the Holy Spirit is preparing preachers to preach.

Preachers are sensitive to the fact that language operates on both the affective and the cognitive levels. This fact is true for biblical language as much as for the language used in the sermon. Reality is perceived through the medium of language. The language of the Bible and the sermonic language have the power to change perception and so change human behavior. Even nonverbal communication is understood and interpreted by means of language, though unspoken; thus, words are still the vehicle. Metaphorical language, too, operates on both the affective and cognitive levels, which is why interpreters need to ascertain which elements in a text serve to inform and which touch the emotions. They need to learn how to use these in sermonizing to move hearers to understanding and experience. When they have made this determination, the structure of the narrative may move from the affective to the cognitive level of meaning, or from the cognitive to the affective level. At any rate, the sermonic goal is to help the hearers go, as they have gone personally, from a surface level of meaning to a deeper level, to the inner being, where real transformation takes place. To be sure, all of this is not done in isolation from a corporate consciousness. The text must be read and studied in terms of the corporate doctrinal/theological story of the whole church, as well as being part of the interpreters' own stories. This means that the interpretation of the text, although contemporary, contextual, and relevant, is not private. It is done in the historical context of Christian, and Seventh-day Adventist, confessional history.

The result of the narrative should be that both interpreters and listeners come to a satisfactory conclusion because of changed perception, that they discover meaning that makes sense and is spiritually moving. As with most storytelling, this discovery occurs as speakers move from figurative, metaphorical language to literal, discursive language, as Jesus often did. The conclusion will either answer questions (doctrinal/philosophical) or bring about a new focus of life (experiential/ontological) or both. As the listeners begin to make sense out of their own life on the basis of the narrative, they will make decisions with respect to ideas and to their response in terms of behavioral change.

The basic structure of the narrative sermon will look something like this: 1. The first part (called the introduction in a typical didactic sermon), in which the goal is to establish a certain mood or tone that will largely determine the nature of the mediating language of the sermon. 2. The second part of the narrative (called the main body in a didactic sermon), in which the textual elements are related to one another, clues to meaning are presented, and the theme or idea is developed in relation to details, creating a unity and progression that is sensible and establishes the value of the text. The goal is to lead to ideation and/or insight, which is the climax of the sermonic narration. Here preachers attempt to surprise listeners with the cognizance they are after. At this point in the sermonic event it is hoped that listeners will respond with comprehension. Meaning is discovered and related transformationally to life. Truth has arrived, and new perception occurs. 3. When truth arrives, narration is over, and the sermon is ended. What is said now (called the conclusion in a didactic sermon) reinforces previously held meaning, introduces new meaning (*insight*), transforms old meaning into new meaning, or enhances old meaning. The biblical story has become part of the listeners' own stories, and the sermon is finished. If that has not happened, preachers may stop talking, but the sermon remains unfinished, because the Word was sent to *do* something as well as *say* something.

Why have I included this chapter about spirituality and the mind, especially as it concerns preachers and preaching, in this book? Because when it comes to spirituality, *as the pulpit goes so goes the church*. There is no better way to close this chapter than with this insightful statement by Ellen White: "The student of the Word finds himself bending over a fountain of living water. The church needs to drink deeply of the spirituality of the Word. Their service to God needs to be very different from the tame, lifeless, emotionless religious experience that makes many believers but little different from those who believe not, very similar in spirit to the unconverted."[10]

Meditation

Focus for a few moments on John 3:16, asking first: "What is this text saying to me?" Then: "What does it mean for me?" Then: "What is it doing in me?" How is God exercising His creative power within you by means of this verse? Do you perceive His power working in your heart? Now draw a picture of your *response* to the verse. Did that exercise help with perception? Are you better able to tell the story in a personal way?

---

[1] I thought I would never see him again. But on the road I travel, the Lord graciously arranged for us to meet again some years later on the sidewalk in front of the library at Andrews University. I apologized for my insensitivity and failure to hear him and understand on the day he came to my office to talk to me about his sermon.

[2] Ellen G. White, *Selected Messages* (Washington, D.C.: Review and Herald Pub. Assn., 1958), book 1, p. 163.

[3] E. G. White, *Testimonies for the Church*, vol. 3, p. 26. (Italics supplied.)

[4] E. G. White, *Thoughts From the Mount of Blessing*, p. 1. (Italics supplied.) She is not urging us to use imagination with respect to anything that might enter our consciousness, but to focus on the scenes presented to that consciousness by Scripture.

[5] Ellen G. White, *Child Guidance* (Washington, D.C.: Review and Herald Pub. Assn., 1954), p. 447. (Italics supplied.)

[6] Ellen G. White, *Evangelism* (Washington, D.C.: Review and Herald Pub. Assn., 1946), p. 663.

[7] E. G. White, *Gospel Workers*, pp. 285, 286. (Italics supplied.) In this passage, the word *soul* obviously refers to the mind.

[8] E. G. White, *The Ministry of Healing*, pp. 130, 131.

[9] E. G. White, *Testimonies for the Church*, vol. 2, p. 605. (Italics supplied.)

[10] *The Seventh-day Adventist Bible Commentary*, Ellen G. White Comments, vol. 7, p. 964.

Chapter 7

HANDLING SPIRITUAL CRISIS

When one listens carefully to the story someone tells about his or her own spiritual journey, some sort of crisis is frequently a part of that story, referred to in terms such as "struggle," "trial," "pain," or "suffering." When the story is told publicly, this component is sometimes not mentioned, even though it was very significant in the experience of a developing spirituality. But in private conversations or sessions with a trusted pastor or trained spiritual counselor, it is sometimes related in great detail—usually, because the one telling the story desperately wants help dealing with it and understanding how the experience is being used by God to shape character. When he or she understands that, a believing faith can accept it for what it is—the indwelling Christ and the Holy Spirit doing their gracious work of transformation, sanctification, and discipline.

Crisis came early for me, around age 10. While playing tag in the dark, I ran into a fence made of a single strand of wire. As a result of the injury, I developed a curvature of the spine that has caused me physical and emotional pain for most of my life. Far into my teens I was laughed at, pointed at, and called "Daffy Duck."[1] Perhaps you can imagine the kind of emotional trauma such jeering and taunting caused. I rarely speak of it, because it is emotionally painful. Nevertheless, it has been a most significant portion of the road I travel.

I dare to speak of it here, even though there is a risk in doing so. Risk, because it is easy to discount as irrelevant, insignificant, self-centered, and even silly what another person considers to be crisis. I hope my experience will be helpful as the introduction for this chapter, dealing with a subject that we would rather avoid. I am so glad (aren't you?) that "the Lord sees not as man sees," and that while "man looks on the outward appearance, . . . the Lord looks on the heart" (1 Sam. 16:7).

Did I learn a spiritual lesson from that experience and trauma? I have to say yes, and I'm still learning from it, even though it was many years before the miracle of a believing faith happened to me. I was already on the road toward it, though I didn't realize it. My "atheist" father,[2] together with some chickens, helped me begin to get a glimpse of it. My early teen years coincided with the years of World War II and the food rationing that was mandatory for everyone. To help alleviate the situation, my father sent for a flock of baby chicks by mail order and turned our garage into a chicken coop. I still remember the day they arrived in three large boxes with holes in the top and sides, so they could breathe. Confined in those boxes for several days, they must have been hungry, as their frantic peeping seemed to imply. My father enjoyed sitting on an overturned pail and watching them as they scrambled for food and water. But as the days went by, he noticed that the chicks were not letting one of their number get to the food. Every time this little chick tried to eat, the others would peck at it and drive it away. In compassion, my father caught it, intending to feed it by hand, when he saw that it had a deformed bill—the top was twisted over the bottom. The deformity didn't prevent the chick from eating or drinking; the other chicks wouldn't let it eat simply because it was different, not normal. First lesson: humans are often just like chickens. My father nurtured that chick, feeding it by hand every day until it matured and began to lay eggs along with the others. It developed into the most productive layer of the flock, but the others never accepted it as one of their own. That chicken learned to trust my father and would always run to him when he appeared. It survived until the war was over, which wasn't the case for most of the others, who eventually found themselves in my mother's stewpot. Second lesson: compassion is productive and rewarding.

My teens were miserable years (made doubly so by the cumbersome orthopedic appliance I had to wear that made my posture even more obvious), but they were sprinkled with some compassionate people who helped me survive. Some stand out in my memory, such as two very special high school teachers who befriended and nurtured me. Another was Curtis Christian, a close friend. He eventually became the police chief of my hometown, Waukegan, Illinois. These individuals were followed by others through the years, some of whom I have mentioned earlier in this narrative. I am overwhelmed by, and so grateful for, the gifts of love and respect that come my way from Shirley, my wife of 55 years, from our two adopted children and their families, together with so many friends and colleagues in ministry, and countless faithful parishioners. This portion of the road I travel has helped me understand the apostle Paul, who speaks of himself as "one untimely born . . . the least of the apostles . . . [and] unworthy to be called an apostle," and declares that "by the grace of God I am what I am, and his grace toward me was not in vain" (1 Cor. 15:8-10).

As with Paul, it is by the grace of God alone that I am who and what I am. The "who" and the "what" provide the answer to the "why."

When the Lord found me, I was such a timid introvert that He had to transform me from the inside out. For this reason the "call" to ministry was a major challenge for me; it would put me in the public eye, making me so much more visible and vulnerable, when my preference was to withdraw and hide. That temptation rears its ugly head from time to time even after all these years, but my gracious Lord always helps me get the victory over it. You cannot imagine how I rejoiced when, in my early Bible reading, I came across the personal crisis story of the apostle Paul (2 Cor. 12:2-10). After acknowledging that he had received "revelations of the Lord" and things that "cannot be told," he said: "So to keep me from being conceited because of the surpassing greatness of the revelations, a thorn was given me in the flesh, a messenger of Satan to harass me, to keep me from becoming conceited. Three times I pleaded with the Lord about this, that it should leave me. But he said to me, 'My grace is sufficient for you, for my power is made perfect in weakness.' Therefore I will boast all the more gladly of my weaknesses, so that the power of Christ may rest upon me. For the sake of Christ, then, I am content with weaknesses, insults, hardships, persecutions, and calamities. For when I am weak, then I am strong" (verses 7-10).

We don't really know what it was that troubled Paul so. We don't have to know. The important thing is how he handled it, and the spiritual lesson he learned in the process. Notice that what Paul calls a "thorn" was *given* to him. Given by whom? He called it "a messenger of Satan." He didn't say exactly that Satan gave it to him, though that could be what he is implying. At any rate, whatever its origin, it was permitted and used by God to teach Paul a valuable spiritual lesson. He needed to learn that no matter his personal circumstances, God's grace would be sufficient and that on that basis he could be content with the situation. When I read those verses, I was inwardly empowered to stop asking God to straighten out my spine and to accept in faith whatever He wished to teach me as a result of it. It hasn't been easy, but you tell me if my response wasn't an exercise in believing faith.

Phases of the Spiritual Journey

During the course of my own spiritual journey, I have identified at least six phases. They could be called transitional points or divine moments. They are:

1. The WOW phase, a time of the *discovery* of God's truth when I first

found the Lord, or rather He found me, and I learned so many new and exciting things about Jesus and the faith.

2. The WHEE phase, a time of *assimilation,* during which new truth discoveries were internalized and became a part of my spiritual experience as I took each new step of faith.

3. The WHAM phase, a time of *confrontation,* with the new confronting the old, the worldview of the kingdom of God confronting that of the fallen world. I was confronted with the changes the Lord asked of me. Like a baby learning to walk, I learned to walk in "newness of life." This is the phase in which new believers discover that they have spiritual enemies—Satan and the flesh.

4. The WOE phase, a time of *struggle,* learning to exercise a believing faith, resulting in obedience to the will and purpose of God.

5. The WHEN phase, a time of *longing,* involving anticipation, expectation, and the hope of glory when Jesus comes again. This phase enlarges and deepens as one grows older, and it becomes clearer that the conflicts, external and internal, will be over and victory finally won. In this phase I discovered what hope was all about.

6. The GRAND WOW phase, which involves *ultimate fulfillment* that is yet to come. The Bible refers to this future promise of fulfillment as the new heaven and new earth that God has prepared for those who have loved Him, worshipped Him, waited for Him, and served Him, for "God himself will be with them as their God. He will wipe every tear from their eyes, and death shall be no more, neither shall there be mourning, nor crying, nor pain anymore, for the former things have passed away" (Rev. 21:3, 4).

Each phase involves change, transformation, often crisis, and always new meaning. The journey is dynamic, not static, and mostly internal. The apostle Paul expressed it this way:

"But whatever gain I had, I counted as loss for the sake of Christ. Indeed, I count everything as loss because of the surpassing worth of knowing Christ Jesus my Lord. For his sake I have suffered the loss of all things and count them as rubbish, in order that I may gain Christ and be found in him, not having a righteousness of my own that comes from the law, but that which comes through faith in Christ, the righteousness from God that depends on faith—that I may know him and the power of his resurrection, and may share his sufferings, becoming like him in his death, that by any means possible I may attain the resurrection of the dead.

"Not that I have already obtained this or am already perfect, but I press on to make it my own, because Christ Jesus has made me his own.

Brothers, I do not consider that I have made it my own. But one thing I do: forgetting what lies behind and straining forward to what lies ahead, I press on toward the goal for the prize of the upward call of God in Christ Jesus. Let those of us who are mature think this way, and if in anything you think otherwise, God will reveal that also to you. Only let us hold true to what we have attained.

"Brothers, join in imitating me, and keep your eyes on those who walk according to the example you have in us. For many, of whom I have often told you and now tell you even with tears, walk as enemies of the cross of Christ. Their end is destruction, their god is their belly, and they glory in their shame, with minds set on earthly things. But our citizenship is in heaven, and from it we await a Savior, the Lord Jesus Christ, who will transform our lowly body to be like his glorious body, by the power that enables him even to subject all things to himself" (Phil. 3:7-21).

The phase cycle is repeated when fulfillment leads to new discovery, and so we press on. One who is engaged in this phase cycle is a participant in spirituality. He or she is being shaped by the Holy Spirit and being conformed to the image of God. I remember a woman in my first parish who came to me with her spiritual struggle. Why she felt she could trust such a young, inexperienced spiritual counselor, I don't know. She told me that her struggle was with impatience. She desperately wanted patience, especially in regard to her husband. She prayed and prayed, but only seemed to have more trouble.

What was I to do? In terms of pastoring, I was not yet dry behind the ears, though my head was filled with theology and psychological theory. Because I didn't know what to say, I thought I would take myself off the hook by quoting the Bible. Did I ever learn something! That turned out to be the best thing I could have done. Why? Because the power is in the Word, not in me or in psychological theory. So I read to her, "We rejoice in our sufferings, knowing that suffering produces endurance" (Rom. 5:3).

Rejoice in suffering? Is it possible? It must be, or Paul wouldn't say it. This kind of persevering patience, as almost everything else, is learned behavior. The Holy Spirit has to do something *in* us to accomplish it. The way we handle spiritual crisis is an inner decision, made possible by the spiritual resources God makes available to us. Was God answering that woman's prayer? She began to realize that He was, and her perception was transformed. We may not always like the means God uses to teach us vital spiritual lessons, but He is sovereign, after all, and in charge of our lives. That's scriptural, too. Yes, God was answering her prayer, but not in the way she imagined. She thought He should, would, take her problem away. Instead, He used it to teach her a valuable spiritual lesson. She needed and wanted patience, and He was teaching her patience through a most effective means. We don't need patience when we aren't experiencing tribulation. It is precisely when there is tribulation in the life that we need patience. And in God's plan of operation it is the tribulation itself that teaches us the patience that we need in order to deal with it. Extremely difficult external situations, especially those over which we have no control, give us the opportunity to grow spiritually, beyond ourselves, in the inner being.

In a spiritual growth crisis, one confronts a critical point in the process, crosses a threshold, and enters a deeper self-awareness and relationship with God. There comes a deeper consciousness of His presence. Crossing critical spiritual thresholds involves: (1) a period of *disintegration,* in which self-confidence and self-righteousness crumble away, (2) a period of *transition,* in which the new principles of confidence in God and in His righteousness alone take their place, and (3) a period of satisfying *integration,* in which those new principles are permitted to transform, guide, and direct one's life. Such is the process of spiritual *trans*formation.

Suffering

The focus of this chapter is on the aspect of crisis called "suffering," in order to be able to see and appreciate its significance in Christian spirituality. By way of example, go back with me to Christmas 1980, when I was alone in the Philippines. Shirley and our children had already gone home to the United States, but I had to complete my term of service. It was rough being so far away from home and family, and I needed to talk about it with someone. So I shared my misery with a colleague. He listened, then handed me a book written by a man who, as a young Jew, spent three years in Auschwitz and Dachau, two of the most infamous Nazi extermination camps. When the war ended, Viktor Frankl discovered that except for one sister, his entire family, including his wife, had all perished in the gas chambers and ovens. How could he find life worth preserving? He writes: "In the concentration camps . . . in this living laboratory and on this testing ground, we watched and witnessed some of our comrades behave like swine while others behaved like saints. Man has both potentialities within himself; which one is actualized depends on decisions but not on conditions. . . . The sort of person the prisoner became was the result of an inner decision, and not the result of camp influences alone. Fundamentally, therefore, any man can, even under such circumstances, decide what shall become of him—mentally and spiritually. He may retain his human dignity even in a concentration camp. Dostoevsky said once, 'There is only one thing that I dread, not to be worthy of my sufferings.'"[3]

Speaking of inmates who became martyrs, Frankl says: "The last inner freedom cannot be lost. It can be said that they were worthy of their sufferings. The way they bore their suffering was a genuine inner achievement. It is this spiritual freedom—which cannot be taken away—that makes life meaningful and purposeful. . . . Here lies the chance for a man either to make use of or to forgo the opportunities of attaining the values that a difficult situation may afford him. And this decides whether he is worthy of his sufferings or not. . . . It is just such an exceptionally difficult external situation which gives man the opportunity to grow spiritually beyond himself."[4]

Few of us have ever experienced such degradation and dehumanization. When I read this, God, who is always near, spoke to me, and my misery melted away. You see, just as Jesus did, we must find our own spiritual crises to be an avenue of His healing power. That's why personal spiritual crisis, which at times involves suffering, is an invitation to ministry, to compassion, and to understanding—an invitation to growth, to knowledge of God and of self. That's why suffering is filled with such promise and hope. It takes a faith born of struggle to see that. Some folks never see it. Why? Because that is not the way humankind naturally looks at and reacts to such things. Long before Frankl wrote his book, Ellen White wrote: "Heaven will be cheap enough, if we obtain it through suffering. We must deny self all along the way, die to self daily, let Jesus alone appear, and keep His glory continually in view. I saw that those who of late have embraced the truth would have to know what it is to suffer for Christ's sake, that they would have trials to pass through that would be keen and cutting, in order that they may be purified and fitted through suffering to receive the seal of the living God, pass through the time of trouble, see the King in His beauty, and dwell in the presence of God and of pure, holy angels.

"As I saw what we must be in order to inherit glory, and then saw how much Jesus had suffered to obtain for us so rich an inheritance, I prayed that we might be baptized into Christ's sufferings, that we might not shrink at trials, but bear them with patience and joy, knowing what Jesus had suffered that we through His poverty and sufferings might be made rich."[5]

"Deny self." "Die to self." Why could she say such things? Because she recognized that suffering is a more powerful force than reason. Reason may convince the mind, but suffering moves the heart. The very source of that truth is the heart of God Himself. "God loved the world so much and so passionately, that He willingly gave His only Son to suffer the cross and die, that whoever believes in Him should not perish but have eternal life" (John 3:16, paraphrase).[6] It was not just the Son who suffered the cross but also the Father, who sent the Son and who knew why the cross was necessary. According to the biblical view of things, love and suffering go together. Love is a synonym for suffering. It is the nature of God's love that it has an eternal capacity to suffer. There is no true love without suffering. The Greek word *agape* (sacrificial love) linguistically describes that reality.

The hymn writer John M. Moore knew what it was like to have a hurting heart. I don't know exactly what his burden was, but his words make it obvious that he knew what suffering is. Words such as "Days are filled with sorrow and care, hearts are lonely and drear." Yes, so they are for many people who are suffering pains of one kind or another, perhaps about which no one else knows. Ellen White understood that too, and wrote, "We are in a world of suffering," and "Difficulty, trial, and sorrow await us all along the way to the heavenly home."[7] She had her share of suffering. The death of two children and of her husband. Physical infirmities of her own. She was misunderstood, vilified—and still is. People were skeptical of her spiritual gift—and still are. She had an awful lot to put up with. But we know what she accomplished, how God used her, in spite of it all. How is it possible for weak, frail human beings, such as you and I, to live successfully with sorrow and care? To actually be overcomers?

Kinds of Suffering

Personal crisis that involves suffering is certainly no respecter of persons. Everyone suffers in some shape or form and in differing degrees of intensity. Pain, disappointment, sorrow, grief, loss—the inevitable response is, Why me? The Bible, together with experience, teaches us that there are three kinds of suffering: (1) the kind that is common to everyone because we live in a fallen, sin-sick world; (2) the kind we bring on ourselves by the way we live, because of habits, addictions, etc., and (3) the kind that God actually allows to come to us. You don't believe He does that? Listen to the following statements:

"God would have His servants become acquainted with the moral machinery of their own hearts. In order to bring this about, He often permits the fire of affliction to assail them that they may become purified. . . . The purification of the people of God cannot be accomplished without their suffering. . . . God takes men upon trial; He proves them on the right hand and on the left, and thus they are educated, trained, disciplined."[8]

"Through his own suffering, Abraham was enabled to behold the Savior's mission of sacrifice. But Israel would not understand that which was so unwelcome to their proud hearts."[9]

"Our sorrows do not spring out of the ground. God 'doth not afflict willingly nor grieve the children of men,' Lamentations 3:33. When He permits trials and afflictions, it is 'for our profit, that we might be partak-

ers of His holiness.' Hebrews 12:10. If received in faith, the trial that seems
so bitter and hard to bear will prove a blessing. The cruel blow that blights
the joys of earth will be the means of turning our eyes to heaven. How
many there are who would never have known Jesus had not sorrow led
them to seek comfort in Him!

"The trials of life are God's workmen, to remove the impurities and
roughness from our character. Their hewing, squaring, and chiseling, their
burnishing and polishing, is a painful process; it is hard to be pressed down
to the grinding wheel. But the stone is brought forth prepared to fill its
place in the heavenly temple. *Upon no useless material does the Master bestow
such careful, thorough work.*"[10]

"A religious *experience* is attained *only* through conflict, through disappointment, through severe discipline of self, through earnest prayer."[11]

"Discipline of self." Suffering in any believer's life is not only an invitation to ministry—it is also an invitation to spiritual growth. Both the
Word of God and the Spirit of Prophecy tell us that suffering has a specific
role to play in the believer's spiritual journey. It may be hard to understand, hard to accept, hard to surrender to that role, but we have to do so
as we search the resources God has given us for truth and for help along
the way, pleading with Him for the spiritual insight and comfort that we
so badly need in the midst of the sorrows and cares of this life. "Like Jesus,
we must be made perfect through suffering."[12]

Suffer With Christ or Without Him

So where do we go when life really gets tough? The hymn writer tells
us: "Troubled soul, the Savior can see every heartache and tear; burdens
are lifted at Calvary, Jesus is very near." It's no use depending on other
people to relieve our hurts. It's not that they don't sympathize or understand. Most often it's because they are not capable of helping us—and
know it. Sometimes they don't know what to say or how to say it, so they
say little or nothing. Many times, even as a pastor, I have been at a loss for
words, especially when called upon to try to help someone experiencing
great tragedy. When we really hurt, the best place to go for comfort and
understanding is to Jesus, who is always very near. Why to Jesus? Because
there is room in His heart for all our burdens, pain, tribulation, and suffering. At times like these it is only Jesus who can adequately heal our souls
with joy. The wounded Jesus knows just how to care for our wounds. Not
only by His own Calvary wounds but from our wounds that He has healed
is His healing power made manifest in a suffering world.

Why is this so? Because He "has borne our griefs and carried our sorrows . . . was wounded for our transgressions; he was crushed for our in-

iquities; upon him was the chastisement that brought us peace, and with his stripes we are healed" (Isa. 53:4, 5). Relying on this, we can become overcomers in His name. Are our eyes so blinded by tears that we cannot see the Savior, who stands so near? Only He can lift the soul above sorrow to peace! "For as we share abundantly in Christ's sufferings, so through Christ we share abundantly in comfort too" (2 Cor. 1:5).

The result of the Christian faith is a transformed life—Christlikeness. To be like Him is to suffer as He suffered, to be given the same kind of eternal capacity to suffer for the sake of truth and for the sake of the world. We cannot overlook the suffering that is part of every great passion. God Himself has shown us what that means. The power of Jesus to heal people like you and me is found in His readiness to suffer for us. Didn't Isaiah say that it is by His stripes that we are healed? (see Isa. 53:5). In the New Testament, Peter underlines Isaiah's words this way: "He himself bore our sins in his body on the tree [for what purpose?], that we might die to sin and live to righteousness. By His wounds you have been healed. For you were straying like sheep, but have now returned to the Shepherd and Overseer of your souls" (1 Peter 2:24, 25).

Are we, who claim to be Christians, becoming incapable of suffering for righteousness sake? As wickedness abounds and increases, love grows cold—so says the Word of God. A callous indifference toward lasting relationships, such as marriage and friendship, prevails today. One who really loves, which is the first fruit of the Spirit, will suffer to maintain a relationship, even though inconvenient. Perfect love lays down life; it is sacrificial. But one can do this only if he or she has first died to sin, self, and the flesh. Slain by His love and resurrected by His love, we can live His life of love. This truth, too, is revealed at the cross. If there has been no death to sin, to self, to the flesh, and to the devil, what we call Christianity is nothing more than baptized paganism. We are, as Ellen White has said, "baptized, but . . . buried alive."[13] Martyrs are those who have already "died," which is why human beings cannot really harm them.

Nobody will stand with Jesus on Mount Zion who has not been with Him in Gethsemane and on Calvary. No one will share in the glories of His resurrection who has not been buried with Him by baptism into His death. Either we suffer with Christ or we suffer without Him. One leads to everlasting life; the other to everlasting death. Suffering with Christ involves the pain of birth, while suffering without Him involves the pain of everlasting death. It's better to die to sin now and be born again than to die later and stay dead forever. This view of the Christian life is not popular, especially in our humanistic age in which plenty of room is made for all the gods and goddesses of immorality, materialism, and greed. If what has been said so far is true, then the fellowship of the church is the place where we share pain. Here is where we help one another see how the grace of God is operating in difficult, even tragic, circumstances. Suffering may be the very thing the Holy Spirit is using for some higher purpose. We can hinder the Spirit's ministry within, by seeking to remove the suffering. Our task as church members and ministers is to allow suffering to be channeled into energy and spiritual power.

Genuine love and suffering are synonymous. One who really loves can put up with a lot. Both love and longsuffering (patience) are fruit of the Spirit, says Paul (see Gal. 5:22). They certainly are not *our* fruit! God has to do a work of grace *in us* in order for us to love the way that He loved, in order for us to demonstrate His kind of patience with one another. The patience/longsuffering the Bible talks about, says my theologian friend Samuel Koranteng-Pipim, "is not passiveness, weakness, cowardice, pessimism, escapism, powerlessness, or even apathy." It is "an inner toughness that surmounts tremendous odds."[14] It's not just giving in, shrugging things off. It is a tough, yet serene, submission to God's will and purpose. It is believing faith. It is living life on a higher plane. It is uncommon. When the Holy Spirit gets hold of us, that's what we become. It's what God does in us that really counts when the chips are down. Retired Admiral Barry Black says that he has "learned to value an individual's interior life more than his or her appearance."[15]

"Love is patient and kind," writes Paul, "love does not envy or boast; it is not arrogant or rude. It does not insist on its own way; it is not irritable or resentful; it does not rejoice at wrongdoing, but rejoices with the truth. Love bears all things, believes all things, hopes all things, endures all things. Love never ends" (1 Cor. 13:4-8). What a mirror to look into!

Remember, a martyr is someone who has already died, "Consider yourselves dead to sin and alive to God in Christ Jesus," says the apostle (Rom. 6:11). Listen to the whole passage from which I quoted earlier in this chapter, in which Paul puts love, grace, justification, faith, peace, suffering, endurance, perseverance, patience, character, hope, and rejoicing in just five verses.

"Therefore, since we have been justified by faith, we have peace with God through our Lord Jesus Christ. Through him we have also obtained access by faith into this grace in which we stand, and we rejoice in hope of the glory of God. More than that, we rejoice in our sufferings, knowing that suffering produces endurance, and endurance produces character, and character produces hope, and hope does not put us to shame, because God's love has been poured into our hearts through the Holy Spirit who has been given to us" (Rom. 5:1-5).

I can't do it. You can't do it. But that doesn't mean it's not possible. God, who is there all the time, can and will do it for us and in us. How do we respond then? What do we do about it? We ask Him to change our hearts—that's what we do.

Meditation

Stop and think. Which phase, or phases, of your spiritual journey have been the most powerful? How did they contribute to your spiritual transformation? Have you been able to find that your own spiritual crises have been avenues of God's healing power?

---

[1] A cartoon character of the time whose posture was bent over, with a prominent Adam's apple.

[2] I put the word in quotes because, although my father was never a church attender, he asked, when he was dying, that "The Old Rugged Cross" be sung for him.

[3] Viktor Frankl, *Man's Search for Meaning* (New York: Pocket Books, 1963), pp. 212, 213.

[4] *Ibid.*, pp. 105-114.

[5] Ellen G. White, *Early Writings* (Washington, D.C.: Review and Herald Pub. Assn., 1882, 1945), p. 67.

[6] God loved the *whole* world. Jesus died for the *whole* world. The Bible does not teach, and Adventists do not believe, what the Calvinists call limited atonement, which holds that Jesus did not die for the sins of the whole world, but only for the sins of the elect, who have been predestined for salvation.

[7] E. G. White, *The Ministry of Healing*, p. 247.

[8] E. G. White, *Testimonies for the Church*, vol. 4, pp. 85, 86.

[9] E. G. White, *The Desire of Ages*, p. 469.

[10] E. G. White, *Thoughts From the Mount of Blessing*, p. 10. (Italics supplied.)

[11] E. G. White, *Testimonies for the Church*, vol. 4, p. 444. (Italics supplied.)

[12] *Ibid.*, vol. 5, p. 71.

[13] *The Seventh-day Adventist Bible Commentary*, Ellen G. White Comments, vol. 6, p. 1075.

[14] *Patience in the Midst of Trials and Afflictions* (Ann Arbor, Mich: Berean Books, 2003), pp. 13, 14.

[15] *From the Hood to the Hill* (Nashville: Thomas Nelson, 2006), p. 214.

Chapter 8

SUFFERING AND OBEDIENCE

In the previous chapter I spoke of three kinds of suffering that the Bible and Christian experience identify. But there is a fourth—the suffering that is inevitable when one takes the Christian life seriously. Speaking of this kind of suffering, Ellen White said of Jesus: "Though His every word and act breathed of divine compassion, His unlikeness to the world provoked the bitterest hostility. Because He would give no license for the exercise of the evil passions of our nature, He aroused the fiercest opposition and enmity." Then she said of us, "*So it is with all who will live godly in Christ Jesus.* Between righteousness and sin, love and hatred, truth and falsehood, there is an irrepressible conflict." That's the reality. Therefore, "persecution and reproach [to express displeasure, to discredit] await all who are imbued with the Spirit of Christ."[1]

Also in the previous chapter I said that love and suffering go together, that love is a synonym for suffering. In the biblical view of things, suffering is also a synonym for obedience. How do we know that? Speaking of Jesus, Paul said that He "made himself nothing" and "being found in human form, he humbled himself by becoming obedient to the point of death, even death on a cross" (Phil. 2:7, 8). Calvary, the cross, is the place in which the relationship between love, suffering, and obedience is unmistakably revealed and demonstrated. Submitting to the cross was an act of loving obedience on the part of the Son of God. Think of it. The Son of God, the second person of the Trinity, who was "in the beginning with God" (John 1:2) and through whom all things were created, made Himself nothing.

The Way to the Place

What was His motive? Love. Love for the Father and love for the world. *That's us.* If acting out that love did not involve obedience, it would never have happened. There is no greater love than this. Yes, it was the will of the Father, demonstrating His love for the world. But it was also

117

a choice Jesus had to make. He made that choice, that decision, that act of surrender, in Gethsemane, where "being in an agony he prayed more earnestly; and his sweat became like great drops of blood" (Luke 22:44). Can we really compare His struggle to obey with our own? "Nevertheless," He said to the Father, "not my will, but yours, be done" (verse 42). Here is the thing that made obedience possible on the part of the Son: not His will (desire), but the Father's. That's our faith struggle, too, is it not? It is not about coming to faith, but about living the faith we profess. Believing faith puts God's will first. Always. No matter what the cost. When the Lord commands us to do something for Him, when we put our whining and complaining alongside His obedience in Gethsemane, there is no comparison. "In view of the infinite humiliation of the Lord of glory, shall we murmur because we can enter into life only through conflict and self-abasement? . . . Man is doing the greatest injury and injustice to his own soul [inner being] when he thinks and acts contrary to the will of God."[2] "Not my will, but yours, be done" is the formula for practicing believing faith. It's the formula for discipleship, for being followers of Christ, for being overcomers. And if we do not become overcomers, we are in danger of being overcome.

Every major decision, and a lot of minor ones, certainly every moral and ethical choice the believer makes, must be prefaced by this formula of faith. Why? Because life is irreversible, and we have to say an irrevocable goodbye to every stage of life. Because we are all looking for a place. Because as people of faith we are on the way to the only place where we will feel completely comfortable and safe, the only place where we will feel secure and protected from disappointments. A place where we know we belong. Jesus said, "My Father's house has many rooms; if that were not so, would I have told you that I am going there to prepare a place for you?" (John 14:2, NIV). Remember, for Him the way to the place that He is preparing for us was through Gethsemane and Calvary. Then He said, "You know the way to the place where I am going"(verse 4, NIV). Do we really know the way? How do we know the way? Because Jesus has shown us the way. Because He *is* the way. What more reliable guide is there to the place for which we are so homesick? But let's not miss the signs that point the way. They say GETHSEMANE, CALVARY, FAITH, LOVE, SUFFERING, OBEDIENCE. The way is the way of Gethsemane and Calvary, which involved love, suffering, and obedience. How did Christ become obedient? Was it natural to that part of His nature that was human?

The Bible says, "During the days of Jesus' life on earth, he offered up prayers and petitions with fervent cries and tears to the one who could save him from death, *and he was heard because of his reverent submission.* Son though he was, *he learned obedience from what he suffered* and, once made perfect, he became the source of eternal salvation for all who *obey* him" (Heb. 5:7-9, NIV). Hebrews 5 begins with faith but ends with obedience. Why? Because we cannot have the one without the other. Genuine, believing faith obeys the One who gives faith. We who claim to be born-again Christians, followers of Christ, need to hear this. "This is how we know we are in him [Christ]: Whoever claims to live in him must [that's an imperative—no other choice, no alternative] live as Jesus did" (1 John 2:5, 6, NIV). Obedience is learned behavior. The evidence proves the reality. How is it learned? Through suffering. Not just any suffering but the suffering that is inevitable when we take the Christian life seriously. It is as much a struggle of submission for us as Gethsemane and Calvary were for Jesus. And His suffering was not for His own sake but for ours, "For as by the one man's disobedience [Adam's], so by the one man's obedience [Christ's] the many will be made righteous" (Rom. 5:19). Ellen White observed, "Many are ruined by their desire for a life of ease and pleasure. Self-denial is disagreeable to them. They are constantly seeking to escape trials that are inseparable from a course of fidelity to God."[3]

Obedience is an unpleasant word and concept today. Why? Because to acknowledge the need for obedience requires acknowledging the reality of its opposite, disobedience. It is the idea of disobedience that postmodernism cannot abide, because to recognize the reality of disobedience is to recognize the reality of God's law and human lawlessness or sin. It is to recognize ultimate "authority," which is another unpleasant word and idea. If there is no ultimate truth, if truth is relative, then there is no ultimate authority. We are answerable to no one but ourselves. *That's frightening.*

If obedience is learned behavior, why is it so hard to learn? Because we must first learn that it is worth learning. Let's rephrase the question and put it this way: Why is it so hard to believe? Because it is so hard to obey. Why is it so hard to obey? Because we see no value in it, especially if believing faith involves trial, tribulation, and suffering. We want all the benefits of salvation, but we don't want to walk the way Jesus walked. We don't want to walk the way of Gethsemane and Calvary, the way of obedience to the will of God. We will discover God's plan for our lives only when we seek for it in His will. That's why Jesus tells us that when we lose our life for His sake, we will find it.

"Blessed [happy] are you when others revile you and persecute you and utter all kinds of evil against you falsely on my account. [*It hurts, but don't be surprised at the source.*] Rejoice and be glad [*Why? Because you must be doing something right . . .*], for so they persecuted the prophets who were before you" (Matt. 5:11, 12).

"If the world hates you, know that it has hated me before it hated you. If you were of the world, the world would love you as its own; but because you are not of the world, but I chose you out of the world, therefore the world hates you. Remember the word that I said to you: 'A servant is not greater than his master.' If they persecuted me, they will also persecute you. If they kept my word, they will also keep yours. But all these things they will do to you on account of my name, because they do not know him who sent me" (John 15:18-21).

"Beloved, do not be surprised at the fiery trial when it comes upon you to test you, as though something strange were happening to you. But rejoice insofar as you share Christ's sufferings, that you may also rejoice and be glad when his glory is revealed. If you are insulted for the name of Christ, you are blessed, because the Spirit of glory and of God rests upon you. But let none of you suffer as a murderer or a thief or an evildoer or as a meddler. Yet if anyone suffers as a Christian, let him not be ashamed, but let him glorify God in that name" (1 Peter 4:12-16).

"Therefore, since we are surrounded by so great a cloud of witnesses, let us also lay aside every weight, and sin which clings so closely, and let us run with endurance the race that is set before us, looking to Jesus, the founder and perfecter of our faith, who for the joy that was set before him endured the cross, despising the shame, and is seated on the right hand of the throne of God" (Heb. 12:1, 2).

Hebrews Clarifies the Way

The book of Hebrews begins by speaking of Jesus as the Son of God, whom God "appointed the heir of all things, through whom also he created the world. He is the radiance of the glory of God and the exact imprint of his [God's] nature ["exact representation of his being," NIV], and he upholds the universe by the word of his power" (Heb. 1:2, 3). He is now seated at the right hand of God (verse 3). Everything has been put in subjection to Him (Heb. 2:8). He is crowned with glory and honor (verse 9). He is the founder of our salvation (verse 10). *Exaltation!* Remember, the way to the place of His exaltation was through Gethsemane and Calvary. God the Father has made the Son "perfect through suffering" (verse 10), not for His own sake, but for ours. That's why He says, "Both the one who makes people holy [sanctifies] and those who are made holy [are sanctified] are of the same family" (verse 11, NIV). We are His brothers and sisters (verse 11). He "partook of the same things" namely flesh and blood (verse 14). He was made "like his brothers in every respect, so that he might become a merciful and faithful high priest in the service of God" (verse 17). He is able to "sympathize with our weaknesses" (Heb. 4:15), because in His humanity He "in every respect has been tempted as we are [but with a major difference], yet without sin" (verse 15). For that reason, we can confidently "draw near to the throne of grace, that we may receive mercy and find grace to help in time of need" (verse 16).

Draw near, not draw away. Sinners like us need His mercy *(withholding punishment though we deserve it and justice demands it)*. Sinners like us need His grace *(giving to us what we do not deserve; His divine gift of faith, power to obey and to overcome, though we do not deserve it)*. Is there ever a time we do not need His mercy and His grace? Is that some of the time or all of the time? Every time is a time of need. Every day. Every hour. Every minute. Every second. The minute we draw near to Him, what do we get? Mercy and grace. Especially in difficult moments and circumstances when we are called to be disciples and stand for God and His righteousness. That help comes in time, *in His time*, and so often just in time, on time. It may be a big thing. It may be a small thing.

After Hebrews speaks of Jesus in such an exalted way, we come to that section from chapter 4:14 to chapter 5:10. It begins with the exhortation "let us hold fast our confession [faith]." We like that. But it ends with obedience. We don't like that. Remember: "Although he was a son, he learned obedience through what he suffered. And being made perfect, he became the source of eternal salvation for all who *obey* him" (Heb. 5:8, 9). We like the idea that He sympathizes "with our weaknesses," that He was tempted just "as we are" (verse 15), that He deals "gently with the ignorant and wayward, since he himself is beset with weakness" (verse 2). But why did Paul have to go and spoil everything by talking about submission and how "although he was [the] son, [Jesus] learned obedience through what he suffered" (verse 8)? What does that have to do with salvation? with biblical religion? It doesn't fit the way we think, so let's just tear it out of the Bible!

And the rest of it: "And being made perfect, he became the source of eternal salvation to all who obey him" (Heb. 5:9). *Tear that out, too!* That's what a lot of folks do with parts of the Bible that they don't like, that don't fit the way we think. How about the text that says when Jesus comes back again "every eye will see Him" (Rev. 1:7)? *Tear it out!* Because some people think it's going to be a secret coming. How about the text that says our bodies are the temple of the Holy Spirit? *Tear it out!* Because we think that what we do with our bodies has nothing to do with salvation or with New Testament Christianity. What about the texts that say that homosexual behavior is sin and that no one who practices such behavior will inherit the kingdom of God? *Tear them out!* Because contemporary culture thinks differently. How about that text in 1 Corinthians in which Paul says that immortality is not something humans have inherently but will be given in the resurrection? *Tear it out!* Why? Because some folks think that the Greek philosophers were more right than the Bible, that there is something inherently good in us that merits living on after the flesh dies. Something called "soul." In Greek thinking, the soul is good, while the flesh is evil. But if the flesh is evil, then Jesus, who took upon Himself human flesh, is evil. But that doesn't make sense, because if He is evil, He cannot be our Savior. How about the words of Jesus: "If you love me, you *will* keep my commandments" (John 14:15)? And "whoever has my commandments and keeps them, he it is who loves me" (verse 21)? Or "whoever does not love me does not keep my words" (verse 24)? First of all, we have to believe what He says (*faith*) and then do what He says (*believing faith*). That requires obedience, doesn't it? Of course it does. But we don't like that. What does obedience have to do with the gospel? with New Testament religion? *Tear it all out!*

What about "remember the Sabbath day to keep it holy. . . . The seventh day is a Sabbath to the Lord your God" (Ex. 20:8, 10)? What does that have to do with salvation? *Tear it out!* While we are at it, we might as well do a thorough job on the rest of the commandments. After all, if we think they belong to the dispensation of the Jews and have no relevance for Christian life, in spite of the fact that the New Testament calls God's law good and holy, then let's *tear them out too!* Out of sight, out of mind. What will happen to people who do believe the Ten Commandments, who reverence them as the absolute standard of God's own righteousness and of human righteousness, as well? Somebody just might come up with the idea that such people are a menace to society. How much shall we tear out of the Word of God? Eventually we get to the last page, where it says, "I warn everyone . . . if anyone takes words away from the words of the book of this prophecy, God will take away his share in the tree of life and in the holy city, which are described in this book" (Rev. 22:18, 19). We might as well *tear that out, too!*

Christless Christianity

We don't become holy by doing holy things; we become holy by yielding to the Holy, by worshipping the Holy, by worshipping Him who is holy. Ellen White says, "True obedience comes from the heart."[4] The crowds that followed Jesus did not want a king who would die on a cross. They would never understand Paul when he said he wanted to know Christ in "the fellowship of his sufferings" (Phil. 3:10, KJV). Nor would they like the idea that if they were to have Jesus as their king, they would have to suffer with Him, deny self, and take up their cross. Deny self? Instead, our culture insists that we exalt self. Paul was thinking of the ultimate fulfillment of those sufferings, the final result, the glorious end, a redeemed world cleansed of all sin and suffering by the blood of the cross. "If we endure, we will also reign with him" (2 Tim. 2:12). He was thinking about the goal and purpose of the gospel—to "bring about the obedience of faith . . . among all the nations" (Rom. 1:5). Those who want a religion that makes them feel good but that makes no demands and calls for no sacrifices can easily find one, but it will not be biblical Christianity. We either suffer with Christ and learn obedience, or we suffer without Him in disobedience. So close is the relationship between obedience and everlasting truth (doctrine) that even He who is the Truth learns obedience.

Today's paradox is that one can be a Christian without really knowing Christ, without following Him through suffering to a life of sanctified obedience and finally to glory. A Christless Christianity. To remain faithful requires faith, not effort—the obedience of faith learned by suffering. This requirement was part of the gospel for Paul as he received it from Christ. Its goal is not this world, but the world to come. Suffering, and the obedience it teaches, is training for eternity. It is dying to this world. Everything selfish is taken away. In this school we are alone with God, not distracted and confused by others. And no one understands as Jesus does. Because no one has suffered for us as Jesus has, and no one will suffer with us as Jesus will. The Danish theologian Søren Kierkegaard writes: "Without suffering one cannot learn obedience, for suffering is exactly the assurance that the devotion is not willfulness, but he who learns obedience learns everything."[5] Here is a crucial question: Why is it that obedience has to be learned through suffering? The answer is that obedience comes through suffering so that we don't get the idea that obedience is something we accomplish for ourselves.

Reduced to the simplest expression, obedience is letting God rule. When we put together what the Bible tells us, we must conclude that there is no obedience without suffering, no believing faith without obedience, and no eternal life without believing faith. Could that be why Jesus asked, "When the Son of Man comes, will he find faith on earth?" (Luke 18:8).

Every born-again Seventh-day Adventist Christian knows, on the basis of both Bible truth and personal experience, that everything we preach and believe centers on Jesus. We stand with the apostle Paul, who said, "For what I received I passed on to you as of first importance: that Christ died for our sins according to the Scriptures, that he was buried, that he was raised on the third day according to the Scriptures, and that he appeared to Cephas, and then to the Twelve" (1 Cor. 15:3-5, NIV). Notice that the authority for belief in the sacrifice of Christ for our sins, and belief in the resurrection power of Christ for newness of life, are the *Scriptures, the Bible.*

We understand, on the basis of Scripture, that both God's law and His grace are united in the gospel of salvation, received through faith in the atoning, substitutionary blood of Jesus alone. This atonement is what He has done *for* us. Justification accomplished by grace and received through faith. It is our conviction that the claims of Christ confront the age in which we live and each one of us. We look at those claims from the perspective of the Word of God, the center of which is the good news of salvation from sin, offered freely to all who put their faith in Jesus Christ.

But we also understand that to be saved *from* sin means more than to be free of the condemnation and guilt that sin produces. It means to be set free from sin's power. By means of the grace offered to us in the gospel, those who put their faith in Christ have been set free from bondage to sin's control. Free from precisely that which would prevent them from living a Christlike life. The grace of God has first set us free *from* something and then free *for* something. Free for what? The Bible says: "For the grace of God has appeared that offers salvation to all peoples. It [the grace of God] teaches us to say 'No' to ungodliness and worldly passions, and to live self-controlled, upright and godly lives in this present age, while we wait for the blessed hope—the appearing of the glory of our great God and Savior, Jesus Christ, who gave himself for us to redeem us from all wickedness and to purify for himself a people that are his very own, eager to do what is good" (Titus 2:11-14, NIV).

According to this scripture, Jesus "gave himself for us" for more than just forgiveness of past sin. For what else did He give Himself? To "redeem us from all wickedness and to purify for himself a people that are his very own, eager to do what is good." The salvation that the "grace of God . . . offers," according to God's Word, involves more than forgiveness for past sin. It involves victory over the power of sin. In order for that to happen, we have to learn something that is taught to us by grace. Grace empowers us to live "godly lives." To really do it. Grace is not just something that heals the broken relationship between God and sinners externally. Grace changes the sinner internally. This is sanctification accomplished by grace and received through faith. It is to be experienced, not just believed.

Yes and No

Separating justification and sanctification, as though they were mutually exclusive, is dangerous to Christian spirituality. Joe Crews, one of our great evangelists, said, "One of the greatest deceptions of the devil in these days is that you can be willfully transgressing God's law and still have the assurance of salvation." Dietrich Bonhoeffer said, "The only man who has the right to say that he is justified by grace alone is the man who has left all to follow Christ."[6] To follow Christ is to become like Christ. Time is running out. The Bible places the whole matter of sanctification, holiness, growth in Christlikeness, into the context of His second coming. Waiting for Jesus to return is not a time of idleness and indolence. Although we are justified by grace and sanctified by grace, there is still something that grace is meant to accomplish *in us,* something that grace teaches us and that we must learn to do. *Yes, do.*

What must we learn to do? We must learn to say no to ungodliness and worldly passions. No is a negative response to ungodliness and worldly passions, but saying no is a most positive response to the will of God regarding ungodliness and worldly passions. To say no to these is to say a resounding yes to living self-controlled, upright, and godly lives. If grace delivers us from the power of sin and empowers us to live godly lives, then we are actively involved, not just passive. God works for us, on us, and in us. "Christ in you" is "the hope of glory," said Paul (Col. 1:27). Knowledge of the truth "leads to godliness" (Titus 1:1, NIV).

Many of us have never learned to say no to ungodliness. Why? Because we resist it. When we are awakened spiritually and first hear the gospel that we are forgiven because of God's grace and that we can do nothing to merit or earn forgiveness, we hear it as marvelous good news. We love to hear it. We say yes to that message. But when we discover that God, by His grace, wants to change us inwardly, we dig in our heels and resist. We want to be loved by God, but we want to stay in control. So we say no to inner transformation. We say no to the wrong thing. And we didn't learn to say it; it comes naturally. But we must learn to say no to ungodliness and worldly passions. How does that learning take place? How does the grace of God teach us to say no?

"If you love your life, you will lose it. If you give it up in this world, you will be given eternal life. If you serve me, you must go with me. My servants will be with me wherever I am" (John 12:25, 26). Follow Him where? To His glorification, which was first the internal wrestling with God's will in Gethsemane, then the suffering and agony of Calvary, then the Resurrection from the tomb and the Ascension to heaven. We have already learned that obedience to God's will is learned behavior and that even Jesus had to learn obedience.

If sanctification is becoming like Christ, then we must walk the way He walked, the way of Gethsemane and Calvary. The Bible identifies sanctification as the "battle against sin" (Heb. 12:4). Part of the good news is that we don't engage in that struggle alone. God the Father is actively involved by exercising His divine discipline. This struggle is how we are taught, and learn, to say no to ungodliness and worldly passion and to say yes to Christlikeness, godliness, and righteousness.

This is grace operating in the form of divine discipline. The Holy Spirit produces Christlikeness, godly living, in us as we submit in believing faith to the Father's discipline. This is sanctification by grace through faith. Legitimate children of God are under His loving discipline. His goal is not just to restore us to fellowship with Him (justification), but to remake us in His image from the inside out (sanctification). Jesus gave Himself for us, remember, not only to "rescue us from everything that is evil" but also to "make our hearts pure. He wanted us to be his own people and to be eager to do right" (Titus 2:14).

Jürgen Moltman wrote, "Not everything that is of fundamental significance for a people can be achieved by reason alone. It has to be bought by suffering."[7] Moltman continues: "Life without passion is poverty-stricken, Life without the readiness for suffering is shallow. We have to overcome both our fear of passion and our fear of suffering. Otherwise hope cannot be born again."[8]

Obedience is learned through suffering—not just any suffering, but the kind that is inevitable if we take the Christian life seriously, the suffering that is part of God's will for us. It is as much a struggle of submission for us as Gethsemane was for Jesus. What kind of suffering was that?

"Let this mind be in you which was also in Christ Jesus, who, being in the form of God, did not consider it robbery to be equal with God, but made Himself of no reputation, taking the form of a bondservant, and coming in the likeness of men. And being found in appearance as a man, He humbled Himself and became obedient to the point of death, even the death of the cross" (Phil. 2:5-8, NKJV).

We are forced to ask: Can there be true spirituality without conflict? What is your Gethsemane—or mine? What is the cross we may have to bear? You and I will find out the minute we start to follow Jesus and share His life. Can you think of any examples of how you have learned to obey God through suffering? Most often it is there that the issue of believing faith is settled. "Therefore lift your drooping hands and strengthen your weak knees, and make straight paths for your feet, so that what is lame may not be put out of joint but rather be healed" (Heb. 12:12, 13).

Yes, obedience is an unpleasant concept and an unpleasant word today. Its opposite is *disobedience,* and the bottom line is lawlessness. "For to this [obedience and suffering] you have been called, because Christ also suffered for you, leaving you an example, so that you might follow in his steps" (1 Peter 2:21). When God's law is used "lawfully" (1 Tim. 1:8), it will bring us to that experience described by John the Baptist as the "baptism of repentance" (Mark 1:4). Only then can one know the joy, the release, the peace, and the freedom of the gospel and praise God in obedient faith. Paul said, "The law came in to increase the trespass" (Rom. 5:20). Why? So that "sin might be shown to be sin, and through the commandment might become sinful beyond measure. For we know that the law is spiritual, but I am of the flesh, sold under sin" (Rom. 7:13, 14).

Transformation of the Sinner

We have a problem with God's moral law, don't we? We don't like it. So we try to figure it out in relation to the cross and have come up with three alternatives. 1. The cross cancels the law, does away with it. But if it does that, what happens to sin and to obedience? There is no sin, and if there is no such thing as sin, there is no need to obey God. 2. The cross changes the law, makes it into something else. In that case, what happens to sin and to obedience? They are changed into something else too. 3. The cross changes God, so that He doesn't really mean what He says. What happens, then, to sin and obedience? God doesn't mean what He has said about them, either.

But the Bible tells us that the message of the cross changes *people,* not God's law! What happens, then, to sin? It is forgiven. The sinner is cleansed of unrighteousness and is empowered by the indwelling Holy Spirit to obey the Father. If the law is not taken seriously, what happens to the gospel? It is not really good news, because it doesn't save me *from* anything. It becomes another form of legalism, and I am saved no matter what I do. I become the authority—a law unto myself. So the law I obey is mine, not God's. *Very clever!* But Jesus asks us, "Why do you call me 'Lord, Lord,' and do not do what I tell you?" (Luke 6:46). You see, the concomitant of cheap grace is easy obedience, or no obedience at all. Grace without obedience is not possible. Neither is obedience without faith. And faith involves struggle, suffering, the cross, and believing. So the real problem is not obedience but faith. How crucial is this? "Without faith it is impossible to please him [God], for whoever would draw near to God must believe that he exists and that he rewards those who seek him" (Heb. 11:6).

Does the Word of God tell us clearly that there is a relationship between obedience and love? Indeed it does. First of all, love is self-giving, not self-centered, and because it is sacrificial it cannot be self-righteous (see John 3:16). Listen to Jesus Himself, who said, "*If* you love me, you

will keep my commandments" (John 14:15), and "This is my commandment, that you love one another as I have loved you. Greater love has no
one than this, that someone lay down his life for his friends. You are my
friends *if* you do what I command you" (John 15:12-14). His love for us
is unconditional, but our love for Him, as well as our professed friendship
for Him, is proven, demonstrated, by obedience. I didn't say that, *He did*.
Furthermore, Jesus makes it unmistakably clear that "because lawlessness
[disregard for the law, refusal to obey] will be increased, the love of many
will grow cold" (Matt. 24:12). The Father's commandments are Christ's
commandments, and Christ's commandments are the Father's. How do we
know that? Because Christ and the Father are One. He has given us the
Father's words, the Father's truth, all motivated by divine love (see John
17; Rev. 14:12). How serious is this? What are the consequences of not
obeying God's truth? "He [God] will render to each one according to his
works: to those who by patience in well-doing seek for glory and honor
and immortality, he will give eternal life; but for those who are self-seeking and do not obey the truth, but obey unrighteousness, there will be
wrath and fury. There will be tribulation and distress for every human
being who does evil, the Jew first and also the Greek, but glory and honor
and peace for everyone who does good, the Jew first and also the Greek.
For God shows no partiality" (Rom. 2:6-11). That's His grace. That's His
mercy. That's His justice. He treats everyone alike, because He Himself is
righteous. The ultimate purpose of the gospel is to "bring about the obedience of faith for the sake of his name among all the nations, including
you who are called to belong to Jesus Christ" (Rom. 1:5, 6). Dietrich
Bonhoeffer, writing about disciples and discipleship, said, "Just as Christ is
Christ only in virtue of His suffering and rejection, so the disciple is a disciple only in so far as he shares his Lord's suffering and rejection and crucifixion. Discipleship means the cross," and "When it comes it is not an
accident but a necessity."[9] Further: "When Christ calls a man, He bids him
come and die."[10]

Why do reborn believers submit and accept the suffering that is a part
of a believing faith? Because on the basis of what has been learned from
the Word of God, they know that "suffering produces endurance, and
endurance produces character, and character produces hope, and hope
does not put us to shame, because God's love has been poured into our
hearts through the Holy Spirit who has been given to us" (Rom. 5:3-5).
Believers actually rejoice in suffering because of what it produces in them
internally. Believers' experiences testify to the truth and reality of what
suffering produces as that truth and reality become part of their spirituality.

Christian joy is not some superficial happiness that is worldly and dependent on outward circumstances. It is inward and is found in the privilege of suffering for Jesus' sake. The suffering that is simply a part of living a Christian life in a world that is increasingly hostile to it is bad enough. The greatest tragedy would be if we did not learn obedience as a result. Suffering directs our attention inward, which is something we resist. We would rather concentrate on *doing* rather than *being*. But it is inwardly that suffering instructs us and that decisions are made, because first we must obey inwardly in order that the outward obedience may be righteous obedience, of believing faith and not of works.

A Personal Illustration

Perhaps another personal story will serve to illustrate what I mean. First John 1:9 says, "If we confess our sins, he [God] is faithful and just to forgive us our sins and to cleanse us from all unrighteousness." Forgiveness is wonderful, provided that it is more than words, if it is actual, real. This is precisely why the Word of God puts forgiveness of sins and cleansing from unrighteousness together. They go together, not just theologically, but experientially. Spiritually speaking, if cleansing from unrighteousness does not accompany forgiveness of sin, what good is forgiveness? If God says He forgives me but does not cleanse me, then I am still the same old person, the person I do not want to be anymore. Feeling good about myself is not good enough.

After almost 10 years of ministry, preaching week after week as a Lutheran minister imbued with Lutheran theology (*at least 500 sermons by then*), I discovered that the gospel involves much more than forgiveness. The day of that discovery turned out to be one of the most crucial days on the spiritual road I travel, because it was part of the process by which God opened the pathway into the Seventh-day Adventist Church. My wife had become a Seventh-day Adventist, and I was desperate. My ministry was falling apart, and I was carrying a load of anger and hatred in my heart that I began to realize would destroy me. No confessing Christian with a believing faith can live with such hatred and anger without it eating away that person's life and spirituality like a cancer. In such a state, I could not face getting into my pulpit again to preach to others.

In utter desperation I went alone to the beautiful sanctuary of Sharon Lutheran Church in Bessemer, Michigan, that fateful day 40 years ago, to talk to the Lord about the situation. Deep within I knew that if I was not cleansed from the sin of anger and hatred, my relationship with Christ would be lost, and my ministry would be over—as well as my relationship with my wife and with the Adventist Christians who had befriended her.

Everything was at stake. My faith. My marriage. My ministry. I truly believe that if what happened that day had not happened, I would not be alive today.

For the first and only time in my life I lay down on my face on the floor of the sanctuary. That will always be a sacred place for me. I could not pray audibly. I could only groan inwardly, as Paul says in a passage that surely must be more than an esoteric theological statement. That passage surely must reflect his own spiritual experience and be designed by the Holy Spirit to help us with ours:

"For I consider that the sufferings of this present time are not worth comparing with the glory that is to be revealed to us. For the creation waits with eager longing for the revealing of the sons of God. For the creation was subjected to futility, not willingly, but because of him who subjected it, in hope that the creation itself will be set free from its bondage to corruption and obtain the freedom of the glory of the children of God. For we know that the whole creation has been groaning together in the pains of childbirth until now. And not only the creation, but we ourselves, who have the firstfruits of the Spirit, groan inwardly as we wait eagerly for adoption as sons, the redemption of our bodies. For in this hope we were saved. Now hope that is seen is not hope. For who hopes for what he sees? But if we hope for what we do not see, we wait for it with patience.

"Likewise the Spirit helps us in our weakness. For we do not know what to pray for as we ought, but the Spirit himself intercedes for us with groanings too deep for words. And he who searches hearts knows what is the mind of the Spirit, because the Spirit intercedes for the saints [believers] according to the will of God. And we know that for those who love God all things work together for good, for those who are called according to his purpose. For those whom he foreknew he also predestined to be conformed to the image of his Son, in order that he might be the firstborn among many brothers. And those whom he predestined he also called, and those whom he called he also justified, and those whom he justified he also glorified" (Rom. 8:18-30).

I know what that kind of inward groaning, that kind of prayer, is like. Without speaking an audible word, I told God all about the anger and hatred that had me spiritually shackled and that was causing inward death. I told Him of the agony I felt, how my heart was so heavy with guilt. I told Him how much I detested the person whom the situation revealed me to be. *The only way to describe the nature of the sin that I had become conscious of is to do so graphically and say that sin is like the smell of one's own excrement. Appealing because it is one's own, and appalling because it stinks.* I told God that I could not go on in the faith, or in ministry, with such a burden of hypocrisy. I told Him of the darkness of my inner being and how I yearned to walk in the light again. I told Him how terribly sorry I was for the anger and hatred in my heart. I begged Him for His mercy and forgiveness and for the grace to forgive others. I was determined not to rise from the floor until He blessed me. It was a major conflict between the kingdom of light and the kingdom of darkness, and though I did not identify it in such terms at that time, it was a most vivid consciousness of the inward dimension of the "great controversy." It was the most critical and decisive moment on the road I travel.

I do not remember how long I lay there. One hour? Two? Then God did what He promises to do, because He is faithful and just. In my inner being I heard and felt His forgiveness wash over me like a refreshing stream. He was present! He was *there*. But that was not all He did in that divine moment. The miracle that is at the very heart of the good news happened. He gave me new life! How? By cleansing me of the unrighteousness, the sin that is the transgression of His law. He took the anger and hatred right out of my heart and made me new again. *He did not do that because I prostrated myself, but because He cared. And because He cared, He was there all the time.* When I finally was able to stand and walk out of the church, it felt like I was floating. I was able to face the next day and the day after that. I could face whatever His will, and His future, was for me. For added reassurance, the Holy Spirit led me to this verse of pure grace: "I know the plans I have for you, declares the Lord, plans for [your] welfare and not for evil, to give you a future and a hope" (Jer. 29:11). He has fulfilled that promise many times since that day.

Because forgiveness imposes commensurate responsibility, something yet remained to be done—immediately, with no delay. I could not go home until the experience was complete and relationships were repaired. "For," as Jesus said, "if you forgive others their trespasses [sins], your heavenly Father will also forgive you, but if you do not forgive others their trespasses, neither will your Father forgive your trespasses." (Matt. 6:14, 15). So it was necessary to drive to the home of the couple that had made such a spiritual impact on my wife and ask their forgiveness for my hateful attitude and behavior toward them. Of course, because they were Christians and imbued with the biblical principles of their faith, that forgiveness was immediately forthcoming. In turn, they asked me to forgive them for all the trouble and agony their witness had caused, which the Holy Spirit had certainly prepared me to grant as well. We have been fast friends ever since, with an unbreakable friendship.

That's what it's all about—the power of the gospel transforming people internally and, at the same time, externally in the way they live. I have spent many hours wondering why the Lord brought me back in retirement, as a Seventh-day Adventist minister, to the same community, Bessemer, Michigan, where it all happened. I think I know now. It was so that He could demonstrate the power of His Word to transform people, even a pastor.

You see, God wants to reveal to the world who His believing people are. He wants to set them free from bondage to the decay inevitable in a life of sin. He wants them to experience the freedom He provides for His believing people. It is because they have the firstfruits of the Spirit that they groan inwardly as they wait for the redemption of their bodies—the whole person. They are saved in that hope. Nothing else has meaning or purpose. Furthermore, the Holy Spirit is present to help us in our weakness. Often we don't know what to pray for or how to pray. But the Spirit does, and He intercedes together with us. The Spirit prays for us by joining in our groanings. God listens to, and hears, the prayer groaning of the Holy Spirit on our behalf. Why? Because God knows that the Spirit is interceding for us. Such Holy Spirit intercession is the Father's will. The outcome of all this is that the Father assures us that whatever happens to those who love Him, it will work out for their good, for they have been called by Him for His purposes. Did you know that we who are believing have been predestined by God to be "conformed to the image of his Son"? To be like Jesus? Talk about predestination.

I want to make something unmistakably clear, especially for anyone who might misunderstand or misinterpret the story just told. *I did not prostrate myself on the floor of the church that day because I was seeking an encounter with a God who is not present, who is hard to find. Nor was I somehow reaching inside myself to find Him. He was already present and had been there all the time. I had known Him by faith for many years. The prostration and the groaning were because of my own sin of hatred and anger, an act of revulsion. I already knew, cognitively, from study of His Word, that He is always present, that He calls, inviting the sinner to confession and repentance, and to receive new life by His grace perceptively. I already knew that He takes the initiative and waits patiently for my response. When I heard His call and responded in the only manner my condition demanded, His Holy Spirit had access to my "inner being" and applied the Word of forgiveness, cleansing, and healing. That which intensified the sense of the Lord's presence was His response of grace and mercy to my response of confession and repentance. That is what we need to concentrate on, not on breathing in and breathing out, or repeating mantras, or staring at a blank wall in order to empty our mind, as some are urging us to do today.*

For Seventh-day Adventist ministers and evangelists, the experience related above should be a vivid reminder that we need to be very sensitive to the spiritual turmoil that can ensue when the truth of the message we preach is recognized, accepted, and internalized. We cannot afford to be indifferent to or aloof from this, but must stand ready to walk with individuals, bearing their burdens, because we have been the bearers of a life-transforming message. We must be ready to help at the precise point at which the spiritual need is most acute. Not to do so would be spiritually irresponsible, which is why evangelism and pastoral nurture, broadly understood to include lay ministry, are the two equal foci of ministry. In order to be able to minister in this way, one must be aware of the inwardness of the faith experience and understand the relationship between *doing* and *being,* that right doing arises out of right being.

It also needs to be said that while such experiences of Christ are genuine elements of spirituality, they must be genuinely part of one's loyalty to Christ in the midst of suffering. Our hope is focused on the soon return of Jesus, when "he will wipe away every tear from their eyes" and there will be no "pain anymore" (Rev. 21:4), when we shall experience a direct encounter with the glorified and reigning Christ. We live in the interim period, which is why such experiences of faith are sometimes necessary. Today we live by a faith rooted in the Scriptures, but "then face to face" (1 Cor. 13:12). During that interim time of faith, apart from sound biblical teaching/truth/doctrine, all we would have is a fuzzy, friendly Jesus.

A significant element in Adventist spirituality is the lifelong internal struggle to stay true to the faith into which we were baptized. We understand that salvation has not been fully experienced apart from the obedience of faith. We may very well be the lone voice in the context of churches capitulating to culture, as they have become increasingly acclimated to culture. Part of the ethos of the time of trouble is that faithful believers are in conflict with the world and worldliness and that they envision the church of Christ as a holy community. In that struggle to stay true to the faith, the value of Christian friends is boundless. Members of that holy community need the spiritual support they can give one another.

Meditation

Spend some quiet time calling to mind some of those events in your life that God has used to teach you how to obey Him. In what ways are you conscious of the purifying process that the Holy Spirit has exercised within you? How have you resisted that process? Why are you thankful for it?

---

[1] E. G. White, *Thoughts From the Mount of Blessing*, p. 29. (Italics supplied.)
[2] Ellen G. White, *Steps to Christ* (Mountain View, Calif.: Pacific Press Pub. Assn., 1956), pp. 45, 46.

[3] E. G. White, *Testimonies for the Church,* vol. 5, p. 70.

[4] E. G. White, *The Desire of Ages,* p. 668.

[5] Søren Kierkegaard, *The Gospel of Suffering* (Minneapolis: Augsburg Pub. House, 1948), p. 56.

[6] Dietrich Bonhoeffer, *The Cost of Discipleship* (New York: Macmillan Co., 1957), p. 45.

[7] Jürgen Moltman, *The Power of the Powerless* (New York: Harper and Row, 1983), p. 63.

[8] *Ibid.,* p. 115.

[9] Bonhoeffer, pp. 71, 72.

[10] *Ibid.,* p. 73.

Chapter 9

THE VALUE OF
CHRISTIAN FRIENDS

The concept of spiritual friendship is certainly not unfamiliar, as my testimony has already demonstrated; nor is it foreign to the Adventist experience of believing faith. It was not foreign to Ellen White, who wrote regarding a minister who was weak "in management," "Brother Hull should confide in Brother Loughborough's judgment, and listen to his counsel and advice." Furthermore, "although it may be humiliating, he [Hull] should give heed to the judgment and counsel of this companion [Loughborough], as a blind man follows one who has sight. By so doing he will escape many dangers that would prove fatal to him were he left alone."[1] That kind of relation is what I would call spiritual friendship. The tenor of her words do not refer to the relationship of a superior ecclesiastical "leader" and an inferior "worker." I believe that her use of the metaphor of a blind man following one who has sight is meant to suggest, not a subservient following, but a trusting relationship between equals in which one can confide in another. She herself was a spiritual friend many times over—even mine and yours—because she understood the need for such friendship, for such a "personal presence."

"Things will go wrong with every one; sadness and discouragement press every soul; then a personal presence, a friend who will comfort and impart strength, will turn back the darts of the enemy that are aimed to destroy. *Christian friends are not half as plentiful as they should be.* In hours of temptation, in a crisis, what a value is a true friend! Satan at such times sends along his agents to cause the trembling limbs to stumble; but the true friends who will counsel, who will impart magnetic hopefulness, the calming faith that uplifts the soul—*oh, such help is worth more than precious pearls.*"[2]

Ellen White's understanding of the need for spiritual friends, especially at a time of personal spiritual crisis, is made vivid when she recalls that as a result of Martin Luther's teaching and preaching a "living faith was taking the place of the dead formalism in which the church had so long been held."[3] Such a spiritual development was resisted. Luther was declared a heretic and brought to trial at Augsburg. At such a time of grave personal crisis he needed a friend, and God provided one.

"At this time, when Luther so much needed the sympathy and counsel of a true friend, God's providence sent Melanchthon to Wittenberg. Young in years, modest and diffident in his manners, Melanchthon's sound judgment, extensive knowledge, and winning eloquence, combined with the purity and uprightness of his character, won universal admiration and esteem. The brilliancy of his talents was not more marked than his gentleness of disposition. He soon became an earnest disciple of the gospel, and Luther's most trusted friend and valued supporter; his gentleness, caution, and exactness serving as a complement to Luther's courage and energy. Their union in the work added strength to the Reformation and was a source of great encouragement to Luther."[4]

In the Seventh-day Adventist experience, spiritual guidance[5] is understood to take place through personal Bible study, corporate worship, the study of the Spirit of Prophecy, Sabbath school classes for all ages, pastoral care and counseling, and incidental relationships with fellow believers. Many of us would find it difficult to think of establishing a spiritual friendship outside of the Adventist circle. We may have a problem in suspecting that anything not born of Adventist piety is not of the Spirit. My own experience has been that while transitioning from the Lutheran to the Adventist understanding of the Christian faith, which certainly involved a change in doctrine and theology, I did not feel the need to abandon the spirituality that was already mine as a Lutheran. For me, it was more an "adding to," rather than starting over or "subtracting from"—not rejecting, but enhancing and enriching.

My own encounter with the need for spiritual friendship took place about 18 months after my initial conversion. Until then, nothing could interrupt the tranquillity of my newfound faith life. Then suddenly I became intensely aware of the warfare that had begun in my inner being between the Spirit and the flesh, as described by Paul in Galatians 5 and Romans 7. We call it the "great controversy" internalized.

I also discovered that I had a ferocious, devious, and determined enemy who was out to make shipwreck of my new life. I discovered that the Christian life is not pie in the sky, but struggle and conflict. I learned, as Joshua and the Israelites learned, that Caanan is a land of warfare as well as victory. Up until then I was content with personal Bible reading, prayer, and public worship. But suddenly I needed to talk with someone who could help me understand what was happening, who could help me learn how to use the faith God had given me together with the means He provides for victory in such a struggle. Someone who knew firsthand—experientially, not theoretically. Someone who had experienced the same thing and overcome. Someone who had grown to maturity as a disciple of Christ. I needed not only a counselor but a friend, one who understood, with whom I could share the deepest thoughts and struggles of my heart, who would not be judgmental or critical, or betray my confidence. Someone who would walk with me on the Way, yet who could listen carefully and ask the kind of questions that probe for reality to help me become more acutely aware of what the Holy Spirit was doing in my inner being. I have learned that a true spiritual friend is one who helps another hear God. A true spiritual friend doesn't just tell another the Way but shows the Way; he or she helps another find the Way and go the Way.

Over the years I have had a number of such spiritual friends, some Lutherans and many more Adventists, as I have already related in previous chapters. Sometimes the relationship has been brief, at times extended, but always beneficial, in harmony with biblical counsel and permission: "Therefore, confess your sins to one another and pray for one another, that you may be healed" (James 5:16). You may have had similar relationships that have proven immensely beneficial and valuable spiritually. For some of us our wives or husbands have served as spiritual friends, helping to provide the insights needed, especially at crisis moments. A deeply devoted wife, God's gift to a man, who has a mature Christian experience of her own, has a way of uncovering experiential truth that is unmatched. Coupled with love and sincere sympathy, and even empathy, she can be invaluable as a spiritual friend. Time and time again my wife has faithfully and perceptively met my spiritual needs in this way. It is my firm conviction that this is one of the primary divine purposes for the institution of marriage between a man and a woman. God's gift of the wife He has chosen, of the husband He has chosen, is part of the sanctification process. "Iron sharpens iron," says the Bible, "and one [person] sharpens another" (Prov. 27:17). The biblical principle applies to Christian marriage, one spouse sharpening another spiritually, assuming, of course, that the marriage union is in harmony with the will and purpose of God, as revealed in His Word. Sanctification is not possible if the union is not in harmony with God's revealed will.

One of the reasons for the neglect of spiritual friendship is the fantastic rise and growth of psychological approaches to the understanding of human behavior, such as the views of Sigmund Freud, with his focus on sex, and Carl G. Jung, with his dream analysis. Within our own Adventist tradition this neglect may be based on both a negative and a positive factor. The negative one is a fear of the subjective side of spiritual experience. The positive one is our heavy reliance on the Spirit of Prophecy for spiritual guidance. It would seem that a "both/and" rather than an "either/or" approach would be the most beneficial.

We are caught in the trap set for us by Western civilization, which has created a split worldview of reality. According to this view, the real world is "out there." Consequently, success is measured by how well one makes it in the "real world." So we have learned to value achievement, objectivity, science, productivity, social class, analysis, and responsible activity. We often hear the advice "If you are ever going to amount to anything, you have to make something of yourself." We become achievers with goals that are always "out there."

This view values the products of the rational mind exclusively and denies the reality of the world within that Paul referred to as the "inner being" (Eph. 3:16). When we speak to one another, it is usually about things related to the "out there." We talk about our work, homes, hobbies, families, goals and ambitions, politics, and sports—always the external. We resist paying any attention to what is going on inside, resist "opening up" and sharing that dimension of life. Often when one tries to do so, he or she is silenced by the comment "That's a private matter!" Or "It's nobody's business!" Or "I don't want to go there!" What is really meant is "I don't want to communicate with you on that level. I don't really want to know you, and I don't want you to know me. Let's keep it superficial and meaningless." The emptiness, loneliness, and fragmentation that result are translated in the church into external activity programs. When we sense a lack of togetherness and belongingness, we design programs and activities to fill the spaces—and still feel alone. We don't *talk* to anyone or with anyone.

What is the "real" world for you? Is it the outer story of your life, filled with activity and work that has become hollow and meaningless? Or is it the inner story? Or is it both? If your focus is on the external, your primary goal, even in an academic program, is to develop the skills necessary for you to be successful "out there" in the things that you *do*. Your focus has to do with becoming something and is usually necessitated by a consciousness of weakness. The tendency is to conclude that the inner life is only fantasy and thus not "real." It shows up in our approach to the Christian life, and for pastors it shows up in their preaching.

How much of the preaching that you hear is devoted to motivating church members to *do* something? How much is focused on helping them *be* something? We see this reflected in an imbalance between evangelism and nurture, between outreach and inreach. If you find yourself caught in this trap that has ensnared so many others, you need a spiritual friend, and you need to be a spiritual friend. As the external dimension of life becomes more complex, the needs of the internal dimension intensify. If they are not given care, the consequence can be physical or emotional illness, theological bandwagoning, spiritual distortion, such as glossalalia, spiritualism, exorcism, the temptation to dabble in Eastern religions, etc., all of which are devastating not only personally but for ministry as well. The result is the blind leading the blind into more blindness and danger. *A bleak picture indeed.* It seems to me that the principle for spiritual friendship is established in the following:

"It is not required of you to confess to those who know not your sin and errors. It is not your duty to publish a confession which will lead unbelievers to triumph; *but to those to whom it is proper, who will take no advantage of your wrong, confess according to the Word of God, and let them pray for you, and God will accept your work [of confession], and will heal you.*"[6]

That's a very significant *but!* It is, therefore, "proper" to establish a spiritual friendship with someone who is trustworthy and will not take advantage of you and of sensitive knowledge gained—who will hear your confession (of sin, faith, struggle, growth) and pray with you and for you. This practice is acceptable to God, who says, "Confess your sins to one another and pray for one another, that you may be healed. The prayer of a righteous person has great power as it is working" (James 5:16). The promise from God is that when we practice this kind of spirituality, the result is spiritual healing for the inner being.

Jesus was not always understood by His "friends," which added to His sufferings, because not being understood can be agony, but He was their patient friend. A spiritual friend is one who is willing to be used by God in the healing of a spiritually wounded person, which involves helping put back together what is broken, helping to bring about rest. The true spiritual friend participates in the kind of environment that allows for healing to take its course, as I have experienced and related in the first chapter. A spiritual friend is not responsible for the healing; that's God's work. But he or she functions like a midwife or a go-between, a spiritual catalyst.

Though his or her own need for spiritual friendship may be acute, it is not easy for a minister to shift from the assertiveness and authority of preaching (verbalizing) to the patience and humility of the sympathetic listener and helper (nonverbalizing). Here the contrast between *doing* and *being* becomes apparent. If our life orientation is "out there," our personal ministry often becomes a form of advice-giving, telling rather than helping, interpreted often as interference and meddling, insensitive and uncaring. Besides, it is dangerous to give advice, because you then become responsible for the success or failure of that advice. If it works, you are idolized. If it fails, you are vilified. Giving advice requires some degree of infallibility, even omniscience, which none of us has. But if our life orientation is inward, then we know that when we are in the company of one who is spiritually distressed, we are in the presence of mystery. This is why some new Adventists have problems with Ellen White's *Testimonies for the Church*. While the general principles are sound, what is good advice for one person may not be applicable to another. In my ministry I have come across this phenomenon every so often. We ministers need to recognize the difference between pastoral care and psychotherapy, for which we have not been trained but in which we are tempted to dabble. Unfortunately, seminary training, with its heavy emphasis on theological knowledge, does not always equip us for pastoral care.[7]

Why is it that although we may recognize that our responsibility and expertise as ministers is in providing spiritual guidance, we spend so much time in pseudo-psychotherapy? Once again, this phenomenon is reflected in much of the preaching we hear that so often is a form of advice-giving or therapy, characterized by words such as *should* and *ought* motivating the hearer to *do* or to *feel* rather than to *be* or to *become*. If you are a Seventh-day Adventist pastor, *Do people come to you for help with the spiritual dimension of their lives? with their struggle with sin, faith, surrender, obedience, suffering, their relationship with God?* If not, if they have been taught to keep such things to themselves, then you have a major spiritual problem on your hands. It should lead you to ask if anything of a spiritual nature is going on in your congregation and cause you to reevaluate your ministry's priorities and emphases.

Can you imagine how thrilled I was as a young pastor when I was able to help a person like that? During my second year in ministry a woman approached me after I had spoken at an evening camp meeting session.[8] She wanted help with a spiritual problem. She desperately wanted to experience God's forgiveness, but could not find assurance. She did not *feel* forgiven. We opened our Bibles to 1 John, and I asked her to read aloud verses 8 and 9 of the first chapter. She read, "'If we say we have no sin, we deceive ourselves, and the truth is not in us. If we confess our sins, he is faithful and just to forgive us our sins and to cleanse us from all unrighteousness.'"

I asked, "Have you confessed your sin to God?"

"Oh yes," she said, "many times."

"Are you forgiven?"

"I don't know!"

I asked her to read the verses again. She did. "Are you forgiven?"

"I don't know!"

"Read them again," I urged.

She looked at me as if to say, *Are you kidding?* But then, after a moment of hesitation, she did read them again. "Has God forgiven you?"

Somewhat hesitatingly at first, then more confidently, she said, "Yes, I believe He has!"

"How do you know He has forgiven you?"

Pointing at the verses, she answered, "Because it says so right here!"

My heart began to pound and leap for joy! After three years of seminary training and more than a year as a pastor, ministry really began for me at that moment. *Nothing can beat that kind of pastoral experience.*

Spiritual guidance requires that we be conscious of both the cognitive and the affective levels of human awareness—the left- and right-brain responses. While we are engaged in the task of passing on in sermons and Bible studies true information about God and His revelation, His will, and the Christian life, we must also be sensitive to the fact that people actually live on the affective level of feelings. Finally, that woman *felt* forgiven. Forgiveness had become experiential. What a spiritual breakthrough for her, as well as for me, in terms of pastoral care. One can have an immense amount of information, yet be troubled by feelings of uneasiness, loneliness, anxiety, guilt, sadness, and uncertainty. While one's left brain is crammed with theological/doctrinal knowledge, the battle between the flesh and the Spirit may be raging within. That is the crucial point. That is where the personal great controversy is won or lost. And that is why every human problem is a spiritual problem.

How we handle such internal problems reveals our own approach to the Christian life. If we are success-oriented, such struggles are seen as obstacles to success for the suffering one and for ourselves. But if we see these struggles as elements of the spiritual life, they become pathways to spiritual growth, victory, and transformation. If we who are pastors become frustrated and impatient with such persons, then perhaps we need some spiritual guidance ourselves. Such folks do take up precious time, which can be very frustrating, especially if one is active and overly conscious of numerical church growth. Transformation of life does not automatically take place following the acquisition of knowledge. How many Bible studies have you given that were followed by no internal change? Such change comes only after the truth struggle has been internalized.

True spiritual friends are those whom God uses to help another to become aware of, and pay attention to, the ways in which God is speaking—to respond to God's speech and, consequently, participate in the relationship that He has initiated. *I am talking about spiritual experience, not ideas.* What I am most interested in, as a pastor, is what *happens* when someone whom I am guiding becomes conscious of being in the very pres-

ence of God. If the relationship that has been established is real, it has dimension, depth, movement, problems, growth, etc., just like any other relationship. It is not something to be simply talked about, but something to
be engaged in. It is helping people get to where they are going, helping
someone find the way, helping someone stay on the way. The focus is not
on externals, but on the inner being. Why? Because all the good and the
bad that folks do comes from within, which points up the need for the
kind of spiritual friendship and guidance we have been talking about.

Who Needs Spiritual Friends?

I don't want to give the impression that spiritual friendship and guidance are for ministers alone to practice. Every Christian believer is called,
and enabled by the Holy Spirit, to live a life guided by the Spirit. The fruit
of the Spirit are for all believers, while the spiritual "gifts" are distributed
by God's sovereign choice.[9] Such friends are not super people, but average
individuals deeply involved in the common human struggle for physical,
mental, and emotional wholeness and survival. Many of these individuals
share the desire for help in knowing that God has been there all the time
in the midst of their struggles and the turmoil of human existence. That
presence, after all, is the point of the marvelous story that Mark tells in his
Gospel (Mark 4:35-41). Jesus and His disciples were together in a boat in
a fierce storm. The boat was filling with water and on the verge of sink-
ing. Everyone was terrified. But Jesus was calmly sleeping, until they woke
Him up and accused Him of not caring. "And he awoke and rebuked the
wind and said to the sea, 'Peace! Be still!' And the wind ceased, and there
was a great calm. He said to them, 'Why are you so afraid? Have you still
no faith?'" (verses 39, 40). The point? That Jesus is with us *in the boat and
in the storm* and will see us through the storms of life. He *is* there.

Because the journey inward can be so painful, I need spiritual friends
who will walk it with me unafraid. That task is the fundamental role of a
Christian minister. The title I like best—better than "Elder" or
"Doctor"—is "Pastor." "Elder" is an ecclesiastical title, referring to one
who holds a spiritual leadership office. "Doctor" is an academic title, referring to one who has successfully completed the requirements for an advanced educational degree. But "Pastor" is a service designation, referring
to those who care for their flock and feed them on the pure Word of God,
as shepherds care for and feed their sheep.

Your pastor, your shepherd, is a spiritual friend who walks with you,
because you are a part of the age of discontent. In spite of the material, secular, scientific achievements of humankind—many of them staggering—
there is in the human consciousness a longing to find meaning in life.

Many people yearn for some kind of inner vision that will show them the way to wholeness. There is a longing that is difficult to put into words, that is deep, mysterious, and often not understood. The charismatic movement, the ecumenical movement, the emerging church movement, initiatives for peace and justice, and interest in encounter groups are all tangible signs of this need and search, as is the growing interest in eastern Asian and Middle Eastern religions, together with the occult. There is a strong feeling of dissatisfaction with the superficiality of so much of contemporary life, and members are leaving mainline churches in large numbers, because the abandonment of *sola scriptura* by these churches underlies a failure to meet those needs. These churches are not just losing their biblical and doctrinal foundations—they have been actively abandoning them![10] Having jettisoned their compass, they have lost their way. The sad thing is that the membership of those churches is unaware of what is happening and the reasons for the decline. Hence the door is open wide for religious phenomena, such as the so-called emerging church. *But the door is also open wide for a church that holds uncompromisingly to the authority of the Bible as the Word of God and unfailingly proclaims its message.* I believe that church is the Seventh-day Adventist Church, provided we remain true to the Word of God come what may. There are only two valid reasons for leaving a church: If it abandons the teachings of the Bible, or if it bows to cultural demands in order to retain members. God's truth is always absolute and uncompromising. It does not accommodate culture; it confronts culture.

For the Christian, this unrest and searching are indicative of the Spirit moving among people and calling them inward and upward. We are being challenged once again to listen to His voice. This is not always easy. It calls for an alertness in the heart, together with a willingness of mind. It requires an openness to the winds of the Spirit, a stilling of the inner chattering and clamoring that so effectively muffles the Spirit's voice, that still small voice that doesn't shout and can be heard most often in silence. "Be still, and know that I am God," says the Lord (Ps. 46:10).

In many Bible passages, such as Luke 13:3 and Acts 2:38, we are called to come to God in repentance. That word too, along with *authority* and *discipline* and *responsibility* and *accountability*, is heavy to hear in an age of perceived absolute freedom. Because of our technological outward orientation, introspection and disclosure of the inward self are repugnant. They even somehow seem unrelated to the idea of a loving heavenly Father. The call to repentance implies that there is something inherently evil in us that requires repentance, which postmodern philosophy rejects. Could God really want us to stand exposed before Him in such a way? Does He really expect us to suffer what is perceived to be the humiliation and degradation of such self-disclosure—especially if we think there is nothing evil to be so disclosed, only good? Yet there it is in His Word. Jesus says, "Unless you repent, you will all likewise perish" (Luke 13:3). Peter, following the practice of his Lord, said to the Jews, "Repent and be baptized every one of you in the name of Jesus Christ for the forgiveness of your sins, and you will receive the gift of the Holy Spirit" (Acts 2:38).

Don't forget that as we look inward, He looks with us, with a loving—not a judgmental—look. Repentance is meant not to embarrass us but to restore us. My children were always unhappy when they had been disobedient. Their unhappiness was unrelieved until I, their father, initiated their confession and repentance and then readily forgave them. What smiles. What joy on their sweet faces. What relief. The inward journey may begin with pain, but it ends in happiness. Happiness described in Scripture as rebirth and newness of life.

"Christ in you" is the hope of glory, said Paul (Col. 1:27). Not intellectual, cerebral, knowledge *about* Him. Not Christological, doctrinal, formulations. Not creedal statements, as important as they are considered to be. Rather, Christ Himself. Not a faith that believes, but a believing faith. It is no accident that John records Jesus as saying:

"Unless you eat the flesh of the Son of Man and drink his blood, you have no life in you. Whoever feeds on my flesh and drinks my blood has eternal life, and I will raise him up on the last day. For my flesh is true food, and my blood is true drink. Whoever feeds on my flesh and drinks my blood abides in me, and I in him. As the living Father sent me, and I live because of the Father, so whoever feeds on me, he also will live because of me. This is the bread that came down from heaven, not like the bread the fathers ate and died. Whoever feeds on this bread will live forever" (John 6:53-58).

These words have always been too literal for us, their true meaning hidden by the clouds of scholastic rationalism. But it is obvious that the relationship of the believer and the Lord is an inward one before it is anything else. It is a relationship demonstrated, described, by the use of words such as *eat* and *drink* and *feeds* and *bread* and *life in you* and *abides in me*.

Christ is the very center of the very center. Strip everything away from the Christian's life, and you should expose Christ at the center. Throughout the history of Protestant theology, justification has been the major concentration, especially for Lutherans, many of whom talk of nothing else. Please do not misunderstand, I certainly do not want to minimize justification—especially given the resurgence and revival of righteousness by faith in the Seventh-day Adventist Church—because it is crucial for a believing faith. But although justification is a crucial doctrinal/theological issue, it is not the whole of the Christian religion. It ought to produce a religious experience in harmony with the truth of it. Ellen White understood this, and, in harmony with both Paul and Luther, wrote "justification . . . means that the heart [the inner being], purged from dead works, is *prepared* to *receive* the blessing of sanctification."[11] Justification is God's preparatory work for the sinner, which makes the inner work of sanctification by the Holy Spirit possible. Once justified, which reestablishes the relationship lost in the Fall, the believer is prepared to receive the gift of being sanctified and thus "made righteous" (Rom. 5:19).

It was the apostle Paul who articulated in his letters the wonderful truth of justification, but when it came to his own religious experience and his own moral character, *union with Christ* was the dominating factor. Again and again we read Paul's words "in Christ" (see, for example, Rom. 6:11). Personal union with Christ in the "inner being" (Eph. 3:16), received by faith and lived in love, is the essence of the Christian religion. It is the most energizing and creative element in Seventh-day Adventist spirituality. United by faith with Christ, the sinner will identify with Christ in His attitude toward sin and in His attitude toward sanctification and holiness. James Stewart writes, "Only when union with Christ is kept central is sanctification seen in its true nature, as the unfolding of Christ's own character within the believer's life; and only then can the essential relationship between religion and ethics be understood. In short the whole meaning of the atonement is here at stake."[12]

Christian life is fellowship with (in) Christ, or it is not Christian life. That fellowship, to be real, has to be an inward fellowship. In the Synoptic Gospels such fellowship is most frequently spoken of as being "with" (Greek, *meta*) Him, whereas Paul (see Eph. 1:1-13) prefers the word "in" (Greek, *en*). The inner nature of the relationship is upheld by Jesus Himself, who said, "For where two or three are gathered in my name, there am I among them" (Matt. 18:20) and, more specifically, "Abide in me, and I in you" (John 15:4). Christ is the believer's new environment. "For to me to live is Christ" is the way Paul expressed that reality (Phil. 1:21). Many believers have experienced the moral and physical vitalization, the verve, the creativeness and exhilaration, the zest and gladness and power, of such a relationship in Christ.

This understanding of the relationship is a decisive challenge to the kind of modern religion that regards Jesus merely as an example. Such a religion does not satisfy the deepest longing of the human spirit for fellowship with the Eternal. The truth is that no shining human example, even that of Jesus, can cleanse a defiled conscience or break the steel-like grip of sin on the inner being of humanity. If all I have is a great teacher, I am left without a Savior and without a Lord. The historical facts about Jesus are clear. The doctrines are true and sound. But the reality of Jesus is a matter of the heart. Only there do we meet Him personally. It is the very purpose of the Sabbath that the chattering of our hearts cease so that we can nurture the inner relationship with Christ. On such a day the words of this hymn can be fulfilled: "Into my heart, into my heart, come into my heart, Lord Jesus. Come in today, come in to stay, come into my heart, Lord Jesus."

Some Christians are suspicious of a faith that emphasizes rational thought at the expense of feeling. Others are suspicious when the emphasis is on feeling at the expense of rational thought. Just as we have one brain with two hemispheres, so we have one faith with two dimensions: thought and feeling. To be whole, we need both *in balance*. If they are unbalanced, our faith experience is incomplete and unreal. We all need the nurture of an inner faith life that is so strong and sure that it breaks the mental ropes that bind us to the world, the kind of believing faith that prepares us to meet adversity. Did you know that the word *hypocrite,* which Jesus applied to the Pharisees who loved outward spirituality, refers to the mask often worn by ancient actors? "As [a man] thinks in his heart, so is he" (Prov. 23:7, NKJV). "For the Lord sees not as man sees: man looks on the outward appearance, but the Lord looks on the heart" (1 Sam. 16:7).

Who needs spiritual friendship? I do. This is the way I see it as a Seventh-day Adventist Christian. I need spiritual friends to help me prepare a place for Jesus in my inner being, as He prepares a place for me in heaven. As I am in His heart, I want Him in mine. On the eve of His betrayal Jesus prayed for those who had received and kept God's Word and for those who will receive that Word through their word, asking "that they may all be one, just as you, Father, are in me, and I in you, that they also may be in us, so that the world may believe that you have sent me" (John 17:21). I need spiritual friends who will not hesitate to share that Word with me, especially at crisis moments in my life. That oneness of fellowship, as we minister the Word of God to and with one another, is a major convincing factor in evangelism. It is manifest evidence of genuine spirituality and is very convincing for those "who will believe in me through their word" (verse 20). That kind of spirituality is as much a part of the message we proclaim as are the words we use in preaching and in personal testimony.

I need spiritual friends to help me toward the place of rendezvous with my Savior and Lord. I am very much aware that it is not inwardness that I need, but Christ. I need spiritual friends to help me pray, and that means more than uttering words. It means awareness and an openness that I instinctively fear, coupled with the willingness to obey the answer. When Jesus' disciples asked Him to teach them to pray (not *how* to pray), He did it by modeling. That demonstration of spiritual friendship is known today as the Lord's Prayer, which He intended to become my way of praying. Learning to pray involves need and desire more than the choice of words. The only way it can be learned is by example, when someone prays with you. I need you praying even more than I need your words. I need spiritual friends, because of my yearning to be a great pray-er, to be holier than I am, a more powerful witness and overcomer. The Bible calls believers "saints" (see 1 Cor. 1:2), calling us to be holy as our Father is holy (see Matt. 5:48). All of us who believe have the potential within to be holier than we are. Isn't that true? To realize this and act upon it is part of the exciting adventure of a believing faith. And we do it in fellowship with Christ. It takes a lifetime to be fully realized, because it is a process, "the Way."

These are the reasons we need spiritual friends. Deep down inside we sense that there is more, much more, than the superficiality of the daily grind. We long for the depths of our being to be evoked, so that our deep may be united with God's deep—His deep riches of wisdom and knowledge. "How unsearchable are his judgments and how inscrutable his ways! . . . For from him and through him and to him are all things. To him be glory forever. Amen" (Rom. 11:33-36). Maturing in a believing faith moves us from abstractions, doctrinal formulations, and creeds, to a Person. In the personal encounter with Jesus, as with any person, especially with one whom you love, you will encounter the conflicts, disappointments, joys, and glories that make the relationship a fulfilling experience. Because the believer knows the hope of glory, which is "Christ in you," he or she is able to look, with eager anticipation and confidence, for the future glory when Jesus comes again.

Does the inner being resist this? Yes, it does, as we know very well when we are honest with ourselves. Here we are face to face with the inner conflict that is part of what Seventh-day Adventist Christians call "the great controversy" between God and Satan, between good and evil, between righteousness and unrighteousness. Paul experienced the reality of that inner controversy. He described it by saying that he was "sold under sin. For I do not understand my own actions. For I do not do what I want, but I do the very thing I hate" (Rom. 7:14, 15). The problem? It is "sin that dwells within me" (verse 17). In a sermon preached by Ellen White to a congregation of Seventh-day Adventists at Lansing, Michigan, on September 5, 1891, she boldly said to the gathered saints in words spoken by a true pietist:

"Unless your *hearts* [inner beings] are *emptied* of sin every day, unless you are sanctified through the truth, you would better not touch the message of God. You cannot cleanse yourselves, but by coming to Jesus in humility, in contrition, surrendering yourselves to God, through the merits of Christ's righteousness you may have an *experience* in the things of God, and taste of the powers of the world to come. You then will have fruit unto life eternal."[13]

The human "soul," or inner being, is like a vacuum; it will suck up whatever is nearest. That's why emptying is so fearful. The inner being, emptied of sin, must be immediately and carefully filled with the things of the Spirit, with the Word of God, with Christ, or it will be filled with worldly trivia. In this way, spiritual life indwells natural life.

The best way to deal with sin is not to try to reform ourselves, but to worship the Lord. While we worship Christ, "who is seated at the right hand of the throne of the Majesty in heaven" (Heb. 8:1) and who at the same time dwells in our hearts by the Holy Spirit, we will not be intrigued by sin. To surrender fully (which I so desperately wish to do when I understand why it is so necessary) may mean a great upheaval in my life. I am afraid of what He may do with me, of what He might ask me to do for Him. I am even afraid of losing my hunger and thirst by being satisfied. Jesus said, "Blessed [happy] are those who hunger and thirst for righteousness, for they shall be satisfied" (Matt. 5:6). He is speaking of a perpetual, continuing, hunger and thirst. As long as I keep on hungering and thirsting for righteousness, I will be satisfied. If I stop hungering and thirsting for righteousness, I will lose it. If I never hunger and thirst for it, I will never receive it. It's so profoundly simple.

Intimacy with Christ cannot be rushed. We must learn to take small bites rather than trying to wolf down large chunks. Time management can change easily into management by time. But I am afraid to stop to pay attention. If I do, I might see the emptiness of my life. This is why fast-lane contemporary religion may outwardly appeal but does not inwardly satisfy. Why not? Because it misses the heart, the inner being. Worship should not be rushed into. If we rush in, we won't want to stay very long, just as the person who grumbles if the worship service goes beyond one hour. Faced with such self-centered whining one Sabbath, I responded with "Do you have anything better to do on the Sabbath?" It is my left brain that needs quieting down so that my right brain (the meditative hemisphere) can be engaged. The mind must slow down to a cleansed level of consciousness. The symbol over a Christian sanctuary is the cross of Christ, not McDonald's golden arches.

Qualities of Spiritual Friends

The purpose of spiritual friendship is to facilitate the fruit of the Spirit in the life of the one befriended. It can be, and often is, a mutual ministry. In fact, it is the most beneficial and fruitful of friendships. It is a gift that God stands ready to give to many more people than currently are open to it. Pastors certainly ought to be such spiritual friends among their people. If they can see that the gift is not restricted to ministers, but is actually given to the entire body of Christ, then pastors will see potential spiritual friends among their people. By modeling such friendship, they can encourage it. Let's call it "mutual ministry." Obviously, this is not possible, nor will it be fruitful, if the members of the body do not trust one another. After all, congregations ought to be communities of faith in which the members learn to love and be loved. The principle established, commanded, by Christ is clear. He said, "A new commandment I give to you, that you love one another; just as I have loved you, you also are to love one another. [For what purpose?] By this all people will know that you are my disciples, if you have love for one another" (John 13:34, 35). Love among God's people, the members of the body of Christ, is the greatest and most productive form of evangelism there is. Jesus said so. Because such love is living proof for "all people" to know that they are Christ's disciples. People can argue about preaching, about doctrines, but they cannot argue with the reality of this kind of love. What does it mean to "bear one another's burdens, and so fulfill the law of Christ"? This is not an ambiguous statement. It is as clear as a bell. We know very well what it means. It means exactly what Jesus says. There is no way around it if we claim to base our faith on His Word. The Spirit of Prophecy enlarges on this principle in a passage about church unity:

"The love of Christ must come [imperative] into the church, and be cherished by every member as a precious plant. If the branches of the vine are united to the parent stock, the same life dwells in them all. In Christ Jesus there is love, and those who are united to Christ will not have merely a tame, common regard as acquaintances, but true, sincere love for one another, because they are endued with the Spirit of Christ. This drawing off from one another is not Christlike, but it is after Satan's order. Love is not a mere simple regard, but a living principle; not a *temporary emotion, but a permanent power.* We drink it in fresh from the fountain of love that flows from the cross of Calvary. We are quickened by this love. 'I in them, and thou in me, that they may be made perfect in one; and that the world may know that thou hast sent me, and hast loved them, as thou hast loved me.' Quickened by this love, the power of the Holy Spirit, we learn to love one another in and through Christ Jesus truly, sincerely, unaffectedly."[14]

This is the living Christ, manifesting His life in His church, when the Christ in me responds to the Christ in you. Nothing, *absolutely nothing*, is more satisfying for pastors to witness, as fruit of their ministry, than this. Imagine how my heart leaped when I heard the camp meeting testimony of a young mother in my congregation who was preparing for baptism. She said, "I have never known a more loving group of people. Their arms are always open wide!" Yes! That's it! That's what the body of Christ is all about. That's what spiritual friendship is all about. Such friends are the kind of people who provide the environment in which spiritual healing can happen. So let's talk a bit about the essential qualities of this kind of people.

Obviously they have to be fellow travelers who are maturing in the faith. It would be difficult—impossible, really—to share one's faith struggles with those who have not experienced any struggles. Certainly it could not be done with non-Christians, who would have no understanding, or sympathy, for the experience. But it could be done with fellow believers who have gone from faith to faith, because those individuals are in a position not only to understand but to be helpful. They are responsive to the prompting of the Holy Spirit and know what—or what not—to say in a given situation. Such people are able to accept the suffering and agony as part of the Spirit's work and are not too eager with advice on how one can get out of it. Rather, they help the individual find God in it, to see His footprints. These kinds of people are sensitive to being a stumbling block to the religious experience. These people are mature enough in the faith to know that answers, and changes, that are deep and lasting do not always come quickly, but usually after struggle and pain. These individuals are patient enough, which is a premier virtue of the remnant people, to wait and to watch for the manifestations of the Spirit and to help others become aware of such manifestations. They have spent some time sorting through the impulses, temptations, weaknesses, and much of the personal and social garbage that makes up life—and out of it have selected some eternal values and principles for the kind of spiritual guidance that helps make sense of it all.

Mature spiritual friends are able to live with a degree of ambiguity and with many unanswered questions, knowing that for some questions there are no answers, at least on this side of the resurrection. Having the patience of the saints, they are content to wait for eternity to reveal the answers. Spiritual friends know that God is going to spend eternity revealing His glory to us and are content for now with the questions, with their own questioning, which saves them from authoritarianism and superiority, and makes them dependent on grace and faith alone. They are not in a hurry, knowing no matter how fast one travels they get nowhere anyway. Nowhere satisfying. Those who are always on the go are not interested in a destination; they are interested in the going. Those who like to travel are ones who like to travel, not be somewhere. "Be still, and know" (Ps. 46:10). True spiritual friends are willing to share the stillness, willing to help someone find it.

Mature spiritual friends are ones who reach out in hospitality. Such hospitality does not change people, but provides the atmosphere in which change can take place. That means giving the gift of their time, even though it may be inconvenient. Sometimes our evangelistic zeal can suffocate persons. They cannot change, because we do not allow them the freedom to change. True spiritual friends will never impose religious views or experiences upon others, but will help them find their own. Jesus reached out to us to meet our deepest spiritual needs, and we can reach out to others as friends, and be friends, in the same way.

We are called to be healers, but the tragedy is that we do not make our healing gifts of support and affirmation available. We stay aloof so often. It takes the grace of God to face our own pain and that of others, and so we substitute advice, counsel, or treatment without having any knowledge of the wounds. Lest you misunderstand, let me be quick to point out that our presence must be not ambiguous, but honest and true. While the love we offer is unconditional and without price, we have to be what we are, Seventh-day Adventist Christians. Concerning what we believe, we have nothing to be ashamed of and certainly nothing to hide or keep to ourselves. We are not neutral "nobodies." As spiritual friends, we are not neutral concerning what we believe and know to be true. But by the same token, love demands that we not be offensively aggressive. That balance requires the grace of God, together with a willingness to suffer inconvenience for the friend. Jesus said, "Greater love has no one than this, that someone lay down his life for his friends" (John 15:13). That truth is reflected in the memorable comment by Dietrich Bonhoeffer: "When Christ calls a man, He bids him come and die." [15] If we believe that, it is imperative to act on it.

True spiritual friends model their lives after that of Jesus and count "others more significant" than themselves. They look to "the interests of others," as the apostle Paul puts it:

"So if there is any encouragement in Christ, any comfort from love, any participation in the Spirit, any affection and sympathy, complete my joy by being of the same mind, having the same love, being in full accord and of one mind. Do nothing from rivalry or conceit, but in humility count others more significant than yourselves. Let each of you look not only to his own interests, but also to the interests of others. Have this mind among yourselves, which is yours in Christ Jesus, who, though he was in the form of God, did not count equality with God a thing to be grasped, but made himself nothing, taking the form of a servant, being born in the likeness of men. And being found in human form, he humbled himself by becoming obedient to the point of death, even death on a cross. Therefore God has highly exalted him and bestowed on him the name that is above every name, so that at the name of Jesus every knee should bow, in heaven and on earth and under the earth, and every tongue confess that Jesus Christ is Lord, to the glory of God the Father" (Phil. 2:1-11).

Talk about evangelism. That's evangelism. It is also a vivid description of Christian spirituality. When God's people live like that among themselves and in the world, how can "every knee" not bow "at the name of Jesus" and finally confess that Jesus Christ is Lord? Such a fellowship is irresistible. *While I was writing these very words, the phone rang. It was a recently baptized member of my congregation, who excitedly shared the news that a friend of hers had just called in distress. After listening to her, she had shared Jesus over the phone. Her friend had accepted Him into her heart then and there. They prayed together, and her friend said she felt so wonderfully uplifted and overjoyed.* That is what spiritual friendship is all about.

Spiritual friends are persons of prayer, those who know the richness of God's forgiveness through silent meditation on the Word of God and through listening for His "voice" as the Holy Spirit impresses the mind and heart. Such friends are companions who themselves may have been hurt and bewildered, sometimes uncertain of their own progress yet having experienced many times the loving but firm influence of God, moving them toward a wholeness and holiness for which we all yearn. The pray-er has perhaps walked in darkness, but with a living hope. Those who have not endured the night of spiritual struggle can hardly empathize truthfully with another crying out to God for help and salvation. Jesus said, "I am the light of the world. Whoever follows me will not walk in darkness, but will have the light of life" (John 8:12).

Jesus understands and is such a sympathetic friend, because He walked through Gethsemane, His darkness. Matthew tells us that He was "sorrowful and troubled," saying to His three companions, "My soul [inner being] is very sorrowful, even to death" (Matt. 26:38). His inner anguish must have been bad, really bad. What did the suffering Savior need at that moment? Friends who would keep Him company. So He asked them to "remain here, and watch with me" (verse 38). That's all. Just to be with Him. What did they do? How did they fulfill His need? They went to sleep. From His suffering heart came a distressed plea, "Could you not watch with me [even] one hour?" Just one hour? So He gave up relying on them. (See Matt. 26:36-44.) How sad. When He needed His friends the most, they failed Him. But He would never fail them. That's grace and mercy. What did Jesus rely on? His own Word: "Blessed are those who mourn, for they shall be comforted" (Matt. 5:4). Paul surely learned that lesson, because he was able to say to the Corinthian believers: "Blessed be the God and Father of our Lord Jesus Christ, the Father of mercies and God of all comfort, who comforts us in all our affliction, so that we may be able to comfort those who are in any affliction, with the comfort with which we ourselves are comforted by God. For as we share abundantly in Christ's sufferings, so through Christ we share abundantly in comfort too. If we are afflicted, it is for your comfort and salvation; and if we are comforted, it is for your comfort, which you experience when you patiently endure the same sufferings that we suffer. Our hope for you is unshaken, for we know that as you share in our sufferings, you will also share in our comfort.

"For we do not want you to be ignorant, brothers, of the affliction we experienced in Asia. For we were so utterly burdened beyond our strength that we despaired of life itself. Indeed, we felt that we had received the sentence of death. *But that was to make us rely not on ourselves but on God who raises the dead.* He delivered us from such a deadly peril, and he will deliver us. *On him we have set our hope that he will deliver us again.* You also must help us by prayer, so that many will give thanks on our behalf for the blessing granted us through the prayers of many" (2 Cor. 1:3-11).

This is what we might call the redemptive mystery. Awareness of this mystery in one's own life is a primary prerequisite for spiritual friendship. If a person has no understanding of, no sympathy for, no sensitivity to, and cannot articulate such spiritual awareness, then, no matter how much doctrinal knowledge and information this individual may possess, he or she will have nothing redemptive to share. As one of my pastoral colleagues says: "No one cares how much you know until they know how much you care." Those who enter into an experience with the Holy Spirit by prayer are permitting love itself to come into their hearts and lives. Their actions then become motivated by love, and they can be expected to be kind, caring, and loving persons—truthfully kind and truthfully loving, so that bold confrontation can occur at times when needed—so that the Spirit of truth can be evoked. There is no room for ungracious behavior in a spiritual friendship, because what is being dealt with are matters of the heart, the inner being. Those who pray much will love much. It is prayer that protects the spiritual friendship from phoniness and superficiality.

Spiritual friends are those who, as the apostle Paul indicates, have the gift of being able "to distinguish between spirits" (1 Cor. 12:10), that is to say, have the ability to distinguish whether the "spirits" are good or bad, evil spirits or the Holy Spirit, and respond accordingly. How does one "distinguish between spirits"? It is characteristic of evil spirits to produce anxiety, sadness, raising obstacles backed by fallacious reasoning that disturb the inner being. Evil spirits can be detected when there is present an inner darkness, inner turmoil, inclinations toward what is base, restlessness arising from temptations that lead to loss of faith, loss of hope, and loss of love.

On the other hand, it is characteristic of the Holy Spirit to give courage, strength, consolation, inspiration, and peace. The Holy Spirit also gives the tears that come with repentance and confession. Such tears move the person toward love of God, whether the tears be caused by sorrow for sin, because of the suffering of Christ, or for any other reason directly related to the praise and service of God. Every increase of faith, hope, and love and all inward joy that attracts one to what is heavenly and to salvation is from the Holy Spirit.

Spiritual friends are able to discern these interior movements, recognizing that the spirit world is an active one and that there are many opportunities for evil spirits or the Holy Spirit to achieve ascendancy in one's life. Because spiritual friends are susceptible too, their sense of insecurity and fear can be increased. Then it is essential to remember that God is the real friend and that we are sinners seeking to discern God's actions through our conversations. Have you ever noticed that at the times you feel threatened during a spiritual conversation, Satan can confuse the issue by leading into an intellectual argument or harangue? Being able to discern the footprints of God can be a subtle process in which one may need the help of a sensitive friend and in which believing faith is exercised. *(Recall the stories I related in the first chapter.)* Of course, this presumes an agreement of confidentiality. A spiritual friend who gossips about a spiritual friend is not a true friend, but a betrayer like Judas.

True spiritual friends must be alert. In a world of cacophonic noises we must be able to hear the sound of a falling snowflake when we listen for the movements of the Spirit. A special effort must be made to resist a drifting concentration. Out of genuine concern, not just duty or obligation, spiritual friends will be alert and attentive. After all, the person who is talking is speaking about personal spiritual reality and life. The listener's choice of words and tone, even facial expressions, are critical. Just recently I was engaged in a deep conversation with some friends, relating a major personal concern, when one of them broke into my narrative with his own agenda. My inner being ached, because it was apparent he was not listening or responding to me. When a person is being too superficial and is not dipping deeply enough, nothing worthwhile is being said, and you need to ask the kind of probing questions that will lead the person to a deeper and more honest appraisal of his or her life in the Spirit.

Jesus commanded us to "love one another as I have loved you" (John 15:12). That command must be obeyed first if we are going to listen to a fellow pilgrim with sympathy and understanding. This love does not mean emotional involvement that would make one ineffectual. But neither does it mean aloofness and distance. The listener must become adept at listening to two things—(1) the words being spoken (language), which involves factual data, and (2) the feelings expressed nonverbally. The listener also needs to pay attention to the feelings evoked within by both of these. Is the language firsthand or secondhand? If secondhand, what does it mask? As a spiritual friend, how do I feel about the language? The Holy Spirit is involved in this listening, and we must learn to respond to the Spirit by responding from the heart and not from the head alone.

Like everything else worthwhile, becoming a true spiritual friend is learned. How? In the school of the Holy Spirit. One is not automatically qualified for this role upon receiving an academic degree or any other kind of training. It requires spiritual maturity, some experience with the spiritual struggle, the battle between the flesh and the Spirit in which a believing faith is victorious. It begins with recognizing the longing in your inner being to go out to others and bring them freedom, peace, and abundant life in Christ. If you happen to be a minister, it rests on a deep dissatisfaction with a skills-oriented ministry designed to make you noticed by others and successful as a professional. Such success helps you climb the ecclesiastical ladder, but brings with it a restless uneasiness because of the intuition that you have not been doing what God has called you to do or to be. Professional success, even advancement, does not satisfy or quench the uneasiness and dissatisfaction. *Call it what it is, guilt.* There is a fascinating passage in 1 Corinthians that we need to consider carefully, whether we are professional ministers or laypersons.

"But I, brothers, could not address you as spiritual people, but as people of the flesh, as infants in Christ. I fed you with milk, not solid food, for you were not ready for it. And even now you are not yet ready, for you are still of the flesh. For while there is jealousy and strife among you, are you not of the flesh and behaving only in a human way? For when one says, 'I follow Paul,' and another, 'I follow Apollos,' are you not being merely human? What then is Apollos? What is Paul? Servants through whom you believed, as the Lord assigned to each. I planted, Apollos watered, but God gave the growth. So neither he who plants nor he who waters is anything, but only God who gives the growth. He who plants and he who waters are one, and each will receive his wages according to his labor. For we are God's fellow workers. You are God's field, God's building. According to the grace of God given to me, like a skilled master builder I laid a foundation, and someone else is building upon it. Let each one take care how he builds upon it. For no one can lay a foundation other than that which is laid, which is Jesus Christ" (1 Cor. 3:1-11).

Did you hear the Word? No matter what position we hold in the church, you and I are only "servants." If there is professional jealousy or strife among the members of the church, we are "behaving only in a human way" and are not "spiritual," but "of the flesh." God's people do not follow human leaders—they follow the Lord, who alone "gives the growth." We just plant and water, following after one another in doing so. Thank God someone laid the foundation in your town, in your congregation. They will get their reward "according to" the work they have done. The foundation is already there, and that foundation is "Jesus Christ" if the work has been done in harmony with His Word and according to His purpose. What then? What is the responsibility of those who come after? It is not to start the work over. It is not to disrespect the work that has been done by previous generations. Yes, "someone else is building upon" the foundation that was laid by others, each new generation of believers. To the young folks who have come after the older folks who have paid the bills up to now, the Word of God lays a solemn charge. It says that each one is to "take care how he builds upon it." Please don't disparage, don't trash what your parents and grandparents have done. Honor it. Thank God for it. Don't start over, but build carefully upon it. How my inner being has hurt when I have heard from the pulpit or read in an article in one of our church publications words that look down the nose at the witness and work of those who planted and watered so faithfully before, who have left a legacy of sacrificial service to build on. The day "will disclose" with what materials the next generation builds, and "the fire will test what sort of work each one has done" in every generation. "If the work that anyone has built on the foundation survives, he will receive a reward" (verses 13, 14). What is the ultimate test? The written Word of God, which is uncompromising and absolute. If we surrender to the prevalent decadent and sin-filled culture, we betray the Lord and His church. Genuine Christian Adventist spirituality is born and nurtured by the truth revealed in the Bible as the Word of God. The seriousness of this truth is underlined in the next two verses when the apostle says, "Do you not know [in spite of all your study, are you ignorant] that you [the church] are God's temple and that God's Spirit dwells in you? If anyone [layperson, pastor, professor, theologian, administrator] destroys God's temple [the church], God will destroy him. For God's temple is holy, and you are that temple" (verses 16, 17).

What do these verses have to do with spiritual friendship? They have everything to do with it, because no one who betrays the Lord and His church by refusing or neglecting to build on the foundation already laid is qualified to be a true spiritual friend. The kind of spiritual friends I have described in this chapter are not like Hindu gurus or personal popes or spiritual directors who tell you what you ought to do. Rather, true spiritual friends are those who are Spirit-sensitive and walk in the Way with you.

Meditation

Have I experienced the value of a spiritual friend, who has helped me bear my burdens and find the Way? Am I prepared to be such a friend myself? Am I able to help someone else hear God? Is Jesus just my example, or do I really believe that He lives in me? Spend some time in meditation before you read on.

---

[1] E. G. White, *Testimonies for the Church,* vol. 1, pp. 437, 442.

[2] *The Seventh-day Adventist Bible Commentary,* Ellen G. White Comments, vol. 3, p. 1163. (Italics supplied.)

[3] E. G. White, *The Great Controversy,* p. 133.

[4] *Ibid.,* p. 134.

[5] "Spiritual guidance" is the phrase we use, rather than "spiritual direction."

[6] E. G. White, *Testimonies for the Church,* vol. 2, p. 296. (Italics supplied.)

[7] One of the most valuable resources currently available for this kind of ministry is Bruce and Dorothy Hayward, *God's Heart Call to Inner Peace* (Berrien Springs, Mich.: LifeSpring Ministry, 2009), lifespringministry@gmail.com.

[8] In the old Finnish Evangelical Lutheran Church, Suomi Synod, they were called Bible camps, because that's where the focus was. But no more.

[9] See 1 Cor. 12:8-11, 28-30; Eph. 4:11-13.

[10] John H. Kaelberer perceptively points out the impact of this on Christian spirituality in his book *The Not So Silent Merger* (Enumclaw, Wash.: WinePress Publishing, 2004). He writes: "The churches that have stood for decades as the 'mainline' denominations of America have drastically changed. Methodist, Episcopal, Congregational, and the United Church of Christ, along with some liberal denominations within the Presbyterian, Baptist, and Lutheran mix, as well as many others, no longer stand doctrinally where they stood just fifty years ago. Following the lead of liberal theologians who have demythologized the Bible, abandoning its authority, denying the miracles of the Virgin Birth and the Resurrection, and trashing as uncongenial any biblical doctrine contrary to the modern day liberated lifestyle, these denominations have betrayed their divine calling to be the true Body of Jesus Christ, the Christian Church which God brought into being at Pentecost. Their membership and finances are no longer where they were even twenty years ago. Christian spirituality vanishes as well and for those old timers who remain within these denominations there are the very haunting questions: 'What is going on in my church? What has happened?'" (pp. 20, 21). Kaelberer also quotes from a study by the Barna Research

Group, pointing out that "in denominations that ordain women, only 15 percent [of their membership] subscribe to a biblical worldview" (p. 108).

[11] Ellen G. White, in *Signs of the Times,* Dec. 17, 1902. (Italics supplied.)

[12] *A Man in Christ* (New York: Harper and Brothers), pp. 152, 153.

[13] Ellen G. White, in *Review and Herald*, Mar. 29, 1892. (Italics supplied.)

[14] Ellen G. White, *The Ellen G. White 1888 Materials* (Washington D.C.: Ellen G. White Estate, 1987), vol. 3, pp. 1141, 1142. (Italics supplied.)

[15] *The Cost of Discipleship*, p. 73.

Chapter 10

BRAIN WASHING
OR BRAINWASHING?

In the first chapter I mentioned that it is hard to communicate when using certain words is like waving a red flag in front of a bull. I also made the appeal that we should not be afraid to use good words. Sometimes the reaction to words can be fierce, a virtual explosion of suspicion that can be seen in the eyes and the body language of the person with whom we are speaking. It can become almost impossible to get past the reaction and allow for friendly, meaningful dialogue.

Words often carry loaded content that produces a reaction similar to what happens when one touches a hot stove. This is certainly true when it comes to the word *tradition,* a word with both negative and positive connotations. After all, there are both good and bad traditions. In the religious world traditions that are not based on biblical revelation, such as the Catholic Mass and the observance of Sunday, have developed historically. By the same token, good traditions that are based on biblical revelation, such as observance of the seventh-day Sabbath, have also developed. Of course, Sabbath observance is a tradition that arouses intense suspicion and accusations of legalism among evangelicals and others. I have said all this by way of introduction to this chapter, because I am going to use, and have already used, the word *tradition* in a positive sense.

The apostle Paul exhorted the church, "So then, brothers, stand firm and hold to the traditions that you were taught by us, either by our spoken word or by our letter" (2 Thess. 2:15). He commended the Corinthian believers for maintaining "the traditions even as I delivered them to you" (1 Cor. 11:2). What traditions was he referring to? The commands of the Lord, the total teachings of Scripture. "If anyone thinks that he is a prophet, or spiritual, he should acknowledge that the things I am writing to you are a command of the Lord. If anyone does not recognize this, he is not recognized" (1 Cor. 14:37, 38). "For I delivered to you as of first importance what I also received . . . in accordance with the Scriptures" (1 Cor. 15:3). Scriptural tradition and none other, especially not a mixing of "traditions." The only tradition that can be relied upon is the *sola-tota-prima scriptura* principle.[1] That which the Bible condemns is "human tradition" (Col. 2:8), for the sake of which "you have made void the word of God" (Matt. 15:6).

Adventist Meditation

Countless times Ellen White underscores the centrality of the revealed Word of God for Adventist spirituality. That fact serves to authenticate and assure the reliability of her spiritual gift for the church. For me, that fact is the most impressive and enduring thing about her ministry. It is the fundamental reason that I trust her counsel. The following passage summarizes that centrality by emphasizing the relationship between faith and hearing God's Word, as well as warning us not to trust human reasoning:

"We need to realize the necessity of exercising that faith which is acceptable to God—the faith which works by love and purifies the soul [inner being]. Without faith it is impossible to hear the Word in such a way as to profit by the hearing, even though it be presented in a most impressive manner. . . . Unless we mix faith with our hearing of the Word, unless we receive the truths we hear as a message from heaven, to be carefully studied, to be eaten by the soul [inner being] and assimilated into the spiritual life, we lose the impression of the Spirit of God. . . . The importance of studying the Word cannot be overestimated. Its promises are large, and full of richness. In no case should we fail of securing the heavenly treasure. Christ is our only security. We cannot trust to human reasoning. The world is full of men and women who cherish deceptive theories, and it is dangerous to listen to them."[2]

We need to hear the Word of God, not the reasoning of those who cherish and promote deceptive theories. God's Word is the only protection from such deception. The only safe mixing is the mixing of faith with the hearing of that Word alone. The Spirit of Prophecy counsel is to meditate on that Word:

"We wish to repeat over and over again, until it is indelibly imprinted upon the heart [inner being], the blessed invitation, Abide in Me. Read the Word, and in the light of a 'Thus saith the Lord,' meditate upon it. Pray until the lesson and meaning of *abiding in* is fully learned, accompanied with its claims and its promises. The Holy Spirit, Christ's representative, is now in our world to bring all things to our remembrance, that His claims shall not be forgotten or neglected. Read the Word and pray. Meditate on the Scriptures until the understanding, the gate to the door to the heart, is opened to comprehend its requirements and our dependence. Those who will wait to hear what the Spirit saith unto them shall not hear in vain. Fix the eye upon Christ alone in quiet waiting upon Him to hear His voice saying, 'Abide in me, and I in you.' "[3]

Understanding of the Word is the gate to the heart's door. Read the Word of God. Pray over it. Meditate upon it. This means to consciously think about the truth it reveals until it is stamped, engraved, imprinted on, and embedded in the inner being. Until it is understood, not just intellectually but experientially. That understanding opens further access to the inner being for the Holy Spirit. Such counsel is faithful to biblical faith and teaching that exclaims, "Oh how I love your law! It is my meditation all the day" (Ps. 119:97). This is to be done by "quiet waiting upon" Christ and with "eyes fixed on Christ."

"The follower of Christ will meet with the 'enticing words' against which the apostle warned the Colossian believers. He will meet with spiritualistic interpretations of the Scriptures, but he is not to accept them. His voice is to be heard in clear affirmation of the eternal truths of the Scriptures. Keeping his eyes fixed on Christ, he is to move steadily forward in the path marked out, discarding all ideas that are not in harmony with His teaching. The truth of God is to be the subject for his *contemplation and meditation*. He is to regard the Bible as the voice of God speaking directly to him. Thus he will find the wisdom which is divine."[4]

The "truth of God" is the "subject" for contemplation and meditation in Adventist spirituality. Nothing else. Discarding ideas that do not harmonize with the teaching of Christ is a vital part of meditative thinking. No lengthy comment on the above quote is necessary. Read it again. It is as clear as a bell. The moment we depart from such counsel we are in deep spiritual trouble. When Seventh-day Adventist Christians speak about meditation, this is what we should mean and should clearly articulate, because if we neglect "the highest source of wisdom—the Word of God," we will not reach our "noblest development."

"That we are in God's world, in the presence of the Creator; that we are made in His likeness; that He watches over us and loves us and cares for us—these are wonderful themes for thought and lead the mind into broad, exalted fields of meditation. He who opens mind and heart [inner being] to the contemplation of such themes as these will never be satisfied with trivial, sensational subjects."[5]

The meditation that is authentic to Adventist spirituality is not a ritualistic emptying of the mind in order to fill it with God's Word. Rather, to meditate is to so fill the mind with God's Word that it crowds out that which should not be there, that which is impure and untrue. If this form of meditation were appreciated and practiced, "there would be an inward rectitude, a strength of spirit, that would resist the temptations of Satan to do evil. A firm, decided will-power is not brought into the life and character, because the sacred instruction of God is not made the study, and the subject of meditation. There is not the effort put forth that there should be to associate the mind with pure, holy thoughts and to divert it from what is impure and untrue."[6]

The only way to divert the mind from the impure and untrue is to fill it with the Word of God. This is washing one's brain with the Word. Such meditation is not "practicing the presence" of God, as some writers suggest. The believer does not need to do that. Why not? Because God is already present. A believing faith knows and understands that He's been there, and is there, all the time. Furthermore, meditation is not a "means of grace," understood as that which conveys, or transfers, grace to the sinner. The only source and manifestation of God's grace is Jesus Christ, who "became flesh and dwelt among us . . . full of grace and truth" (John 1:14). It is through Christ, and Christ alone, that we have "obtained access by faith [alone] into this grace [alone] in which we stand" (Rom. 5:2). Not through mystical rituals.

By way of clarification, the words *meditation* and *contemplation* are related terms. For Adventists, "to meditate" means to focus one's thoughts on the Word of God and to contemplate means concentrating on spiritual things. Contemplation is not a state of mystical awareness. Both meditation and contemplation focus on the Word of God. The Spirit of Prophecy counsel is "It would be well for us to spend a thoughtful hour each day in *contemplation* of the life of Christ. We should take it point by point, and let the *imagination* grasp each scene, especially the closing ones."[7] Notice that this is a process of *thinking,* not a process of emptying one's mind. It is a thoughtful use of the imagination, thinking about what the Word of God says in reference to the life of Christ. Can we use the imagination? Of course. God created us with imaginations. But imagination is used to help us grasp, take hold of, and understand what we read in the Bible in the process of meditation/contemplation. To what end? The passage continues: "As we thus dwell upon His great sacrifice for us, our confidence in Him will be more constant, our love will be quickened, and we shall be more deeply imbued with His spirit." There is always a lesson, a teaching, to be learned by study of the Word that produces an authentic experience of believing faith, which has spiritual consequences. The passage continues: "If we would be saved at last, we must learn the lesson of penitence and humiliation at the foot of the cross."

The Spirit of Prophecy
No doubt you will agree that we need a form of spirituality that is

based on, and consistent with, our own Seventh-day Adventist tradition. You will also agree, I trust, that we must find such a spirituality, if we are to find it at all, in our own religious tradition and not somewhere else. This has certain important implications. For us the problem is compounded today by the idea of the theological and cultural pluralism of a world church that has managed, in spite of its diversity, to build and maintain a strong sense of unity and oneness. Virtually half of the membership of the Seventh-day Adventist Church, perhaps even more, has spiritual roots in other Christian traditions. Furthermore, the majority of the church's members live outside of North America. All of these persons bring with them individual and collective memories that retain certain spiritual images. In their transition to Adventism they have abandoned some former beliefs and practices as they have discovered additional biblical truth, but they have not scrapped everything in their spiritual past. That which is retained and enhanced is what Ellen White calls "Bible imagery," which has "a transforming influence upon mind and character."[8] All of this contributes to the richness of Adventist spirituality. This is certainly true in my case.

My spiritual roots are in Lutheranism, more specifically, in Finnish Lutheran pietism. Those roots are still there. I have not rejected the pietism on which I was nurtured spiritually for many years, in spite of some distorted criticism of pietism that I have heard. It was that tradition that formed the biblical basis upon which my subsequent Adventist spirituality has been shaped. After all, the roots of Adventism itself can be traced back through Methodism and Moravianism to pietism. When I began to seriously read the works of Ellen White, my first impression was that she represents the best of pietism. That insight helped immensely in providing the confidence I needed in my critical investigation of the Spirit of Prophecy, which over the past 40 years has become a vital portion of the spiritual road I travel.

What is the most important single factor that has contributed to what others see as the strange, pervasive, and strong cohesion of the Seventh-day Adventist Church? Outside of a common faith in Jesus Christ as Savior and Lord, it is the life, ministry, and writings of Ellen G. White. It is strange how, at the time in our denominational history when our tradition could best serve us, there appeared a movement to discredit Ellen White by questioning the authenticity of her prophetic gift and literary work. I believe there is a great need among us today to know her as our spiritual godmother. Don't misunderstand. I am not talking about veneration, which would be repugnant to her. When I first visited Oak Hill Cemetery in Battle Creek, Michigan, where she is buried, I was struck by the fact that her resting place is as unassuming as can be, in spite of her major role in the founding and growth of the Advent movement. Just to the left of the central family monument is a small stone marker engraved with the simple word *Mother*. She sought no special place or honor. She did not hunger for fame above virtue. Her own life, with its pains and triumphs, is eloquent testimony that she was one of those rare individuals able to distinguish between unworthy motives that serve self and generosity that serves others. Her legacy is not a marble memorial tomb, but the prophetic insight, the wisdom, the spiritual counsel, admonition, and exhortation found in her voluminous writings. She lived and worked for one purpose, and one alone: to point suffering humanity to the only source of healing power, the Lord Jesus Christ. Those who visit her grave come not as pilgrims doing homage, but as faithful believers determined to follow her example in Christlike service. They do not honor her so much as they honor the faith she confessed, and draw inspiration from the memory of her long life of unfailing ministry. Her life and witness shaped, and continues to shape, Adventist spirituality. Her last words were "I know in whom I have believed." She was a humble woman who, fully surrendered to her Lord, was made powerful by the indwelling Christ. She was spoken of as a "mother in Israel" by one of the orators at her funeral. I think of her as an insightful and perceptive spiritual friend, a vital and most positive influence in our tradition and in my life.

Ellen White is the critical link between ourselves and our past. Her writings do not, as some would suggest, constitute a fence across the road of developing spirituality. Rather, they are a fence along the side of that road, protecting a pluralistic church from veering off the biblical path doctrinally, either to the extreme left or to the extreme right, in its search for an authentic spirituality. From the very beginning of the Christian tradition there has been a constant battle with all the forces seeking to pervert the faith. One of the major purposes of the Spirit of Prophecy is to illuminate, and give us confidence in, the earliest periods of Christian history as revealed in Scripture, and to inspire us with insight into major events that highlight victories in the development of Adventist spirituality, such as the Reformation and the story of the Waldensian struggle to maintain biblical faith in the midst of religious persecution.

The Spirit of Prophecy, with its roots firmly planted in the biblical revelation of God, was given to help us live as Christians in an ever-changing culture that once could be spoken of as "Christian," but can be no longer. To so live, we must rely on the same sources that made it possible for the early Christians to live faithfully in pagan cultures. They were the first believers after Christ; we are the last believers on the edge of eternity—a minority in a world and in a sin-sodden culture that are not hospitable to biblical Christianity. Today's culture is one in which the major subject of consideration and conversation is human sexuality, not biblical spirituality. This is one of the major contributors to the social pathology of our times, tragically supported and even promoted officially by some mainline Protestant denominations in spite of unequivocal biblical counsel.[9]

We have much to learn from the formative years of the early church. But we have much to learn from the formative years of the Advent movement as well. In order to discover, or rediscover, an authentic Seventh-day Adventist spirituality, we must go back to the sources. For us, those can be only the Bible and the Spirit of Prophecy. To abandon either of these would be to short-circuit the search and would run the risk of coming up with an inauthentic spirituality. Today, because of the erosion of biblical truth and a deep surrender to that truth, we can learn far more from those such as the Waldensians and those in our own history who once were, or still are, branded as heretics than we can from the "orthodox" who have judged them and us.

A spirituality for our time cannot be borrowed from the East or from any other source. We must forge it ourselves with the resources we have been given by God—Scripture and the Spirit of Prophecy. As Adventist Christians, we have the same freedom as did the early believers to create an authentic form of spirituality, but for the shape or form of that spirituality we must turn to one another and to our immediate predecessors in this post-Christian century. Who are they? I can tell you who they have been for me. I still value their witness, their thinking, and their spiritual influence, for they represent unmistakable direction signs on the road I travel.

Literature

I have noticed in listening to stories of personal spiritual journeys that they have three things in common: (1) the witness, encouragement, and counsel of significant persons, such as grandparents, parents, other relatives, friends, neighbors, Christian believers, teachers, respected leaders, etc.; (2) circumstances, events, especially crises of one kind or another—things that have happened that have proved to be transitional and transformative; (3) literature, often books purchased or received as gifts. I have already shared with you some of the persons and events that have served to shape my own spirituality. Literature, especially books, has certainly been extremely vital as well. Some of them I bought myself, but many were providentially given to me as gifts. The books I mention below are those that have been most significant and influential for me.

During the formative years of my own search I was helped by authors such as O. H. Hallesby, a Norwegian Lutheran pietist and a professor on the faculty of the Independent Theological Seminary at Oslo, Norway, three of whose books were instrumental for me. In his book *The Christian Life,* which I purchased in 1956, Hallesby discusses the reality of sin, what it means to be converted and awakened to faith in Christ, the power of faith, and the fellowship of God's people as the center of inner spiritual power for the superhuman task of mission. *Under His Wings,* which I also purchased in 1956, discusses the depths of the Christian life. It is a book for the believer struggling against sin, a guide to godliness and the holy life. Then there was *Religious or Christian,* which was a Christmas gift to my wife from her pastor brother and his wife. It came into my hands upon our marriage in 1955. These books were written in the 1930s. At that time Hallesby was already critiquing what he calls the blending of religions, Protestant syncretism, intellectual religiosity, aesthetic religiosity, moralistic religiosity, and calls for a scriptural Christianity.

Another important book form me was *A Faithful Guide to Peace With God,* by C. O. Rosenius. I can't recall whether I purchased it or if it was given to me, or the date it came into my possession. Rosenius was born in 1816 and became an influential pietist in the Lutheran Church of Sweden. He occupies a place similar to John Wesley in England, John Knox in Scotland, and Hans Nielsen Hauge in Norway, all of whom fought the rationalism and worldliness threatening the spiritual life of the church of their day. The concern of Rosenius was for truth in the inner person, experiential truth. The burden of the book was to help people find the way to peace with God. It is to Rosenius that I attribute my understanding of the relationship of law and gospel.

Then, of course, there was Martin Luther, especially his commentaries on the Sermon on the Mount, Romans, and Galatians, which helped me understand what happened to me in terms of justification, when the Lord found and converted me in 1953. Luther helped me translate the right-brain experience into left-brain language. Add to this Luther's *Large Catechism,* which helped me focus on the centrality of the gospel, the dynamic of the written Word of God, an understanding of how the Christian ethos functioned during the period of the Reformation, and how trust in God is the fulfillment of the commandments.

During my Lutheran seminary days my spiritual struggle was with the impact and influence of liberal theology represented by neoorthodoxy and theologians such as Rudolph Bultmann, Karl Barth, and Emil Brunner. A major corrective for me was *Pia Desideria,* by Philip Spener, who was one of the early founders of pietism. His book came into my hands at a critical moment. It had originally sparked a spiritual revival in Europe in reaction to rationalism and dead orthodoxy following the Reformation, and influenced religious life for almost two centuries in Scandinavia and Finland. That book helped me gain a spiritual perspective amid the neoorthodoxy and Social Gospelism in the Lutheranism of the late 1950s and early 1960s. I will leave for the next chapter a discussion of this book, and the strong impression it made on the development of my own spirituality during the formative years.

In 1957 I bought a copy of Dietrich Bonhoeffer's classic, *The Cost of Discipleship*, which was first printed in English in 1948. From Bonhoeffer I learned what discipleship really means, and it served to keep me surrendered during my own subsequent spiritual crisis. From him I learned about Christian suffering in relation to the cross of Christ and to discipleship, as well as the hidden or inner character of the Christian life. This was not simply reactionary, or emotional (subjective), pietism, but a sophisticated theological treatise with a deep and abiding spirituality that Bonhoeffer's own martyrdom authenticated.[10]

Then there was A. W. Tozer's *The Knowledge of the Holy*, which is the only book in my library in which almost every sentence is underlined. Tozer helped me understand God the Father as a divine being. The book made a major contribution in the development of a theocentric/Christocentric spirituality. Tozer discusses, in 23 chapters, the attributes of God and their meaning in the Christian life. His book has one major weakness—it lacks a chapter on the righteousness of God.

Then there was a little book of just 79 pages, *The Inward Knowledge of Christ*, published in Helsinki in 1957. It consists of a translation of the writings of Paavo Ruotsalainen (1777-1852), with an introduction by my spiritual friend Walter J. Kukkonen. With this book I plugged in significantly to my spiritual roots in Finnish Christianity. Ruotsalainen was an uneducated farmer who became a major figure in the spiritual awakenings in Finland from 1809 to the end of his life. His ministry was dedicated to helping people cultivate a relationship with Jesus Christ, not letting either sins or piety get in the way. Christ is confronted in solitude, said Paavo, otherwise one is in danger of bypassing Him for the sake of spiritual entertainment. What must be practiced is a constant waiting and yearning for Christ in the inner being. For Paavo, no external form of piety could be a condition of a living faith. He was unwilling for the direction of the spiritual life to be taken out of the hands of Christ and put into the hands of pious people, no matter how good their intentions might be. In his view, not even prayer was at the center of Christian life; Christ Himself was the center. In 1844 Paavo broke with a minister friend, Fredrik Hedberg, who was teaching that people should consider themselves saved because Jesus had died for the whole world and because they had been baptized (as infants). In Paavo's view believers are not in charge of their salvation. Instead, by means of His Word, God takes charge, convicts of sin, reveals Christ to the sinner, justifies the ungodly by grace through faith, and gives His Holy Spirit to dwell within. This is what Paavo meant by the inward knowledge of Christ. He maintained that we must never allow the external elements of Christianity to replace the inward knowledge of Christ.

In 1958 I bought a copy of *A Man in Christ,* by James S. Stewart. He discusses union with Christ as the vital element in Paul's religion. This book, too, made a great impact on me in the midst of liberalism, neoorthodoxy, and the Social Gospel. It is a theological/exegetical study of the reality of the indwelling Christ. It was important to me in the face of Albert Schweitzer's *Quest for the Historical Jesus* and served to authenticate theologically the reality of the inner knowledge of Christ.

These books, in addition to the Bible, served to prepare me to face the crisis that was coming in my spiritual journey in the late 1960s and early 1970s. The things I had learned and assimilated from writers such as these, contributing to the shaping of my spirituality, made it possible for me to become a Seventh-day Adventist and to find the spiritual heritage, in a refreshingly renewed version, that was being abandoned in subsequent Lutheran church mergers.

I need to insert here the story of an event that took place during my Lutheran seminary days. As it turned out, this incident had a major influence in laying the theological foundation for my eventual transition to Adventism. It was a series of lectures by Granger Westberg, professor at the University of Chicago Divinity School. His lecture on the nature of humans, in which he showed from Scripture that the human being does not have a "soul" distinct from the body that lives on after death, rang a lot of bells for me, because my own reading of the Bible had already posed serious questions regarding the dualism in Catholic and much of Protestant (Lutheran) theology.

But no writer or theologian has had such a seminal influence on my developing spirituality as Ellen White. I am still processing the impact of her writings on my life. Because of my long-held views on revelation/inspiration, I have not been touched negatively by the debate about her and her writings that has devastated the faith of some Adventists. I have continued to appreciate her as a spiritual friend, concentrating on both the theological content and the spiritual intent of her material.

One does not read long in the Spirit of Prophecy before one becomes aware of its overriding spiritual concern—that the reader come to know Christ personally, become like Christ in attitude and character, and be prepared for His return. If the purpose of spiritual friendship is to affirm faith, explore the nature of the faith relationship, and confront with respect to areas needing change in attitude and character, then Ellen White fills the bill. She was not elected to the position she held in the Seventh-day Adventist Church. She was called to it, appointed by the sovereign choice of God Himself. Her spiritual authority was direct, and God used her mightily. Begun with only a handful of people, the church that she helped found and continues to guide by means of her writings now numbers more than 16 million members and counting, baptizing an average of more than 3,000 people every day. Her spiritual impact has been astounding. She was appointed to fulfill an unpopular mission and do a work refused by others. Her own spirituality would not allow her to refuse, no matter the consequences. This is why I have not hesitated to quote extensively from her works in this book.

Two Faith Traditions

I see two major faith traditions that contribute to the shaping of Adventist spirituality. The first, which I have already alluded to and which is substantive relative to the faith experience of Seventh-day Adventists, is pietism. The general emphasis within the pietistic tradition has been on group Bible study, prayer gatherings, the nurture of a believing faith within the context of biblical doctrine, concern for the ethical manifestations of Christlikeness, and spiritual awakening.[11] I recognized this tradition in the writings of Ellen White and in the faith and mission of Adventist believers, as well as in their lifestyle. Historically, the roots of Adventist spirituality can be traced back through post-Reformation pietism. This is why, aside from doctrinal truth, I have felt spiritually comfortable among Adventist believers and in its ministry. Both Adventist doctrine and spiritual experience are in harmony with Scripture.

The other faith tradition shaping Adventist spirituality is eschatology, the return of Christ that ushers in the final events of human history. Eschatology is the faith tradition that embodies the theology, the spiritual experience, and the mission of the Seventh-day Adventist Church during the climactic events that precede and encompass the return of Jesus and its consequences. Adventist spirituality views the world, culture, and historical events from this eschatological perspective. This is what frees the Adventist believer from hopelessness and despair as world events press down and tempt us to wander aimlessly in the gloom of a long night. There is no hope in a salvation that is bound to this world, and thus this world has no eschatological anticipation.

What does it mean to be a Seventh-day Adventist Christian living during the last days of earth's history? In what sense do both realities, the believing faith of Seventh-day Adventist Christians together with their consciousness of the last days, serve to shape Adventist spirituality? The faith of such people has two essential foci: They have put their faith in Jesus Christ, and they keep the commandments of God. That is the fundamental essence of biblical Christianity, of Adventists' eschatological faith. In other words, their faith in Christ is demonstrated before the whole world by their obedience to God the Father. "Here is a call for the endurance ["patient endurance," NIV] of the saints, those who keep the commandments of God and their faith in Jesus" (Rev. 14:12). What is the reality demanded, the primary character trait required, for such a time? It is patient endurance. This patient endurance is not just the ability to withstand adversity, to put up with it, to remain firm and steadfast in spite of it; it has to do with patience, enduring calmly without complaining. And what is the eschatological mission of the church living in the last days? Although it responds to the Lord's commission to "make disciples of all nations" by the preaching/teaching of His Word, its mission is not to change the world politically or socially. Its mission is to introduce people to Jesus Christ, who changes persons from the inside out, so that they are prepared for His return. The spiritual benefit of faith in the good news of Jesus' return is that Seventh-day Adventist Christians are people who have learned to live in hope. Because of their fervent belief in, and expectation of, the imminent return of Christ, they have a long view of life.

One of the best ways to illustrate this is to tell another story. Recently it was necessary for me to have cataract surgery and lens implants in both eyes. I was amazed at the results. Since my teen years I have been nearsighted and have needed glasses for distant sight. I could see to read without glasses, but could not drive a car without them. After the surgery everything was changed. Now I need glasses to see close, but my ability for distance sight is 20/20. The finely tuned focus of the faith lens on the scriptural message of Christ's return is what produces the long view. In the Bible we get a clear, undistorted picture of Jesus, which climaxes with the glorious fulfillment of His promise that "all the tribes of the earth . . . will see the Son of Man coming on the clouds of heaven with power and great glory" (Matt. 24:30). "Turn your eyes upon Jesus," invites the hymn writer, "look full in His wonderful face; and the things of earth will grow strangely dim in the light of His glory and grace."

I have never had a problem with the so-called delay in the return of Christ. Why not? Because I believe the Bible, which tells me not to overlook "this one fact . . . that with the Lord one day is as a thousand years, and a thousand years as one day" (2 Peter 3:8). God is infinite, limitless. It is virtually impossible for a limited, finite human mind to grasp this reality. No statement of human speech can adequately express His infinitude. We see time as an unrelenting enemy, devouring our days. But God does not hurry. He has no deadlines. For Him, there is only what His Word calls the fullness of time. Believing faith rests on the Lord's promise "Surely I am coming soon."[12] And answers, "Amen. Come, Lord Jesus!" (Rev. 22:20). The promise is enough. Patient waiting for Him to fulfill His promise is a major component of Adventist spirituality. Thank God for His patience with us. He is "not slow to fulfill his promise as some count slowness, but is patient toward you, not wishing that any should perish, but that all should reach repentance" (2 Peter 3:9). Let's leave the timing to Him and busy ourselves with "what sort of people ought you to be in lives of holiness and godliness, waiting for and hastening the coming of the day of God . . . waiting for new heavens and a new earth in which righteousness dwells" (verses 11-13).

Change We Can Really Believe In

The year 2009 witnessed a major historical event in the history of the United States—the inauguration of the first African-American president. It was inevitable, but I never thought I would live to see it. Some folks are saying that his inauguration was the moment America changed. The truth is that change had already taken place, and that change made Barack Obama's election possible. What Americans really celebrated at his inauguration was the hope and determination that racism will no longer be a major factor in our social/political life. The hope that racism is finally done. Over. Past. Buried. Those that have used racism as a political/economic weapon, making money and political hay by keeping it alive, have suffered a great defeat. That's good for all of us.

President Obama's campaign slogan was "Change we can believe in." Candidates for public office, from all parties, learn pretty fast how to use political rhetoric to convince us to vote for them. They are good at making sweeping promises and leading us to believe that the world will be at peace and everyone will prosper if only they are elected. The student of the Bible hears it all with a great deal of skepticism, knowing that the moment a new president enters the oval office reality sets in and everything looks different. Adventist Bible believers are leery of change for the sake of change. Because we live in an ever-changing world, we recognize that change at times is desperately needed. But we also know that there is good change and bad change. Right change and wrong change. We are in favor of change that is the fulfillment of Bible truth, change that produces righteousness rather than licentiousness. But we are wary of change demanded by those who "have become callous and have given themselves up to sensuality, greedy to practice every kind of impurity" (Eph. 4:19). Why? Because "that is not the way you [we] learned Christ!—assuming that you have heard about him and were taught in him, as the truth is in Jesus, to put off your old self, which belongs to your former manner of life and is corrupt through deceitful desires, and to be renewed in the spirit of your minds, and to put on the new self, created after the likeness of God in true righteousness and holiness" (verses 20-24).

That is change we can *really* believe in! Right? Notice that Paul said that sensuality and greed for impurity are not the way we who claim to believe "learned Christ." Not learned *about* Him, as though He was a subject to be discussed, but learned *Him*. The contrast between verses 19 and 20 is dramatic. Living as verse 19 describes is not the way followers of Christ live, because they have "learned Christ"! There is a dramatic, visible difference between the lifestyle of the believer and that of those who "have become callous," who are hardened and thickened like a callus. When I was a bricklayer, I developed calluses on my fingers and hands by handling rough brick and cement blocks. Because of the calluses, I could no longer feel the irritation and pain. To become calloused means to feel no emotion, no sympathy. It means being indifferent to the suffering and needs of others. Finally, it means not to care anymore.

Some people call this text Paul's morality passage, saying that it doesn't fit the flavor and intent of the gospel or the times. They say it should be ignored, together with the Ten Commandments, as being irrelevant to the contemporary Christian life. That's quite a change, isn't it? What do you think Paul would say about that? He would say, But that's not the way you "learned Christ." He would say, If that's the way you think, then you have never really "learned Christ." He would say that putting off the "old self" and putting on the "new self" that is created in the "likeness of God in true righteousness" is *change* that we can really believe in. Transformational change. After all, we are "not [to] be conformed [molded] to this world [to its ways of thinking and doing]" but instead be "transformed [changed] by the renewal of [our] minds" (Rom. 12:2). That's a change in the way we think by the power of the gospel! Change that we can really believe in transforms the way we think. For example: Anyone struggling with an addiction can overcome it when they *stop* thinking about it the way they did before they learned Christ and instead think about it as that which "belongs to your former manner of life" (Eph. 4:22). It's over with. Instead, think of it in terms of the "new self." Christ is not just an external, objective name. He strengthens us "with power through his Spirit in your inner being." The inner being is where change that we can really believe in oc-

curs. For what end? "So that Christ may dwell in your hearts through faith
. . . to know the love of Christ that surpasses knowledge, that you may be
filled with all the fullness of God" (Eph. 3:16-19).

That's what it means to "learn Christ." If you are a believer in Christ,
a follower of Christ, don't waste time debating with the "old self" about
how you are going to live today. Instead, think again. Decide that you will
live today, and every day, in ways that fit your transformed character. In
ways that demonstrate that you have learned Christ. Put on a lifestyle that
is not dominated by the carnal nature. Keep thinking that way, and thinking that way will become the most natural way to think. That is change
you can really believe in! God's people live differently. They "put off" (as
in getting rid of old, dirty, worn-out clothes) their "former manner of life"
that is "corrupt [morally perverted, rotten] through deceitful desires
[wants]." One of my college professors used to say that some Christians are
like lampposts. They don't smoke or drink, but they stay out all night. His
point was that one may be addicted not to alcohol or nicotine, but to other
things, such as greed (as opposed to generosity). How we use money can
be as corrupt and addictive as anything else.

In an article on surviving the current financial crisis I found this: "One
reason the economy is in such shambles is because people borrowed more
than they could reasonably afford. They were led to do so by the greed of
lenders."[13] But is all the fault on the side of greedy lenders? How about
greedy borrowers, who borrowed knowing they could not, or even would
not, pay it back? Today the credit-card debt is astronomical. The problem
is greedy people, whether they are rich or poor. Both have the same corrupt human nature and are equally greedy. The poor want what the rich
have, and the rich want more than they have. Both want to keep what
they have. Some folks are actually blaming capitalism and want the system
changed. But history demonstrates that changing political or economic systems does not change people. The Bible tells us that it is people that need
to be changed. Politically, the issue is between conservatives and liberals.
Mike Huckabee, former governor of Arkansas and a recent presidential
candidate, is right when he points out that conservatives want less civil
government and liberals want more civil liberties. But what is needed is
more civil people![14] Good kids raised by good parents with virtues instead
of vices. Kids that will contribute to the welfare of all, rather than expect
everyone else to make life easy for them. That's why Adventist congregations have the faith, the courage, and the determination to make the sacrifices necessary to support elementary and secondary parochial schools.

Change that we can really believe in is an inside job. Only God the
Holy Spirit works from the inside. He doesn't coerce. He doesn't force His

gifts on anyone. They cannot be earned. Cannot be produced. Cannot be achieved. They can only be received. He gives them, but only to those who will accept them, appreciate them, and use them for His purposes. It's like a Christmas present that is freely given but is not yours until you accept it. What does that require? Willingness. Appreciation. Thankfulness. Openness to receive what God chooses to give. It's not a matter of getting what's outside inside by human effort, but of getting outside what God puts inside by His grace. One of those spiritual gifts is generosity. Speaking of the spiritual gifts, Paul says, "Let us use them" (Rom. 12:6). For ourselves? No. Let us use them in serving God and others, as "one who contributes, in generosity" (verse 8). Generosity is the opposite of greed. God promises to meet our needs, not our greeds. Our country does not need more greedy people. It needs generous people. In terms of our witness, the way we handle money is very revealing. Generous giving is the most powerful and convincing witness of the gospel. "Each one must give as he has decided in his heart, [but] not reluctantly [grudgingly] or under compulsion [the need itself is motive enough], for God loves a cheerful giver" (2 Cor. 9:7). Scary? Listen to God's promise. "God is able to make all grace abound to you, so that having all sufficiency in all things at all times, you may abound in every good work. . . . You will be enriched in every way for all your generosity, which through us will produce thanksgiving to God" (verses 8-11). People will "glorify God because of your submission flowing from your confession of the gospel of Christ, and the generosity of your contribution for them and for all others, while they long for you and pray for you, because of the surpassing grace of God upon you. Thanks be to God for his inexpressible gift!" (verses 13-15).

Data reveal that only a few on the fringes of mainstream Christianity behave with their money as if they believe the Word of God is true. Data also reveal that very few Christians practice the biblical tithe, and that conservative Christians are the greatest givers. Economic hard times do not change the biblical principles of tithing and giving. This is no time to be stingy with God. In tough times Christian generosity is needed all the more, because it shows the world that it is God's grace, not a big checkbook balance, that is the source of our security. What people read in the Bible they need to see in the church— change that can really be believed in. That, too, is descriptive of Adventist spirituality.

Meditation

Ponder this: If the Word of God is the "highest source of wisdom," can I gain anything of transforming spiritual value by meditating on anything else? Can I find an authentic Adventist spirituality if I abandon the only sources that can produce it and look elsewhere? In what ways do I consciously discard ideas that are not in harmony with God's truth? Now, read on.

---

[1] Fernando Canale, *Basic Elements in Christian Theology* (Berrien Springs, Mich.: Andrews University Lithotech, 2005), p. 28. This threefold emphasis underscores the importance of the scriptural tradition *alone*, the *total* scriptural tradition, and the scriptural tradition *primarily*.

[2] E. G. White, *The Upward Look*, p. 75.

[3] E. G. White, *In Heavenly Places*, p. 277.

[4] E. G. White, *The Acts of the Apostles*, p. 474. (Italics supplied.)

[5] E. G. White, *Child Guidance*, p. 509.

[6] Ellen G. White, *Fundamentals of Christian Education* (Nashville: Southern Pub. Assn., 1923), p. 132.

[7] E. G. White, *The Desire of Ages*, p. 83. (Italics supplied.)

[8] Ellen G. White, *Counsels to Parents, Teachers, and Students* (Mountain View, Calif.: Pacific Press Pub. Assn., 1913), p. 172.

[9] Such as the action, in August 2009, of the Evangelical Lutheran Church in America, approving the ordination of noncelibate homosexual clergy and same-sex marriage, in spite of the biblical prohibition of gay practice among God's people. As the delegates met in Minneapolis, Minnesota, a sudden, unannounced, and unpredicted tornado suddenly descended on the area of the assembly hall, damaging the roof and knocking the cross off the steeple of the host church next door. No tornado had hit downtown Minneapolis for 90 years. Was this a modern theophany? One pro-gay pastor is reported as saying, "Let's stop leaving people behind, and let's be the family God is calling us to be." Instead, how about "Let's stop leaving the Word of God behind, and let's be the people His Word calls us to be"?

[10] For testimonies regarding Bonhoeffer's martyrdom, see the foreword by the bishop of Chichester and the memoir by G. Leibholz in *The Cost of Discipleship*.

[11] While this has been nurtured, beneficially, among Lutherans in Germany, Denmark, Sweden, Norway, and Finland, it needs to be said that it has been resisted by Lutheran "orthodoxy," which has historically been fearful of the subjective side of Christian experience. It has even been referred to as "mystical fanaticism." On the contrary, supporters of pietism saw it as integrating faith with daily life, as a corrective to the idea that head knowledge of doctrine is in itself true Christianity. Such knowledge must result in spiritual transformation of the person of the believer. One of orthodoxy's criticisms of pietism was that it emphasized sanctification over justification. The emphasis, orthodoxy insisted, should be on what Christ has done *for* us, rather than on what He does *in* us. However, the truth is that it is not an either/or matter, but a both/and matter. This is why "orthodox" Lutheranism has never understood the need for a "born-again" experience, even though Jesus said, "Unless one is born again he cannot see the kingdom of God" (John 3:3). This is why "orthodox" Lutheranism focuses on sacramentalism, rather than on evangelism, with respect to church growth. The major emphasis in orthodoxy has been the objective and external preaching of the Word and the administration of the sacraments. Ellen White comments on John 3:3, "The change that must come to the natural, inherited, and cultivated tendencies of the human heart is that change of which Jesus spoke when He said to Nicodemus, 'Except a man be born again, he cannot see the kingdom of God.'. . . He virtually said to Nicodemus, it is not controversy that will help your case. Arguments will not bring light to your soul. You must have a new heart, or you cannot discern the kingdom of heaven. It is not greater evidence that will bring you into a right position, but new purposes, new springs of action. You must be born again. Until this change takes place, until all things are made new, the

strongest evidence that could be presented would be useless" (*Christ Triumphant*, p. 233).

[12] The New King James Version rendering is "I am coming quickly," which puts the emphasis on the manner, not the timing, of Christ's return.

[13] *Adventist Review*, Jan. 8, 2009, p. 17.

[14] *Do the Right Thing* (New York: The Penguin Group, 2008), p. 23.

Chapter 11

THE ROAD BEHIND

One of the most well-known and oft-repeated statements by Ellen White is "We have nothing to fear for the future, except as we shall forget the way the Lord has led us, and His teaching in our past history."[1] Although she was referring to the history of the Advent movement, her words certainly apply to the personal history of every Christian believer. If one is following a recognized road, it is very comforting when the Lord brings to mind the way He has led in the past, because it produces confidence in the way He will lead in the future. Some things we may forget until His Spirit opens our memory. In the previous chapter I mentioned the influence of pietism on the shaping of my developing spirituality and the fact that I discovered that pietism in the literary works of Ellen White, which helped to make possible my transition from the Lutheran Church to the Adventist Church. In this chapter I want to share the story of how the grace of God was preparing me for that eventuality.

That story begins with an event that occurred early in 1958, when I was a student at Northern Michigan University. Graduation was coming in June, and I had to decide which Lutheran theological seminary to attend. I wanted to go to Luther Theological Seminary, in Minneapolis, Minnesota, which had the reputation of being theologically conservative. However, the Finnish Evangelical Lutheran Church was in the process of merger negotiations with three other Lutheran bodies and had already moved its seminary from Hancock, Michigan, to the campus of Chicago Lutheran Theological Seminary in Maywood, Illinois, a western suburb of Chicago. That seminary had the reputation of being theologically liberal, and for that reason I did not want to go there. So I filled out an application for Luther Seminary, sealed the envelope, put a stamp on it, and stuck it in my briefcase, intending to mail it on my way to class the next day. As I approached the mailbox, I took the application out of the briefcase and was about to drop it in the slot when something stopped me. I remember standing there unable to mail it and then putting it back into my briefcase.

This happened every day for more than a week! Finally I got tired of it, filled out an application to Chicago Lutheran, and the next day, with no hesitation, popped it right into the mailbox!

I have often thought of that event, with no satisfactory answer as to why it happened that way, wondering what the spiritual significance might be. No answers ever came—until 50 years later, on October 30, 2009, when I awoke early in the morning and spent two hours recalling that unusual event and pondering its meaning. My wife and I had returned the previous day from a shopping trip in Duluth, and while I was driving home it occurred to me that the next Sabbath would fall on October 31. In the medieval church that day was known as the Feast of All Saints. It was also the day, in 1517, that Martin Luther nailed his ninety-five theses to the big wooden door of the Castle church at Wittenberg, Germany. Intended as the basis for theological debate, the theses set off major controversy all over Europe. Recalling that date may have jogged my subconscious memory. At any rate, during those two early-morning hours the meaning of the 1958 mailbox event began to emerge.

I know now why it was God's plan that I attend the Chicago seminary. It was because only there could I come under the influence of two men, Professors Walter Kukkonen and Karlo Keljo, who represented the theological and spiritual ethos of Finnish Christianity, which, unbeknown to me at the time, I would need many years later during my transition to Adventism. From them I learned the historical facts about my own spiritual heritage.

Historical Background

The Christianizing of Northern Europe began in A.D. 823 when the Catholic archbishop Ebo of Reims went to Denmark to preach the gospel. Three years later the man who became known as the apostle of the northland, Ansgar, arrived in Denmark. By 829 he was in Sweden, where the door to Christian missionary work was open. During the next decades little progress was made. But in 960 the king of Denmark was converted to the Christian faith, which was a major event in the establishment of Christianity in Scandinavia. By that time Norway also had felt the impact of Christian missionary activity. Another major event was the baptism, in 1008, of the Swedish king, Olof Skötkonung. With the cooperation of the monarchs of Denmark, Norway, and Sweden, the pope established the bishopric of Lund in 1104, giving it spiritual oversight of all the churches in Scandinavia. The stage was set for the conversion of Finland.

Historians recognize 1155 as the date when Christianity officially came to Finland from Sweden, although there had been earlier contact with

Christians and the Christian faith along trade routes to Northern Europe and to Scandinavia across the Gulf of Bothnia and the Baltic Sea via the Åland Islands (*Ahvenanmaa,* in Finnish). Under the leadership of King Eric, a crusade was sent that included a bishop named Henrik (Henry), who became the patron saint of Finland and the founder of the Church of Finland. Legend has it that Henry was killed on the ice of Lake Köyliö by an irate peasant named Lalli, dramatizing the fact that the encounter between the pagan culture and the new Christian culture was not without violence and antagonism, as the populace were forced to decide between pagan beliefs and the new faith. One consequence was the incorporation of some elements of the new into the old faith. For example, the sign of the cross, the virgin Mary and other saints, and even Christ Himself were adopted as new means for achieving the old pagan objectives. There are stories told about how some of the pagan Finns accepted baptism, but then washed it off in the heat and steam of their saunas!

In 1229 Pope Gregory IX took Finland under his personal protection, and it was incorporated as one of the states in the most powerful empire of that time, the Roman Catholic Church. On January 25, 1291, the first election of the bishop of Finland took place on Finnish soil, and the first Finn, Magnus I (Maunu), was consecrated at Turku. By 1323 the missionary period had ended, and the medieval period began, which was a time of consolidation and steady growth. It was also a period of greater papal control over the church in Finland. By the end of the Middle Ages the Church of Finland had brought almost all of the people within its sphere of ecclesiastical influence. The only places without churches were the wilderness areas of vast forests and lakes in central Finland and Lappland.

Since the eleventh century, Sweden and Russia had struggled for control of Finland. The Swedes wanted to convert the Finns to Catholicism, and the Russians wanted to convert them to Eastern Orthodoxy. Finland became part of the Swedish kingdom in 1323, and the Church of Finland was incorporated into the Church of Sweden. (In 1809 Russia occupied Finland until 1917, when Finnish independence was declared.) The power struggle throughout Europe between church and state in the Middle Ages involved Sweden/Finland as well, and resulted in efforts on the part of secular rulers to establish national churches. This factor played an important role in the Reformation.

By the end of the Middle Ages the church was the biggest landowner in Finland, and the bishop was the biggest businessman, which was a constant source of irritation. The bishop was also a major political figure, sharing in the rule of the country by his membership on the council of the Swedish king, which gave him a voice in the election of the monarch.

Perhaps the most unique feature of Finnish Catholicism was the fact that preaching was encouraged, in spite of the fact that the Fourth Lateran Council of 1215 prohibited preaching without specific papal permission. The major contribution in this area was made by the Dominican preaching friars, who traveled from parish to parish preaching in the language of the people. The Bible was not available to the people, but there was the preaching of the gospel which produced faith in Jesus Christ. The preaching friars served to acquaint the people with the Scriptures, another significant factor in the Reformation. The religion of the average Finn during the medieval period was largely one of fear regarding the dangers of hell and purgatory and one of devotion to the sacraments, which supposedly protected them from such dangers. Another factor that played a major role in the coming of the Reformation was the practice of the Finnish bishops to send young men to study in foreign universities. In this way contact was made with the leaders of the Reformation in Germany.

Reformation Comes to Finland

The Reformation in Finland did not come as a great upheaval, but emerged gradually over a period of time, yet not without struggle and controversy, including controversy between crown and ecclesiastical figures over control of the church and even an attempt by one of the Rome-leaning kings to restore elements of the Catholic Mass to worship services.

The Reformation in Finland began, however, as a purely spiritual movement, and the first to preach the evangelical faith was a native son, Peter Sarkilahti, who returned around 1523 after studying in Germany. In his preaching he was an uncompromising evangelical, with the desire to free his people from the idolatry of the Papacy. He died in 1529, but not before planting the seed of the new faith in the heart of a young man named Michael Agricola, who was destined to become the Reformer of Finland. Between 1532 and 1550 at least eight Finnish students went to study under Luther and Melanchthon at Wittenberg. Agricola was one of them. He heard Luther's lectures on the Bible and participated in discussions conducted by Luther. Of even greater influence on him were Luther's sermons as well as his writings in the university library collection. A letter that Luther wrote on Agricola's behalf to the Swedish king, Gustav Vasa, indicates personal knowledge of the student. One can conjecture that Agricola may have been one of the students privileged to dine at Luther's table, thus hearing his "table talks." Agricola's days at Wittenberg coincided with the most illustrious years of Melanchthon's teaching career, which began in 1518 in both the theological and philosophical faculties. In spite of the regard Agricola had for Luther and his teaching, the thought life of the Finnish Reformer was closer to that of Melanchthon. Therefore, he reflected an attitude toward Rome not as violent as Luther's. He was influenced by Melanchthon's humanism and wanted to build rather than tear down. However, like Luther, he was a man of prayer, with absolute dependence on the Word of God.

While he was at Wittenberg, Agricola started the project that became his greatest contribution to the Finnish people and the most important factor in the Finnish Reformation—a translation of the New Testament into the Finnish language. When he returned to Finland, he filled an important assignment in the cathedral chapter in Turku and so shared in its administration. In that capacity he was able to experience firsthand the growing control of the church by the Swedish crown, as well as the rapid evangelical developments within the church. Meanwhile, knowing that a Finnish New Testament would mean nothing to people who could not read, Agricola published an ABC book around 1542. In 1548 his New Testament was published. The main texts used were the Greek translations of Erasmus, Luther's German Bible, and the Swedish translation of 1526. In addition he later managed to translate about one fourth of the Old Testament, but could not complete it for financial reasons.

When it came to the central doctrines of evangelical Christianity, Agricola was fully in accord with Luther. He carried the Reformation fight to what he considered the two chief enemies of biblical Christianity—Papacy and paganism. He condemned those who worshipped Mary, as well as those who sought to earn salvation through mediators other than Jesus Christ. He died on April 9, 1557, while returning from Moscow, where he had gone to help preserve peace between Sweden and Russia. With the death of Agricola and King Gustav Vasa (September 29, 1560), the first phase of the Reformation in Finland came to a close.

Reformation Takes Hold

The second phase began with a controversy over the doctrine of the Lord's Supper. Calvinistic thinkers understood it as a memorial feast, and the followers of Luther emphasized its sacramental character. In 1565 the issue was resolved when the Reformed doctrine was rejected in favor of Luther's position. The Calvinists were allowed to remain in the country, however, since it was believed by the king and the church that they had no power over individual consciences. This policy became a permanent feature of the Swedish/Finnish Reformation and certainly reflected the democratic nature of the fiercely independent Finnish spirit and character. Here were the seeds of religious liberty and tolerance in Finland.

The 1560s saw great strides in the improvement of the economic status of the clergy and in the deepening of their spiritual ministry. Much was accomplished in raising the level of preaching in the churches. Increasingly, the Bible and the Lutheran Augsburg Confession became the norm for doctrine and preaching. Archbishop Laurentius Petri insisted that the Word of God and the gospel be the creed and norm of the church. As time passed, more and more people came to appreciate the religious, and national, treasure they possessed in the new faith. Controversies produced a generation holding deep "Lutheran" convictions. A summit event was the church assembly meeting at Uppsala in 1593, acknowledging the "pure and saving Word of God" as the foundation of doctrine and faith. At the same time, the three ecumenical creeds (the Apostles', the Nicene, and the Athanasian), together with the Augsburg Confession, were adopted as the confession of the Swedish/Finnish Church. By this action the Church of Sweden/Finland officially took its place among the Lutheran churches of Europe.

As has already been mentioned, the Reformation in Finland was more a process than an event. The turn from Catholicism to the Evangelical faith was gradual rather than sharp. One reason for this may have been Finland's geographical isolation from the continent. However, the most decisive factor was the *inner nature* of the Reformation movement in Finland, which exhibited a spirit greatly different from that of the German Reformation. It remained closer to Luther's original position that the highest guide for the individual Christian's faith life is the Word of God. By 1571 it was required that pastors examine all communicants to make certain that they knew at least the Ten Commandments, the Apostles' Creed, and the Lord's Prayer. In spite of this official confessional basis, there remained among many of the illiterate and uneducated general population some superstitions associated with elements of Catholic rites and ceremonies. Besides that, drunkenness, licentiousness, "Sabbath-breaking," and insolence toward the clergy flourished. However, good seed had been sown during the Reformation era, and spiritual harvest would eventually follow.

The Period of Orthodoxy

After the chaotic, crucial years, Finland, as elsewhere in Europe, moved toward doctrinal and ecclesiastical orthodoxy. The two characteristic features were (1) adherence to the "pure doctrine" as defined in the confessional writings of Lutheranism, and (2) loyalty to the officially established institutional church. The first filled the vacuum created by the rejection of tradition in the formulation of doctrine, and the second resulted from reliance on secular rulers (such as the king and his council) within the Lutheran Church in the absence of anything comparable to the Catholic hierarchy. While the crown resisted the development toward confession-alism, it was anxious to adopt the German system of ecclesiastical polity, which gave the secular ruler ultimate authority in the church. The Church of Sweden/Finland had entered the seventeenth century without a rigid confessional basis or a formal ecclesiastical structure. But the elements and leaders for both were at hand, and in the course of time the church became a national (state) church, but with sole authority in various aspects of its in-ternal life.

Attention was again given to raising the level of preaching, and direc-tion was focused on the structure and content of effective sermons. Preachers were to avoid irrelevant issues and were not to preach according to their own whims. The Word of God was to be rightly divided, with the law primarily used to frighten the stiff-necked and the gospel to comfort the sorrowful. Sermons must be carefully prepared so as to reflect this twofold balance. Preparation was to be focused not just on sermons them-selves, but also on the personal faith life of the preacher, which meant that the preacher was to live by the Word of truth. In this way the faithful were to be prepared for battle against the devil, the world, and the flesh. In their sermons the preachers sought to uncover the literal meaning of Bible texts, with little use of allegory. Coupled with this was the indoctrination of the people in the content of the Christian faith, accompanied by examinations in the Lutheran catechism. The result was a strong doctrinal/theological biblicism that would characterize the development of the Reformation brand of Finnish Christianity.

One of the major figures serving as a forerunner of pietism in Finland was John Gezelius the Younger,[2] who had become friends with Philip Jacob Spener of Germany, with whom he carried on an extensive corre-spondence for many years. In 1679 Gezelius was appointed full professor of theology in the University of Turku. In the spirit of Spener, his empha-sis was on the importance of a personal faith life. He pointed out the pedantic side of the scholastic sermons of the day and underscored the need for a spiritual revival in the midst of what he considered to be a degener-ate Christianity. He called for simpler, heartfelt, and devotional preaching with repentance and surrender to God as the goal.

In 1686 Gezelius broke his connection with Spener as his attitude toward the pietists grew cold and he became less tolerant of Calvinisn. As vice chancellor of the university he did not permit any independent re-search or freedom of thought and tightened the shackles into which ortho-doxy had bound free investigation. Because he was unable to distinguish between the radical and churchly pietists, he attacked on a wide front. Although in his personal life, and even as a teacher of preachers, he reflected the spirit of pietism, as a churchman and administrator he was a rigid representative of orthodoxy, meaning salvation based on belief in right doctrine, as opposed to pietism's insistence on the need for a personal relationship with Christ based on a born-again experience. By 1686 two ideals of Lutheran orthodoxy had been reached—the adoption of the full confessional stance of orthodoxy and the establishment of a state church. The effect was that freedom of religion was now understood as freedom to practice the Lutheran faith without any interference from other religious groups. The church did not hesitate to use civil authority to enforce its decrees and its discipline. If anything can be learned from the period of orthodoxy, it is that faith and piety cannot be legislated. Still, this period was not completely void of personal faith and spiritual life. In fact, without the existence of such faith and life it would be hard to explain what happened in the eighteenth century. In spite of its rigidity, there was in orthodoxy that which provided a point of contact for pietism.

Pietism and the Awakening

As has been mentioned, the pietist movement was divided between the radical and the churchly pietists. The radicals accused the established church of apostasy, because they felt it was a Babylon that held souls captive. Some called for the total rejection of Lutheran doctrine. The churchly pietists wanted an awakened church, with a restoration of spiritual life and piety. The view of the latter was that true doctrine should, in practice, lead to repentance and a living faith. Given the nature of the church at that time and the rigidity and spiritual deadness of orthodoxy, it can be understood why pietism was initially introduced in Finland in a radical form. After all, when masses of warm air collide with cold air, violent storms are unavoidable.

While the official church fought against the new religious movement, spiritual awakenings took place among the people. Some prominent lay leaders played major roles in seeking to make the church into an institution that would promote and sustain spiritual life. The whole story of the awakenings covers roughly 120 years, from the late seventeenth to the early nineteenth centuries. It was a struggle for freedom of conscience and for awakened hearts to take the Bible seriously in matters of both personal and congregational life. Sadly, some bypassed true repentance and the way of grace in favor of self-righteousness and self-chosen pious practices that led to all forms of carnality. Often the Word of God was pushed aside in order to make room for revelations and visions. Yet there were those among the awakened who pointed to the absolute authority of the Word of God, and because of wise leadership and guidance the movement was retained within the church to its spiritual benefit. The story of the Church of Finland in the eighteenth century is one of new spiritual life among both the clergy and the people, which served to keep the revivals and awakenings alive within the church.

Pietism, and the revivals and awakenings it produced, represented the desire of the people to remove control over the shaping of personal faith and spirituality from the clergy and return it to the Holy Spirit. This was initially resented by the clergy, who enjoyed ecclesiastical power and who resisted and opposed the awakening movements—until they too began to experience spiritual revival and saw the benefits it brought to the people, to their parishes, and to the nation.

The following statements provide the essence of the theology of Finnish pietism:

• Too much time is spent preaching *about* "the gospel" and too little about Christ.
• We are saved by a Person, not by a doctrine.
• Faith justifies us and clothes us with the righteousness of Christ.
• Faith is both being possessed by Christ and a dissatisfaction with the spiritual status quo, a yearning for spiritual gifts not yet received.
• Faith is not a mere confession of lips, but an ethically compelling power.
• Only the morality that is the fruit of faith is of any value.
• If the Bible is not seen as God's Word, there is no faith and no forgiveness of sin.
• Faith is a power received from above, and not a theory, always walking and never resting.
• Without the fruit of faith, Christianity is meaningless.
• The power of new life is experienced in the tribulations God sends His children. God sustains the believer in the inward conflict, and this is the ultimate assurance of God's grace.
• The believer must deny the world and bear the cross.
• Christianity is life with God, entered by an inner experience of faith and new birth.
• True repentance is inward, the expression of a contrite heart.

More could be said, but this list is enough to taste the flavor of the Finnish pietism that produced powerful awakenings and revivals.

Finnish Christianity is characterized by biblicism on the one hand and pietism on the other. My spiritual heritage, therefore, is a strong and stubborn faith in, and reliance on, the doctrinal authority and integrity of

Scripture, coupled with the kind of believing faith those doctrines are meant to produce. This is also what I have seen in the writings of Ellen White. Professor Kukkonen, with whom I share the same spiritual heritage, understood its significance in my life and wrote of it in this way:

"God works in mysterious ways to lead His people along roads they would never choose to goals they consciously avoid but unconsciously seek with their whole beings. That is what happened to my former student C. Raymond Holmes, and through him to me. It became clear to me as I listened to his story that he found our Finnish Lutheran spiritual heritage in a refreshingly restored version when he left the Lutheran Church to follow his wife into the Seventh-day Adventist Church. This is evident in his book in which he describes the spirituality of some Christians as a state of having been *baptized but buried alive*. Quoting Ellen G. White, Holmes wrote, '"The new birth is a rare experience in this age of the world. This is the reason why there are so many perplexities in the churches. Many, so many, who assume the name of Christ are unsanctified and unholy. They have been baptized, but they were buried alive. Self [ego] did not die, and therefore they did not rise to newness of life in Christ."'

"When I read it, I was struck by the similarity of White's insight into baptism and Luther's statement in his *Small Catechism*: 'It signifies that the old creature in us with all sins and evil desires is to be drowned and die through daily contrition and repentance, and on the other hand that a new person is to come forth and rise up to live before God in righteousness and purity forever' (*The Book of Concord* [2000], p. 360). Holmes summarized White and Luther in a single sentence: 'The greatest spiritual lesson any believer can ever learn is that it is God's will to transform daily life into daily death and then daily death into daily spiritual life.'"[3]

Adventist spirituality, like that of the pietist heritage of the road behind, is intensely aware of the warfare between God's kingdom and the demonic kingdom, a warfare that rages not in the cosmos but in the human heart, in the inner being. Christian life is seen in terms of this spiritual conflict, for which spiritual weapons are needed—prayer, meditation on and study of the Word of God, the invaluable counsel of the Spirit of Prophecy, and personal devotion, together with corporate worship, which is the heartbeat of the church.

It was Kukkonen who introduced me to Philip Spener's *Pia Desideria* as one of the reading requirements for his seminary course on Finnish Christianity. Spener was born on January 13, 1635, hence his span of life was roughly a hundred years after Luther's. After completing theological studies, he was ordained and wrote a dissertation for the Doctor of Theology degree, and became pastor in Frankfurt am Main. In his later years he was one of the sponsors at the baptism of Nicholas Zinzendorf (1700-1760), forming a link with the man who became the founder of the Moravian Church, through which Adventism traces its roots to pietism. The motivation for the publication of Spener's book was the deplorable spiritual condition of the Reformation church as a result of the period of dead orthodoxy, which he referred to as "wretched conditions." He appealed to his fellow clergy and scholars:

"Let us remember that in the last judgment we shall not be asked how learned we were and whether we displayed our learning before the world; to what extent we enjoyed the favor of men and knew how to keep it; with what honors we were exalted and how great a reputation in the world we left behind us; or how many treasures of earthly goods we amassed for our children and thereby drew a curse upon ourselves. Instead, we shall be asked how faithfully and with how childlike a heart we sought to further the kingdom of God; with how pure and godly a teaching and how worthy an example we tried to edify our hearers amid the scorn of the world, denial of self, taking up the cross, and imitation of our Savior; with what zeal we opposed not only error but also wickedness of life; or with what constancy and cheerfulness we endured the persecution or adversity thrust upon us by the manifestly godless world or by false brethren, and amid such suffering praised our God."[4]

Though born in the United States of Swedish/Finnish ethnic heritage, I had the strangest feeling on my first trip to Finland that I was coming home. Could anthropologists be right when they talk about "ethnic memory"? The road was already there long before I began my spiritual journey or knew the direction it would take and what the destination would be. The primary impact of the pietism with which I am most familiar, and which I have found articulated in the Spirit of Prophecy, is that true biblical doctrine produces an inner-faith experience that is prerequisite to sharing that faith, to evangelism, and church growth. Should the Seventh-day Adventist movement lose sight of what biblical doctrine is intended to accomplish, both objectively and subjectively, its message would become powerless and its mission crippled. We must always maintain a balance between that which is given doctrinally and that which is experienced inwardly. Objective doctrinal truth and experiential believing faith are not mutually exclusive, and we must consciously avoid language that implies they are.

I think the best way to conclude this chapter is to let my wife tell the story of how she rediscovered the value of her spiritual heritage during the Mission Institute at Andrews University, which we were required to attend prior to our service in the Philippines, and which, she says, "turned

out to be another milestone in my spiritual journey." She described it this
way:

"Since my decision to become an Adventist I had felt geographically
disconnected, emotionally dislocated from my past, and severed from my
identity as a Lutheran Christian. As a Sabbathkeeper I was separated from
numerous meaningful connections with extended family and former
friends, all of whom I loved dearly. Precious associations were suddenly
nonexistent or awkward. The symbol and substance of Lutheranism was
relinquished forever, I thought. The texture of daily life, the array of in-
tangibles, once supporting me no longer contained the same strong, familiar elements. I had zealously leapt into the full acceptance of Adventist
doctrines and clung to them tightly, the future stretching before me.
However, I felt like some vital part of me was missing.

"The Mission Institute was an enormous help in many practical ways.
Of inestimable value was the orientation to new cultures through lectures,
books, films, and interaction with other mission candidates.

"The outstanding blessing, however, was that those weeks recon-
nected me with my missing past! Adventism need not, after all, cancel or
replace my Lutheran heritage. No longer need I lament the 'death' of my
community of origin. By means of the anthropological and biblical lectures
of Dr. Russell Staples, in particular, my feet rested once again on my religious substructure, my foundation! Healing forces were set in motion. In
effect, Dr. Staples said that a missionary makes his best contribution when
true to self, using God-given gifts to the fullest. I learned that loving people of a different culture means honestly accepting them as they are, as well
as fully being who I am. Mission Institute began the process of restoring
the 'ultimate meaning metaphors' I had absorbed in my childhood and
Lutheran past. . . .

"[The process of grafting] is an amazing parable of what the heavenly
Gardener did for me during the Mission Institute! He skillfully reattached
me to the half from which I had been severed, my root system. The combination of both parts would be a new and unique person, one who might
be termed a 'Lutheran Adventist Christian.' I was handed back my heritage
as a gift and charged to stand firmly on it. My new community of faith
must include my community of origin. It would have its own unique challenges and disappointments, joys and rewards. I was to be what I had
always been, yet walk in the new light He gave me, and use it all for His
glory!"[5]

Meditation

Now, ask yourself: Knowing how God has led in my life, how confident am I that He will lead me in the future? How truly thankful am I for the ways in which God has led His people in the past? In what ways am I a beneficiary of that history?

---

[1] E. G. White, *Life Sketches*, p. 196.

[2] At the age of 34 he was appointed superintendent of Ingria. In his efforts to convert the people, many of whom were Finns, from Greek Orthodoxy to the Lutheran faith, he clashed with Russian authorities. Nevertheless he was successful, and by 1684, 3,000 families had converted. By 1686 whole parishes had turned to the evangelical Lutheran faith. The population of the area continues to be Lutheran even after more than two centuries of Russian rule. It is in Ingria that the Suomi Free Conference, an independent association of ethnic Finns within the Evangelical Lutheran Church in America, has its most effective mission work today.

[3] Walter Jacob Kukkonen, *The Gate to the Beyond Within* (Tucson, Ariz.: Polaris Press, 2001), pp. 124, 25. His quote is from my book *Baptized but Buried Alive*. Kukkonen was a dear and cherished spiritual friend, yet I found myself troubled by his fascination with the psychology of Carl G. Jung. Unfortunately, we never found time for a discussion of this or for an understanding of the meaning of his comment, "This is what happened to my former student . . . and through him to me."

[4] Philip Jacob Spener, *Pia Desideria,* trans. Theodore G. Tappert (Philadelphia: Fortress Press, 1964), pp. 36, 37.

[5] Shirley S. Holmes, *No Turning Back*, p. 134.

Chapter 12

A DEEPER LIFE

Simply by observation alone, one has to come to the conclusion that genuine Seventh-day Adventists are some of the most disciplined Christians on the face of the earth. I will go into the details of that observation later. But first I want to introduce the subject of spiritual discipline. So let's talk about it.

Spiritual Discipline

Ellen White used the phrase "spiritual discipline" in the booklet *Christian Education,* published in 1893. Later it was reproduced in *Fundamentals of Christian Education,* a collection of articles published in 1923. Here is the passage as it appears in both sources:

"It is true that the simplicity of true godliness has to a large degree been lost from the church, and many of those who profess to be followers of Christ have become so blinded that they think that gain is godliness, and they devote their powers to the things of time. They do not realize that all their intellectual ability has been purchased by Christ, and that they should devote to Him the best results of their thought, that His cause may be advanced. But instead of giving their sharp, clear ideas to advance the cause, to strengthen and bless the church, they devote all their powers to the advancement of their own interests. They do not gather with Christ, but lead away from Him by their words and acts. They surround their souls with an atmosphere that is deleterious to spirituality. They profess to be followers of Christ, but they do not know Him by an experimental [experiential] knowledge. They do not practice religion. They do not seek to be Christians in the same way in which they would learn a trade. They profess to believe advanced truth; but it is evident that they keep it in the outer [external] court; for it has no sanctifying power on life and character. They do not realize how much is at stake; for the salvation of their own souls and that of others is imperiled. They do not realize that in order to be a savor of life unto life they must be under *spiritual discipline* and training, learning in the school of Christ. Without this *spiritual discipline*, they become inefficient, ignorant, and undeveloped, and see no necessity for the *spiritual training* and knowledge which would qualify them to hold positions of influence and usefulness. If they do not consecrate themselves wholly to God, becoming learners in His school, they will do haphazard work that will result in injury to the church."[1]

This statement is profound, and we need to spend some time unpacking its meaning and implications.

It is apparent that the primary concern of this passage is for the spiritual condition and welfare of the "followers of Christ," and, by extension, for that of the church, which is God's institutional instrument for His mission in the world. If the members of the body of Christ are spiritually weak, the body itself is weak. Conversely, if the body is weak, so are the members. The major weakness of the body is the loss, to a large degree, of "true godliness." That loss, which injures the body, is attributed to a number of spiritual weaknesses in members "who profess to be" followers of Christ:

1. They have become blinded, perhaps by the fact that they have prospered financially and otherwise, thus mistakenly concluding that prosperity itself indicates godliness and so devoting more and more—no, *all*—of their energies to the accumulation of such perceived evidences of godliness.

2. They have lost sight of the fact that everything they are and have, all of their intellectual ability that has resulted in such prosperity, belongs to Christ, whom they claim to follow.

3. They have lost sight of the fact that the best results of their abilities should be devoted to Christ in order to advance His cause, not theirs.

4. They have lost sight of the fact that instead of advancing their own personal interests, their thinking and planning and energy should be devoted to the service of Christ.

5. Their words and acts lead them away from Christ, rather than, together with Him, leading others to saving faith.

6. As a consequence, they have surrounded their whole beings with an atmosphere "deleterious" to spirituality. By "deleterious" she means a poisonous quality that destroys their own spiritual lives and the mission of the body. *A very serious condition!*

What is the spiritual problem? They do not know Jesus "by an experimental knowledge," by which she means a knowledge derived from personal experience. A living faith. A believing faith. Consequently, they "do not practice religion." Why not? Because without a knowledge of Jesus experientially, inwardly, it is not possible to practice the Christian religion.

There is sometimes a big difference between what one believes and the way one lives, between doctrine (what is believed) and religion (the way it is lived). One can profess to believe "advanced truth" and not allow it to penetrate to the inner being where real transformation takes place, relegating it instead to the external, to the "outer court," where it has no sanctifying power on life and character. Let's pause here and see what else Ellen White says about those who claim to have been given advanced truth for these times:

"When we see the fruits of righteousness in those who claim to have advanced truth, as we claim to have it, then there will be a course of action which testifies that we have learned of Christ."[2]

The proof, then, of having received advanced truth is demonstrated by the course of action it produces.

"There are many in the church who at heart belong to the world, but God calls upon those who claim to believe the advanced truth, to rise above the present attitude of the popular churches of today. Where is the self-denial, where is the cross-bearing that Christ has said should characterize His followers?"[3]

"The world watches to see what fruit is borne by professed Christians. It has a right to look for self-denial and self-sacrifice from those who claim to believe advanced truth."[4]

"Let believers and unbelievers see in the life of those who claim to have a knowledge of advanced truth a steady, clear, strong light shining forth in zeal, in devotion, in nobility of character, in their dealings with men."[5]

"Why is it that those who claim to believe advanced truth live so far beneath their privileges? Why do they mingle self with all they do? If they will cast out self, Jesus will pour into the thirsty soul a constant supply from the river of life."[6]

Self-denial. Cast out self. This is radically different from the contemporary self-centered me-me-me way of life.

"This is an age of almost universal apostasy, and those who claim to hold advanced truth mislead the churches when they do not give evidence that their character and works harmonize with the divine truth. The goodness, the mercy, the compassion, the tenderness, the loving-kindness of God are to be expressed in the words, deportment, and character of all who claim to be children of God, especially in those who claim to be messengers sent by the Lord Jesus with the word of life to save the perishing. They are enjoined by the Bible to put away all that is harsh and course and rough in their character, and to be *grafted into Christ*, the living vine. They should bear the same quality of fruit that the vine bears. Thus only can the branch be a true representation of the preciousness of the vine."[7]

"Man is required to surrender self, to submit to be a child of God, to submit to be saved by his grace, and when this is done, divine agencies co-operate with the human agent, and the character is *transformed*. It is in the surrender of the will that the line of demarcation between a child of God, an heir of heaven, and the rebellious, who refuse the great salvation, is distinctly drawn."[8]

"The Lord of heaven has bestowed abundant labor upon the human race. The Holy Spirit operates upon the man as the leaven operates upon the meal. It is man's part to submit to be operated upon, to allow his will to be brought into conformity to the will of God."[9]

This is spiritual transformation. According to Elbert Hubbard: "If your religion does not change you, then you should change your religion." In an age of "almost universal apostasy" the Seventh-day Adventist Church, to which she speaks, must lead "the churches," rather than mislead them, by unmistakable evidence that both what they are inwardly and the way they live outwardly harmonize "with the divine truth." This is what Ellen White means by "present truth." She makes the connection between Bible doctrine and believing faith unambiguously clear. For example, in unhesitating and straightforward counsel to parents, she says:

"I am filled with horror as the condition of families professing present truth is opened before me. The profligacy of youth and even children is almost incredible. Parents do not know that secret vice is destroying and defacing the image of God in their children. The sins which characterized the Sodomites exist among them. The parents are responsible, for they have not educated their children to *love and obey* God. They have not restrained them, nor diligently taught them the way of the Lord. They have allowed them to go out and to come in when they chose, and to associate with worldlings. These worldly influences which counteract parental teaching and authority are to be found largely in so-called good society. By their dress, looks, amusements, they surround themselves with an atmosphere which is opposed to Christ.

"Our only safety is to stand as God's peculiar people. We must not yield one inch to the customs and fashions of this degenerate age, but stand in moral independence, making no compromise with its corrupt and idolatrous practices."[10]

Moral independence takes faith and courage. Standing as God's peculiar people, the external dimension of spirituality, means loving and obeying God, which is the internal dimension of spirituality. She makes the relationship between the internal and external dimensions of spirituality very obvious:

"There is hope for every one of us, but only in one way—*by fastening ourselves to Christ* and exerting every energy to attain to the perfection of His character. This goody-goody religion that makes light of sin, and that is forever dwelling upon the love of God to the sinner, encourages sinners to believe that God will save them while they continue in sin and know it to be sin. This is the way that many are doing who profess to believe present truth. The truth *is kept apart from their life,* and that is the reason it has no more power to convict and convert the soul. . . . The lives of many show that they *have no living connection with God. . . . They have no part or lot with Christ.*"[11]

Goody-goody religion does not suffice. "Those who believe present truth," she says, "are to *practice the truth, live the truth.* They are to study the Word *and eat the Word,* which means eating the flesh and drinking the blood of the Son of God," internalizing Christ who is the living Word of God. "They are to bring that Word, which is Spirit and life, into their daily, practical life. It is the bread from heaven, and it will give life to the world."[12] Her words are a vivid example of tough love long before that expression was commonplace. Disciplined Adventist Christians appreciate her motherly love when she tells us that we have "the standard of piety altogether too low" and come "far short of Bible holiness" and "give way to the risings of self."[13] Statements such as these go straight to the heart of Adventist spirituality, which is precisely why the Seventh-day Adventist Church does not baptize a person unless there is at least some evidence of inner transformation demonstrated by righteous living.

Now let's return to the problem, the need for an "experimental" (experiential) believing, faith. How is that need met? The members of the body "must be under spiritual discipline and training, learning in the school of Christ." Why? Because without such spiritual discipline "they become inefficient, ignorant, and undeveloped [spiritually]." Furthermore, without such spiritual discipline, they see "no necessity for the [kind of] spiritual training and knowledge" that alone qualifies for positions that influence the membership of the body and that are useful (fruitful) in the mission of the body. This is an imperative. If the branches are to be like the Vine into which they are grafted, they "must" be under such spiritual discipline and training, the purpose of which is to inwardly produce the kind of total consecration to God that will strengthen the body, rather than weaken it.

Who Does the Disciplining?

Given the truth of the above, we must now ask the questions: Who

does the disciplining? Do we discipline ourselves by means of some esoteric, ritualistic techniques? What does the Bible say?

"Therefore, since we are surrounded by so great a cloud of witnesses,
let us also lay aside every weight, and sin which clings so closely, and let
us run with endurance the race that is set before us, looking to Jesus, the
founder and perfecter of our faith, who for the joy that was set before him
endured the cross, despising the shame, and is seated at the right hand of
the throne of God. Consider him who endured from sinners such hostility against himself, so that you may not grow weary or fainthearted. In
your struggle against sin you have not yet resisted to the point of shedding
your blood. And have you forgotten the exhortation that addresses you as
sons?

'My son, do not regard lightly the discipline of the Lord,
    nor be weary when reproved by him.
For the Lord disciplines the one he loves,
    and chastises every son whom he receives.'

"It is for discipline that you have to endure. God is treating you as
sons. For what son is there whom his father does not discipline? If you are
left without discipline, in which all have participated, then you are illegit-
imate children and not sons. Besides this, we have had earthly fathers who
have disciplined us and we respected them. Shall we not much more be
subject to the Father of spirits and live? For they disciplined us for a short
time as it seemed best to them, but he disciplines us for our good, that we
may share his holiness. For the moment all discipline seems painful rather
than pleasant, but later it yields the peaceful fruit of righteousness to those
who have been trained by it" (Heb. 12:1-11).

God the Father does the disciplining. He takes the initiative. Why?
Because we need it, and He is a good Father who cares about His children.
We are subject to Him, as are all children to their earthly fathers. When
He disciplines us, God treats us as His legitimate children. Our struggle is
against sin, so we must endure, accept, yield to, His discipline for our spiritual welfare. We submit to His discipline. In fact, we welcome it, praise
Him for it, and invite Him to continue exercising His discipline in our
lives. Why? Because we appreciate the outcome, the results. Such willing
endurance is the exercise of believing faith, which is also obedient faith.
Consider this: "You shall therefore love the Lord your God and keep his
charge, his statutes, his rules, and his commandments always. And consider
. . . the discipline of the Lord your God, his greatness, his mighty hand and
his outstretched arm, his signs and his deeds. . . . For your eyes have seen
all the great work of the Lord that he did" (Deut. 11:1-7). We need His
spiritual discipline to protect us from self-righteousness, from ourselves.

Why? Because we cannot take the credit for that which only God's discipline produces.

For what ultimate purpose do His people submit to His discipline? That they might share His holiness and experience righteousness as the fruit of His loving discipline. This is the way Christian believers experience spiritual transformation, becoming Christlike in character—not by rituals such as sitting cross-legged on a cushion, staring at a blank wall repeating a mantra, or by any other liturgical rituals. The kind of spiritual discipline spoken of in the Bible and the Spirit of Prophecy is the exercise of God's discipline carefully chosen and applied for each individual believer. It is by means of His "training of the heart and mind that spiritual strength is gained, that weak points of character are made strong."[14]

Just how does the believer submit to God's discipline? Hebrews 12 tells us. We submit by laying aside every weight and sin. By running the race of faith with endurance. By looking to Jesus, who endured the cross for us. By not growing weary or fainthearted. By not seeing God's discipline as a matter of indifference, nor as alien to His love. By recognizing God's motive as being for our good. By accepting it as part of our training as His disciples. The word *discipline* comes from the same root as the word *disciple,* so God is actually busy "discipling" us when He is "disciplining" us. In brief, we submit to God's discipline by viewing it as our good Father's way of molding character. "But such a character is not the result of accident; it is not due to special favors or endowments of Providence. A noble character is the result of self-discipline, of the subjection of the lower to the higher nature—the surrender of self for the service of love to God and man."[15] Here, Ellen White is talking about God's discipline of the self. Self-discipline is the surrender of self to His will. He's there all the time. Believing faith knows He is present and can hear His voice.

"Through all our trials we have a never-failing Helper. He does not leave us alone to struggle with temptation, to battle with evil, and be finally crushed with burdens and sorrow. Though now He is hidden from mortal sight, the ear of faith can hear His voice saying, Fear not; I am with you. 'I am He that liveth, and was dead; and, behold, I am alive forevermore.' Rev. 1:18. I have endured your sorrows, experienced your struggles, encountered your temptations. I know your tears; I also have wept. The griefs that lie too deep to be breathed into any human ear, I know. Think not that you are desolate and forsaken. Though your pain touch no responsive chord in any heart on earth, look unto Me, and live."[16]

"Jesus, our Redeemer, man's representative and head, endured this testing process. He suffered more than we can be called upon to suffer. He bore our infirmities and was in all points tempted as we are. He did not suffer thus on His own account, but because of our sins; and now, relying on the merits of our Overcomer, we may become victors in His name. God's work of refining and purifying must go on until His servants are so humbled, so dead to self, that, when called into active service, their eye will be single to His glory."[17]

"A religious *experience* is attained *only* through conflict, through disappointment, through severe discipline of self, through earnest prayer."[18]

"The pruning will cause pain," she said, "but it is the Father who applies the knife. . . . The husbandman prunes away the harmful growth, that the fruit may be richer and more abundant."[19] The Father's discipline produces "godly grief" in the believer. As He exercises His divine discipline, we are "grieved into repenting," because "godly grief produces a repentance that leads to salvation without regret, whereas worldly grief produces death" (2 Cor. 7:9, 10). Worldly sorrow is devoid of repentance. "Those whom I love," says Jesus, "I reprove and discipline, so be zealous and repent" (Rev. 3:19). Why? Because "unless you repent, you will all likewise perish" (Luke 13:3). Evidently repentance is an ongoing part of the sanctification process. Luther understood this, which is why the first of his famous ninety-five theses declares: "When our Lord and Master Jesus Christ said 'Repent,' he willed that the whole life of believers should be one of repentance." Romans 12:3 says that faith is a gift of God. So also is repentance. In response to Peter's preaching concerning the baptism of the Holy Spirit, some of the Gentiles declare, "So then, even to Gentiles God has granted repentance" (Acts 11:18). So let us use the gifts of grace that God has given us and in faith repent of our ungodliness and worldly passions, so that we are enabled to live godly lives. The proof of it will be found in our relationships. With family. With friends. With fellow church members. In the way we treat people. The way we speak to people and about people. The "I" and "me" talk will come to an end, and we will talk about Jesus, and be "eager to do good" (1 Peter 3:13, NIV). He disciplines us for our good, so that we can do what is good. Does the Bible say what it means and mean what it says? We have only two choices. Either we believe the Bible or we don't. There is no third possibility. Why? Because truth is the issue. Just as there is no such thing as a half-lie, so there is no such thing as half-truth. If there were, it would not be the truth. Everybody has to decide; our eternal destiny depends on it. Either the Bible is true or it is not. There can be no halfway position. If it is not true, there is no salvation, no kingdom of heaven, no hope. If it is not true, this world and the life we live in it is all there is. *How depressing the thought.* The Bible says, "By their fruits you will know them" (Matt. 7:20, NKJV). Not by their words, but by their fruits. I remember my father saying of an incompetent bricklayer who talked a good job, "He's all mouth; he can't lay brick in a barrel."

God gives us faith and then empowers us by the indwelling Holy Spirit to be believing. Then like the good, loving, caring Father that He is, He teaches us to be obedient. Obedience means living "under grace." It means to live by faith, obtaining "access by faith into this grace in which we stand, and we rejoice in hope of the glory of God" (Rom. 5:2). He fulfills His promise that He "who began a good work in you will bring it to completion at the day of Jesus Christ" (Phil. 1:6). Death seals, forever, what we have become. Then comes rest until the trumpet sounds and the "mortal puts on immortality," and God "gives us the [final] victory through our Lord Jesus Christ" (1 Cor. 15:54, 57). Because we have such promises from God, "let us cleanse ourselves from every defilement of body and spirit, bringing holiness to completion in the fear of God" (2 Cor. 7:1). Do we have divine help in this? Yes, we do. The Lord has given His apostles, prophets, evangelists, pastors, and teachers, to the church "to equip the saints for the work of ministry" (Eph. 4:12). What is that ministry? It is "building up the body of Christ, until we all attain to the unity of the faith and of the knowledge of the Son of God, to *mature manhood*, to the measure of the stature of the fullness of Christ, so that we may no longer be children, tossed to and fro by the waves and carried about by every wind of doctrine, by human cunning, by craftiness in deceitful schemes. Rather, speaking the truth in love, we are to *grow up* in every way into him who is the head, into Christ, from whom the whole body, joined and held together by every joint with which it is equipped, when each part is working properly, makes the body grow so that it builds itself up in love" (verses 11-16).

This has been deeply imprinted on my Adventist consciousness, because it is true to Scripture. My personal experience in the fellowship and ministry of the Seventh-day Adventist Church has been wonderfully positive, and I praise God for what He has done for, in, and with me.

Discipline Observed

I began this chapter by saying that by observation alone one can conclude that Seventh-day Adventists are some of the most disciplined Christians on the face of the earth. It's manifested in the way they live, their stewardship of time and means, their devotion to mission. This was most impressive to me as I began to become aware of the nature of the spiritual life of this body of believers. I am talking about the way Adventists demonstrate awareness of purpose. The way they study the Bible and the Spirit of Prophecy, which is the Adventist form of meditation. The way they worship, which is informed and motivated by the biblical seventh-day Sabbath. Their reliance on prayer. Their determination to share their faith, evidenced in their stewardship of means and generosity. Surrounding it all is what Adventists call "the health message," which, when taken seriously, enables them to give maximum attention and energy to all the other aspects of their lives. Of course, these are all external manifestations, but the remarkable worldwide growth of the Seventh-day Adventist Church would not be possible apart from internal realities.

I am reluctant to refer to these manifestations as "spiritual disciplines," because the term suggests that they are things one does in order to reach, or find, God. We should, instead, speak of them as "faith responses" to the God who is there, and who has been there all the time—responses to His grace and discipline. He has revealed Himself in His Son, Jesus Christ, who indwells the believer by the Holy Spirit. These responses do not put us in the place in which change can occur. Rather, they bear witness to what God the Holy Spirit has already accomplished within the believer. I also hesitate to refer to them as "means of grace," because the Bible says that "the Word became flesh and dwelt among us, and we have seen his glory, glory as of the only Son from the Father, full of grace and truth" (John 1:14). Furthermore, "grace and truth came through Jesus Christ" (verse 17). Jesus Himself is the means of grace. We need Jesus, not rituals. Jesus is not found in rituals. He is the living Word, found in believers, who demonstrate a believing faith that is in harmony with the written Word of God.

Faith Active in Love

Perhaps the best way to illustrate what I have been saying in this chapter is to let a recently baptized member of the Seventh-day Adventist Church contribute. She is a professional woman with a deep and sincere Christian faith, based on disciplined study of the Bible. The spiritual road she has traveled has taken her on a denominational search that has led to a home in the fellowship of the Seventh-day Adventist congregation in Bessemer, Michigan. In spite of her love for the written Word of God, she always felt that "something was missing" until her inquiry into Adventism exposed what was missing from her understanding of Scripture. I recall, as we studied at the dining room table in my house, how her jaw would drop and her eyes open in astonishment, as she exclaimed more than once, "How come I never saw that before!" She was captivated by Bible truth. She has since become an extremely capable, insightful, articulate, and animated Sabbath school teacher. But objective, cerebral, Bible truth was not the whole picture.

Sometime after her baptism, as I began work on this book, I asked her if she would share with me the characteristics—distinguishing traits or qualities—of Adventist church members that impressed her and contributed to the faith transition she had experienced. I hope you are as thrilled as I was with her response. She prefaced her list by saying, "My observations of the characteristics of the church may or may not be unique to my situation. I was blessed to come into a small body of believers whose love not only for Jesus but also for one another was clearly present. The following traits were especially evident in the lives of those who were spiritual leaders within the congregation." Her list included: seekers of the truth, students of the Word, self-disciplined, dedicated to prayer, obedient to the Word of God, doers of the Word, humble, loving, heart knowledge versus head knowledge, mission-minded, not sanctimonious or pretentious, sincere, not overbearing. She subsequently added practicing a healthy lifestyle to the list. "Essentially summed up by the fruit of the Spirit: love, joy, peace, patience, gentleness, goodness, faith, meekness, and temperance."

Stewardship needs to be added to this list—stewardship, understood in broad terms to include the biblical principle of tithing and generous offerings for the local and worldwide mission work of the church, care for the physical body of the believer, which is the temple of the Holy Spirit, and care for the environment of God's created world.

She concludes with these words: "Recognizing that each person is at a different place in their walk with the Lord, fruit borne varies with the individual member. However, by and large, as I have met other Adventists outside of my small, local congregation, they too exhibit these characteristics." Need any more be said, except "Praise the Lord!"? What Adventists call "the message" works! It works from the inside out. This is believing faith. This is evidence of spiritual transformation. This is walking in "newness of life." This is life on a higher plane. "Faith active in love" is perhaps the most descriptive way to characterize a faith that responds positively to the Lord's discipline, reflective of a deeper "discipled" life. I also asked this woman how she would characterize the message preached by the Seventh-day Adventist Church in comparison to what she had heard preached in other churches she had attended. Her answer was that it was "complete" and had greater spiritual "depth."

Adventist Christians *do not* believe that the above characteristics are meritorious in any way. They are not the cause of justification or of sanctification, which result from the cross of Christ and His ministry in the heavenly sanctuary as high priest. Rather, such characteristics are the fruit of God's grace and mercy first in the "inner being" and consequently in the outward manifestations of a believing faith. A faith that really works! Also it needs to be made clear that Adventist Christians, while they rejoice in the fruit of faith, do not believe that the manifestation of such characteristics is the criterion for truth. Truth is found in the historical revelation of God in His written Word and in the Christ of the Bible, who is the living Word of God. The believer's trust can be confidently placed in both, not in the inward communion with God, as promoted by mysticism, or in the spiritualistic idea that truth is found within every person. Although Adventist Christians are as concerned about spirituality as much as anyone else, they insist that true spirituality must be rooted firmly in the Word of God. For this reason they are careful not to elevate discipline above biblical doctrine/truth. At the same time, they do not want to make a big mistake by putting so much emphasis on doctrine that reformation of life is neglected. Balance is always needed, theologically and experientially.

Healthy Lifestyle

The Adventist concern for a healthy lifestyle is not just a peculiar invention of Seventh-day Adventists. It is scriptural and is taken seriously. Why? Because we believe the Bible, which says, "Beloved, I pray that all may go well with you and that you may be in good health, as it goes well with your soul" (3 John 2). The gospel is not just the good news of salvation and eternal life; it is also the good news *about* the good life. This too is part of the grace and mercy of a loving God. It is part of a believing faith that actively, consciously, chooses to participate in the exercise of God's will for physical health. Anything else is a rejection of *sola scriptura*. God's promise is connected to His commands. "If you will diligently listen to the voice of the Lord your God, and do that which is right in his eyes, and give ear to his commandments and keep all his statutes, I will put none of the diseases on you that I put on the Egyptians, for I am the Lord, your healer" (Ex. 15:26). Do what is right in His eyes. Pay attention to His commands. Keep all His statutes. The results are good, not bad. This kind of faith response to the Word of God is *not* legalism. Only a rebellious, self-willed mind would think so. Because He is a God of grace, God's concern for humankind includes both His gift of eternal life and the quality of life He makes possible on this side of the resurrection. This is why Seventh-day Adventist Christians understand that ministry is for the whole person and that every aspect of life is touched and transformed by the gospel. They rejoice in that understanding and experience. They rejoice not only in the spiritual benefits of the gospel but also in the physical benefits of a healthy lifestyle. Consequently, they do not hesitate to teach "that every practice which destroys the physical, mental, or *spiritual* energies is sin, and that health is to be secured through obedience to the laws that God has established for the good of all mankind."[20]

Is there a struggle and conflict with this? You bet there is. There was for me. This part of the road I travel was bumpy for a while—until I finally got it. I was raised on meat and potatoes, but thanks to the Lord, I have been a vegetarian for the past 40 years. *What possible connection,* I asked myself, *can there be between justification, faith, forgiveness, salvation, the gift of eternal life, and a healthy lifestyle?* Many church members, confessed believers in Jesus Christ, live as though there were no such connection, ruining their health, and often their families, by addiction to nicotine, alcohol, and illegal drugs, plus other debilitating lifestyle habits. Why? Because the distorted theology they have been taught allows them to thumb their nose at the will of God for human life. They attend church services to worship the Lord and repeat, as part of the ritual, "Bless the Lord, O my soul, and forget not all his benefits, who forgives all your iniquity [sin], who heals all your diseases, who redeems your life from the pit, who crowns you with steadfast love and mercy, who satisfies you with good so that your youth is renewed like the eagle's" (Ps. 103:2-5). Then they leave the sanctuary, light up a cigarette, and head for the bar. They bless the Lord, who forgives sin, and then go and live in it. They bless the Lord, who redeems from the pit, and then go wallow in it, thinking that everything is OK. What a delusion! Yes, Jesus forgives sin, but He also cleanses the forgiven sinner from unrighteousness (see 1 John 1:9). Yes, Jesus heals the sick and the lame, but then He says, as He said to the lame man healed at Bethesda, "See, you are well! Sin no more, that nothing worse may happen to you" (John 5:14).

As a Lutheran seminary student and ordained minister, I was steeped in justification by faith and the gospel of forgiveness. I do not recall, as a seminary student, hearing a single lecture on sanctification. When one student raised the subject in class, the professor, typically stuck on justification, responded, "That's synergistic." He meant that the human being cannot contribute anything to salvation, which is true. But the saved do not live in deliberate sin. The apostle Paul makes that indelibly clear. First, there is the gospel of grace and then the response and the results:

"But God, being rich in mercy, because of the great love with which he loved us, even when we were dead in our trespasses, made us alive together with Christ—by grace you have been saved—and raised us up with him and seated us with him in the heavenly places in Christ Jesus, so that in the coming ages he might show the immeasurable riches of his grace in kindness toward us in Christ Jesus. For by grace you have been saved through faith. And this is not of your own doing; it is the gift of God, not a result of works, so that no one may boast. *For we are his workmanship, cre-ated in Christ Jesus for good works, which God prepared beforehand, that we should walk in them"* (Eph. 2:4-10).

What could be more clear? Salvation is by grace alone, received by faith alone. It is all a gift of God. In no way is it the result of what we do. However, those saved by grace through faith are God's workmanship, re-deemed and re-created by Him for "good works." There is a big differ-ence between the "works" of verse 9, and the "good works" of verse 10! Simply put, the power of grace changes, transforms, the sinner from the inside out. That's the only way it can be done. But it is done! At least, it is meant to be done. But in order for it to be manifest, God sanctifies the forgiven sinner by developing a Christlike character within by means of His Word and the power of the Holy Spirit and the indwelling Christ. The Spirit of Prophecy puts it this way in the following graphic description of a life transformed by grace. No one anywhere has said it better.

"To the heart that has become purified [by the converting power of God], all is changed. *Transformation of character is the testimony to the world of an indwelling Christ.* The Spirit of God produces a new life in the soul [inner being], bringing the thoughts and desires into obedience to the will of Christ; and the *inward man* is renewed in the image of God. Weak and erring men and women show to the world that the redeeming power of grace can cause the faulty character to develop into symmetry and abun-dant fruitfulness.

"The heart that receives the word of God is not as a pool that evapo-rates, not like a broken cistern that loses its treasure. It is like the moun-tain stream, fed by unfailing springs, whose cool, sparkling waters leap from rock to rock, refreshing the weary, the thirsty, the heavy-laden. It is like a river constantly flowing and, as it advances, becoming deeper and wider, until its life-giving waters are spread over all the earth. The stream that goes singing on its way leaves behind its gift of verdure and fruitful-ness. The grass on its banks is a fresher green, the trees have a richer ver-dure, the flowers are more abundant. When the earth lies bare and brown under the summer's scorching heat, a line of verdure marks the river's course.

"So it is with the true child of God. The religion of Christ reveals it-self as a vitalizing, pervading principle, a living, working, spiritual energy. When the heart is opened to the heavenly influence of truth and love, these principles will flow forth again like streams in the desert, causing fruitfulness to appear where now are barrenness and dearth.

"As those who have been cleansed and sanctified through a knowledge of Bible truth engage heartily in the work of soulsaving, they will become indeed a savor of life unto life. And as daily they drink of the inexhaustible fountain of grace and knowledge, they will find that their own hearts are filled to overflowing with the Spirit of their Master, and that through their unselfish ministry many are benefited physically, mentally, and spiritually. The weary are refreshed, the sick restored to health, and the sin–burdened relieved. In far-off countries thanksgiving is heard from the lips of those whose hearts are turned from the service of sin unto righteousness."[21]

For this reason Seventh-day Adventist Christians are into a healthy lifestyle. It is part of bearing witness to the transforming power of the grace of God. Yes, we are "health nuts"! What's wrong with that? It's better than being an alcohol nut. Or a nicotine nut. Or any other kind of nut. What's wrong with avoiding illness—and by so doing testifying to the "inexhaustible fountain of grace and knowledge"? As a seminary professor of mine so eloquently put it: "A Christian is like an oak tree; he starts out as a nut and grows from the inside." Just as forgiveness is not really real to one who has not accepted it by faith, so healing is not really real to one who refuses to stop sinning by God's grace. The discipling/discipline of the Father produces a deeper spiritual life.

Meditation

After some thought, take paper and pen and describe your present spiritual life, based on what you have read so far. Then ask: Have I been devoting all my abilities to personal interests, rather than to the cause of Christ? Am I just a churchgoer for whom God's truth is an external rather than an internal matter, resulting in not practicing the religion of Christ that I profess to believe? Does my faith really work? What inner transformation still needs to happen in order for me to be the person God wants me to be? Am I willing to yield to the Father's discipline so that I can share His holiness?

---

[1] Ellen G. White, *Christian Education* (Battle Creek, Mich.: International Tract Society, 1893), p. 136; *Fundamentals of Christian Education*, pp. 254, 255.

[2] Ellen G. White, *Faith and Works* (Nashville: Southern Pub. Assn., 1979), p. 63.

[3] E. G. White, *Fundamentals of Christian Education*, p. 289.

[4] E. G. White, *In Heavenly Places*, p. 316.

[5] Ellen G. White, *Reflecting Christ* (Washington, D.C.: Review and Herald Pub. Assn., 1985), p. 206.

[6] *Ibid*, p. 304.

[7] E. G. White, *Testimonies to Ministers*, pp. 151, 152. (Italics supplied.)

[8] *Review and Herald*, Mar. 24, 1896. (Italics supplied.)

[9] Ellen G. White, *Manuscript Releases* (Silver Spring, Md.: Ellen G. White Estate, 1993), vol. 14, p. 145.

[10] E. G. White, *Child Guidance*, p. 449. (Italics supplied.)

[11] E. G. White, *Christ Triumphant*, p. 81. (Italics supplied.)

[12] *Ibid.*, p. 247. (Italics supplied.)

[13] Ellen G. White, *Christian Experience and Teachings of Ellen G. White* (Mountain View, Calif.: Pacific Press Pub. Assn., 1922), p. 104.

[14] E. G. White, *Ellen G. White 1888 Materials*, p. 583.

[15] E. G. White, *Education*, p. 57.

[16] E. G. White, *The Desire of Ages*, p. 483.

[17] E. G. White, *Testimonies for the Church,* vol. 4, p. 86.

[18] *Ibid.*, p. 444. (Italics supplied.)

[19] E. G. White, *The Desire of Ages,* p. 677.

[20] E. G. White, *The Ministry of Healing*, p. 113. (Italics supplied.)

[21] E. G. White, *Prophets and Kings* (Mountain View, Calif.: Pacific Press Pub. Assn., 1917), pp. 233, 234. (Italics supplied.)

Chapter 13

"LET NO ONE DECEIVE YOU"

Although we should not be paranoid about the contemporary interest in spirituality, at the same time we need to be alert. After all, God's Word does caution us concerning deception, saying, "Let no one deceive you with empty words, for because of these things the wrath of God comes upon the sons of disobedience" (Eph. 5:6). Be careful! But being careful is not enough. Take action as well. "Therefore do not become partners with them [those who would deceive you]" (verse 7). Why not? Because "at one time you were darkness, but now you are light in the Lord" (verse 8). What must we do if we are light in the Lord? "Walk as children of light (for the fruit of light is found in all that is good and right and true), and try to discern what is pleasing to the Lord. Take no part in the unfruitful works of darkness, but instead expose them" (verses 8-11). Those verses say it all.

There are warning signs, red flags, that we must be aware of if we are to be faithful to the message and mission God has given to the church of the last days. Here is one of them. In the introduction to a book that analyzes the theology and teaching of Rick Warren, the author makes the observation that Warren's theology has "infiltrated almost every Christian denomination," including "Conservative Baptist, American Baptist, Southern Baptist, Reformed, Lutheran, Episcopal, Nazarene, Methodist, Christian and Missionary Alliance, Foursquare Church, Presbyterian, Vineyard, *Seventh-day Adventist*, United Pentecostal Church, Church of God, Evangelical Free, Calvary Chapel, and a host of community and non-denominational churches throughout the United States and the rest of the world."[1] The Seventh-day Adventist Church too?

Can it be? If so, we need a revival of confessional responsibility at all levels of church life. In order to have something significant to say about faith, about life in this world, we first have to be certain about what we are saying. We must be careful that we do not turn wine into water. Being progressive does not necessarily mean discovering something "new" or different. It may mean rediscovering our own Adventist tradition and telling the story in new ways. If our mission is to evangelize the world and continue the Reformation, then only the message that can accomplish that mission deserves our attention and our allegiance. All of us—laity, administrators, pastors, evangelists, theologians, teachers—must dedicate ourselves to the shaping and renewing of the consciousness of our church. Luther once observed:

"If I profess with the loudest voice and clearest exposition every portion of the truth of God except precisely that little point which the world and the devil at that moment are attacking, I am not confessing Christ, however boldly I may be professing Christ. Where the battle rages, there the loyalty of the soldier is proved, and to be steady on all the battlefield besides is mere flight and disgrace if he flinches at that point."[2]

Confessional Responsibility[3]

Part of the road I travel was the great privilege of serving on the faculty of the Seventh-day Adventist Theological Seminary at Andrews University. Conscious of the enormous responsibility that entailed, I found it necessary to consider the following: Because God has charged the church and its educational institutions with guarding the truth (see 1 Tim. 6:20), what should be their attitude toward views that attempt to explain away the facts of the faith? Should they not resist any misleading modification or destruction of the church's beliefs? The church is not obligated to grant the widest liberty to all opinions or practices, to challenge no teacher or teaching. What is so confidently called "academic freedom" is not an end in itself. The purpose of the church's teaching ministry is for "building up the body of Christ, until we all attain to the unity of the faith and of the knowledge of the Son of God, to mature manhood, to the measure of the stature of the fullness of Christ" (Eph. 4:12, 13). There are some ideas that are wrong, that contradict Scripture, and there are some teachers who are wrong. A confessional school is not a place where no one can ever be wrong, or it would be a place where no one can ever be right. Academic freedom does "not include the license to express views that may injure or destroy the very community that supports and provides for" denominational teachers.[4] The Adventist teacher will go beyond investigation of all views and show students where the truth lies as confessed by the church. Confessional responsibility requires that the personal beliefs of the teacher harmonize with those of the church.

In other words, Adventist teachers of all academic disciplines have a pastoral duty from which academic freedom does not absolve them. They do not speak only for themselves but for the body of believers. Academic freedom and confessional responsibility are not mutually exclusive. Academic freedom must always be subordinate to confessional responsibility. Why? Because heresy often hides behind academic freedom. We must always remember that without freedom of thought and inquiry no one could ever come to the faith. Yet at the same time we must assert that without the preservation of the faith, no amount of freedom of thought will bring a person to know the truth. The most stable and lasting growth in the church occurs when confessional responsibility is paramount. We must always appeal for our scholars and students to reach as high as possible intellectually, but always in the context of strong, unshakable convictions and beliefs. Someone has said that bigotry is the anger of those who have no convictions. Many who have lost the faith would promote passionately the evolution of Adventist spirituality into something they can accept, which poses the grave question: Must those who believe most ardently give way to those who believe less so and, finally, to those who do not believe at all?

The moment our Adventist educational institutions cease to stand for something definite, the cause is lost and the reason for their existence collapses. Many great universities, such as Harvard, Princeton, and the University of Chicago, originally founded by Christian denominations, became secularized and apostate because the confession of faith was abandoned. By virtue of their mission, academic institutions supported by the Seventh-day Adventist Church are confessional institutions with a bias regarding revealed truth. *In such schools, responsibility for the preservation and propagation of that truth defines the limits of academic freedom.* The apostle Paul did not fashion his message to suit any particular culture or social group. He preached the same message to the young and to the old, to men and women, to the educated and the uneducated. He didn't take a survey, analyze the results, and adapt his message accordingly. For Paul, meeting spiritual needs took precedence over meeting what is referred to euphemistically today as "felt needs." Though Paul was "all things to all men," he did not adapt his message, because it had been given to him by Christ. He would preach the same message to our generation that he preached to the upwardly mobile people of his time. Divine revelation, not human need, determines doctrine and truth. If we were to fail in our confessional responsibility, the spirituality that would result certainly would not be genuinely Adventist or biblical spirituality.

Turning East

In the early 1980s, about the time I was invited to the faculty of our seminary at Andrews University, I acquired a copy of *Turning East: The*

Promise and Peril of the New Orientalism, by Harvey Cox,[5] who was a professor at Harvard Divinity School at the time. I didn't read very far before abandoning it, because I had no interest in Eastern religions—not even to the point of trying to understand why some people left the Christian faith for Eastern cults. The Christian faith that I had entered into by choice, first Lutheranism and later Adventism—satisfied my inner needs for truth, love, acceptance, and hope. Cox's book has been reposing in my library ever since, and now, after almost three decades and motivated by writing this book, I have read the whole of it. Age has dried and cracked the binding, and pages are falling out. But it has caught my attention, because we are faced today with a crisis of spirituality and because some Adventist Christians are evidently being attracted by the emerging church.[6]

Cox tells the story of a Sunday afternoon in which three young people knocked on his door. The two young men had shaved heads, wore saffron-colored robes, bead necklaces, and sandals. White lines were painted on their faces, and drums hung around their necks. The young girl wore a sari, with small cymbals on her fingers. They asked if they could come in and talk to him about Hare Krishna. It turned out that one of them had grown up in a Protestant home; one came from a Catholic family; one was born a Jew. When they left, they presented Cox with a copy of a Hindu scripture and went on their way, chanting and tinkling down the street.

Cox was puzzled and intrigued by that encounter. As a Christian theologian, he wanted to discover what provoked such an Eastern religious revival. He wanted to know what it was that caused these young people to abandon traditional religious life for the sake of a new spiritual movement.[7] So he recruited some of his students, and together they began to do a serious study. Casting aside suspicions, they attended meditations, lectures, worship gatherings, and study groups. Devouring large quantities of Krishna literature, they watched, listened, and taped meetings. In the early stage of the research they wanted to experience Krishna life in order to be as thorough as possible in their study. Unfortunately, as time went on, Cox became personally attracted by what he was observing, and his "scholarly restraint disappeared."[8] He insists that he remained Christian, but His Christian faith became more and more syncretistic as he absorbed some of the religious practices and rituals he was observing. As he put it, the investigation "became a discovery."[9] He freely admits that "once one starts down the road of 'participation,' almost anything can happen."[10] He became a Christian practicing Buddhist meditation[11]—which, of course, is an oxymoron.

Chapter Five, "Meditation and Sabbath," is one of the most fascinating chapters in *Turning East.* In it Cox attempts to justify certain forms of

Eastern meditation that he had adopted, while at the same time claiming he had not accepted Buddhist philosophy. An unusual evangelical, he admits that the seventh-day Sabbath was not invented by the Jews, though he refers to the "Jewish Sabbath." Rather than tracing its origins to the biblical account of Creation, and thus to the Creator, Cox attributes the Sabbath to "the religious milieu of the ancient Near East."[12] He became captivated by the Sabbath, because he saw in it the biblical equivalent of Buddhist meditation. He writes, "It nurtures the same kind of awareness that [Buddhist] meditation nurtures, for Sabbath is not just a day for doing nothing. It is a particular form of consciousness, a way of thinking and being that strongly resembles what the Buddhists call 'mindfulness.'"[13]

As part of his research Cox spent an entire Sabbath, from sundown on Friday to sundown on Saturday, with a rabbi and his congregation. He concludes the chapter by saying that he had found in Buddhism not only a way of meditating, but also a way of integrating that practice into his own Protestant religious tradition, through his experience of spending that Sabbath day with the rabbi. "I had learned what it means to be a Christian who practices a 'Buddhist' form of meditation—from the Jews."[14] He says so many perceptive things about Sabbath that one wonders why he did not absorb into his own spirituality the biblical practice of seventh-day observance, as he did with the practice of Buddhist meditation. He plaintively asks, "Can we ever regain the glorious vision of Sabbath as a radiant queen, a jeweled sovereign who comes to visit bringing warmth and joy in her train?"[15] But then he goes on to say why he thinks such a recovery is not possible, citing the need for either a "religiously unified culture—which we obviously do not have—or a tight and self-conscious subculture, which Jews once had but do not have any longer." What is needed, in Cox's view, "is a form of Sabbath observance which can be practiced in the modern, pluralistic world, which can function on an individual or a small group basis, but which restores the lost dialectic of action and repose, of intervention and letting be." Obviously Cox knew little or nothing about either the Seventh-day Adventist practice of Sabbath observance or the spirituality that sustains it. What was his answer to the need that he recognized and its lack of fulfillment that he laments? Because he did not see the possibility of a common Sabbath being recovered, he concluded that the form of meditation he learned to practice "could become a modern equivalent of Sabbath." He concluded that such meditation can serve to restore the "insight that despite all the things that *must* be done in the world—to feed and liberate and heal—even God occasionally pauses to draw breath."[16] This is the kind of interpretation that emerges when *sola scriptura* is abandoned and religious traditions are mixed.

In light of what I am trying to do in this chapter, the most disturbing section in Cox's book is his discussion of the reasons some people were turning East. He identifies them as mostly young, between the late teens and early 30s, with the 20s most frequently being the turning time. The majority of those turning to Eastern religions were educated, from middle-class and upper-middle-class affluent families. Cox makes a startling observation, quoting a study of the Hare Krishna movement, that "the large liberal Protestant churches whose church school attendance declined even more during the 1960s than their adult membership contribute most to the membership of the Hare Krishna movement."[17] Why? Cox wanted to know, and so did I.

As he and his students interviewed individuals to find out what they could about their inner motivation, a common pattern emerged. 1. Those looking to Eastern religions told stories of loneliness, isolation, and searching for supportive communities. A major motivation was the need for *simple human friendship*. 2. Another motivation was the search for a "real personal encounter with God" and an inner peace that Cox identified as *immediacy*, a religious experience apart from "ideas and concepts." Some of those they interviewed said that they had a problem with what they considered to be an abstract, cerebral approach to religion. They described a contrast between "direct experience and mediated teaching." 3. Some were looking for *authority*. They wanted to "find truth, to lay hold on a message or teaching they could believe and trust." They were "refugees from uncertainty and doubt." A *guru,* or teacher, who exhibited the power of wisdom and/or charisma was a major emphasis. Cox attributed this need to "the dissolution of conventional moral codes, the erosion of traditional authorities." The hunger was for simplification and assurance. They wanted fewer and less-demanding choices. 4. Some of the most educated said that Eastern religions seemed more *natural*, feeling that the religious traditions of the Western world were outworn. They viewed Western Christian civilization as corrupted by money and power, and were attracted by Eastern peoples, "who have never been ruined by machines and science, who have kept close to their ancestors' simplicity, their inner feelings, and the given rhythms of nature and the cosmos." *One wonders what these individuals would think of Eastern Asia, especially China, 10 years into the twenty-first century. In many ways Asia is moving out of its ancient past.* 5. A small number, mostly women, said they were trying to get away from *male chauvinism,* from what they considered to be the male domination of Western Christianity, in which a "male god creates a man who is supposedly led astray by a woman." A religion in which there is a "male Christ and twelve male apostles" plus male popes, bishops, and priests.[18] 6. Some turned East out of a concern for "health, ecology, and the conservation of the planet's dwindling resources." Many of these followed a vegetarian diet, seeing a significant relationship between what one eats and the condition of the spiritual life.

Cox's reflection on the above motivations for turning East is very perceptive:

"Below the surface of the quest for companionship and felt experience, and in addition to the other pressures that motivated them, it is possible that some of the East Turners of today are simply doubtful about the prospect of 'making history,' and prefer to sit it out. If this is true, and I believe it is, then it puts the challenge of the Turn East on a profound theological level. Why, given the calamitous history of this [the twentieth] century, should we not be skeptical about the prospect of making history? Why not simply let things be? Surely the result could not be much worse than the result of centuries of Western history making?

"Or could it? I believe the current wave of skepticism about the human prospect and about our capacity to influence history is mainly the result of the modern assumption that human beings are fully responsible for everything that happens, that there is no higher intelligence or grander purpose at work in cosmic evolution and human history. The Turn East is the logical outcome of the death of God [in human consciousness]. This represents a curious twist in intellectual history. It was once argued by secular humanists that positing the existence of a deity makes human beings lazy, that they will merely sit back and let God do it. The other side of that coin, however, is that when the tasks become enormous and the challenges nearly overwhelming, it is not the presence of a cosmic ally but the lack of one that drives people to despair.

"This seems to be where many people who were once confident they could make a difference find themselves recently. The impact of biblical religion brought the idea of history and human responsibility for it into existence. But in its original version, this responsibility was to be exercised under the judgment and promise of God. In the modern and secular form of historical faith, God disappeared from the picture. Humankind was left with history to make but without cosmic support or any final source of accountability. . . . No wonder some people simply want to resign . . . without God now nothing seems possible."[19]

Why have I included this examination of *Turning East* in this narrative? Because I believe it is relevant to the current appeal of the emerging church movement. The major danger with the emerging church is that it is very eclectic when it comes to doctrine. What its adherents are after is a "new" expression of the Christian faith, a global community that permits any and all expressions of that faith. It is a radical ecumenical approach that allows for all beliefs and practices, even though they are not supported by the Bible. Its theology comes not from the Bible but from eclectic experience. When that experience conflicts with the Bible, the Bible is adjusted to fit the experience or simply ignored. But if we don't need the Bible for the revelation of Christ, we replace the authentic Christ with a human fabrication. "Faith" then rests on an illusion. Not only is the authentic Christ replaced by an illusion, but consequently a genuine Christian spirituality will not emerge. I am reminded of this perceptive statement by Mike Huckabee: "When an organization can't even focus on its focus, it is hopelessly lost."[20] Speaking of Luther and the other Reformers, Ellen White wrote:

"The experience of these noble Reformers contains a lesson for all succeeding ages. . . . In our time there is a wide departure from their [the Bible's] doctrines and precepts, and there is need of a *return* to the great Protestant principle—the Bible, and the Bible only, as the rule of faith and duty. . . . The same unswerving adherence to the Word of God manifested at that crisis of the Reformation is the *only* hope of reform today."[21]

The question is: Who will stand firm, united on Scripture and the authentic Christ revealed in the Bible? I believe that the Seventh-day Adventist Church has emerged from within Protestantism and is being prepared by God for this very hour. Its witness is global. It has a common cause. Furthermore, it constitutes the true ecumenical movement designed to call God's people to a unity based on Scripture, not on eclectic compromise. I believe that the Seventh-day Adventist Church is the genuine emerging church, having appeared during the nineteenth century just when it was needed most, calling renewed attention to the Bible as the Word of God, protected and guided in that mission by the Spirit of Prophecy, which lifts up Christ and references the Bible on virtually every page. This belief, this conviction, is a vital component of my own spirituality and shapes my worldview. I do not need an "unconscious" worldview. I need a conscious worldview, one that I am acutely aware of because God's truth has touched and shaped my inner being. God, who is there all the time, is at work in His world, among His faithful people, and in our time. Ellen White's words are so prescient, so perspicacious:

"Men in this age of the world act as if they were at liberty to question the words of the Infinite, to review His decisions and statutes, endorsing, revising, reshaping, and annulling, at their pleasure. If they cannot misconstrue, misinterpret, or alter God's plain decision, or bend it to please the multitude and themselves, they break it. We are never safe while we are guided by human opinions; but we are safe when we are guided by a 'Thus saith the Lord.' We cannot trust the salvation of our souls to any lower standard than the decision of an infallible Judge. Those who make God their guide, and His Word their counselor, follow the lamp of life. God's living oracles guide their feet in straight paths. Those who are thus led do not dare judge the Word of God, but ever hold that His Word judges them."[22]

Cox's investigation should pose this question for the Seventh-day Adventist Church: What was/is lacking in the Protestant churches, especially our own, that results in such an exodus? It should also cause us to ask such questions as: Why should anyone have to search elsewhere than the fellowship of the Seventh-day Adventist Church for simple human friendship? What is wrong if the doctrines we preach and teach do not produce a genuine religious experience and spirituality? Has our approach to biblical faith been abstract, cognitive, and cerebral, with no appreciation for, and little experience of, the affective dimension of that faith? Once the truth is found, is it demonstrated by a faith that is active in love to God and to all humankind? How can anyone trust the message we preach if they cannot trust those who preach it to be unwaveringly true to it?

The value of Cox's book lies in its exposure of the weakness of the churches, not of the biblical faith they supposedly espouse. The story he tells should serve both as a warning to "let no one deceive you" (Eph. 5:6) and as a stimulus to reaffirm the Reformation and for a revival of "the faith that was once for all delivered to the saints" (Jude 3). God is perceived as dead by human consciousness, and consequently He has disappeared from history. And a major reason for this perception is that scholars and theologians of mainline Protestantism have eagerly adopted a method of Bible interpretation in which doubt predominates over faith.[23] During my lifetime I have heard it said that as far as American consciousness is concerned, God is dead. If that is so, who is responsible for His demise? It is necessary, apologetically, to be critical of Catholic and Eastern mysticism and of the theology of the emerging church movement. But we also have the responsibility to be brave enough to take a good look at ourselves and ask why some Seventh-day Adventists have been attracted to this perspective. Where, and how, have we failed them so as not to keep them in our fellowship? In our theology and in our ministry, have we been too cerebral, giving little or no attention to nurturing a believing faith in the "inner being" (Eph. 3:16)? Have we failed to produce the kind of believer and spiritual professional who is able to meet this reality demand?

Example

Early in 2006 a lecture series was held at Luther Seminary,[24] in St. Paul,

Minnesota, during which two of the presenters were former presiding bishops of the Evangelical Lutheran Church in America. One said that "sin enters in when humankind speaks about what God said [presumably in the Bible] rather than when it talks about God." His implication? That one can talk authoritatively about God with no reference to what He has said in Scripture. The other speaker, describing how the church should use the Bible and using the illustration of a tricycle, said, "The church uses the Bible as the big front wheel, responsible for steering." The back two wheels are "tradition" and "reason," which are what provide "stability." He said that the church should use the Bible "in light of tradition" and "reason" and also in light of the "witness of the Bible today." He spoke of his skepticism as a young man about the Roman Catholic use of tradition, then added, "Most of us, I believe, have come to recognize that we cannot understand the Bible apart from tradition."[25] His implication? That stability in the faith does not come from the Word of God alone, *sola scriptura*, but from human tradition and reason. Sound familiar? It always has been the position of the Catholic Church that when the Bible conflicts with tradition, it is most reasonable to follow tradition. It is a major shock to read such views uttered by ecclesiastical leaders of a church that bears Luther's name! For me, it is very sad, too. But such sad, shocking evidence confirms that God, who is there all the time, has shown so clearly the road He wanted me to travel. His footprints are unmistakable.

In vivid contrast to this modern view is Luther himself. During the national crisis in Germany called the Peasants' War, Luther was lecturing on the book of Jonah (1526). He turned the thoughts of the people to Scripture, "to feast our hearts, to strengthen, to comfort, and to arm them, lest fatigue and lassitude subdue us in our daily struggle. May God grant me grace that we, by His Word and the comfort of Scripture, may be refreshed and invigorated to fight [for His truth] with ever greater courage." The devil together with "mad bishops and princes . . . purpose to expel God . . . and to exterminate His Word. . . . [The devil] senses that the Day of Judgment is looming and is therefore determined in a final assault to employ his full power against Christ and His Word." Luther talked about God's miraculous preservation of Jonah for his mission, then said: "Jonah is also an object of comfort for all who administer the Word. It teaches them not to despair of the fruit of the Gospel, no matter how badly it appears to be devoid of fruit." Jonah is dispatched by God on a seemingly impossible mission.

"That such a mighty king and such a powerful kingdom should be moved, converted, and frightened by the words of one weak individual . . . and by a message which the king did not even hear—he heard of it

THE ROAD I TRAVEL

only as a report. . . . His [Jonah's] conversion of the city of Nineveh with
one sermon is surely as great a miracle as his rescue from the belly of the
whale, if not an even greater one. For just as the whale had to spew Jonah
forth in obedience to the words of God, so Jonah by the Word of God also
tore the city of Nineveh from the belly and jaws of the devil, that is, from
sin and death."[26]

Unity on Scripture implies unity of interpretation, the loss of which
among Protestants has its roots in the Enlightenment of the seventeenth
and eighteenth centuries. In turn, this loss had a devastating intellectual impact in Germany by the nineteenth century. Human reason was deified,
the reality of sin replaced with the inherent goodness of humanity. The results? Faith in the authority of the Bible gradually eroded as the historical-
critical method of interpretation was increasingly adopted. The point?
Divergent views regarding biblical interpretation cannot be maintained
while at the same time insisting that unity amid doctrinal diversity is possible.

Where Is God?

The story is told of a missionary teacher who asked the members of his
class, "Where is God?" The Catholic students pointed upward to heaven,
and the Hindu students pointed inward to their hearts. Which is the correct response? The first reflects belief in the transcendence of God, that He
is above the world of humankind, hence remote. The second response reflects belief in the immanence of God, that He is present and active in the
world of humanity. The biblical witness is that God is both transcendent
and immanent. Philosophically the reality of God's immanence has been
distorted into pantheism and panentheism. Pantheism is the idea that God
is everything; He is identified with His creation, including human beings.
Panentheism is the idea that everything is God, including human beings.

Because God is seen to be either transcendent or immanent, above humanity or within humanity, both Catholic and Eastern mysticism use rituals to attempt to reach Him, to make contact. In Catholicism it is by
means of the liturgy (sacramental rituals, the saying of the rosary, confession to a priest, absolution, etc.) that such contact is made with the God
who is above.[27] In Buddhism and other forms of Eastern religion it is by
means of the rituals of meditation (including silence, contemplation, breath
prayers, emptying of the mind, etc.) that such contact is made with the
God who is conceived to be within all human flesh.

But what does the Bible teach? The Bible view is that the transcendent
God (Isa. 6:1; Eze. 1) has revealed Himself in His Son, Jesus Christ (2 Cor.
5:19), and that He who has seen the Son has seen the Father (John 12:45).

Furthermore, contact with Father and Son is established by grace through faith alone (Rom. 4:16). God the Father has taken the initiative and revealed Himself in the person of His Son, which initiative is called His "grace." We are justified "by his grace as a gift, through the redemption that is in Christ Jesus, whom God put forward as a propitiation by his blood, to be received by faith" (Rom. 3:24, 25). Justification is the gift of God offered to the sinner by grace *alone* and received by faith *alone*. This establishes a saving relationship.

The Bible also testifies that "Christ in you . . . [is] the hope of glory" (Col. 1:27). God the Father, God the Son, and God the Holy Spirit are one. To receive the Son by faith is to receive the Father and the Holy Spirit. How does the transcendent God come to indwell the believer? When the sinner hears the Word of God, which includes both law and gospel, the moral law of God (the Ten Commandments) convicts of sin, leading to confession, repentance, and surrender to Jesus Christ as Savior and Lord. Having achieved access to the inner being of the repentant sinner, Christ comes to dwell within by the Holy Spirit. This is not achieved by the practice of rituals, but is received by faith.

One does not need to go to Mass or sit cross-legged on a cushion staring at a blank wall, saying "breath" prayers or reciting mantras in order to make contact with the God who is above or who is within. Rather, God Himself takes the initiative and makes contact with us. One does not need to empty one's mind in order to find one's self, as Jungian psychology suggests, nor to find the god within, as New Age and Eastern mysticism suggest. What is needed is to fill the mind with the Word of God. Why? So that God's truth can purge our minds of all the trash forced upon it by the "sin that dwells within me" (Rom. 7:17). The Word of God has the power to purge the mind from the influence of the flesh, culture, and religious traditions that are not harmonious with that Word and that contribute to the shaping of a secular worldview. In this way we are enabled to think with the mind of Christ—think God's thoughts that will shape a biblical worldview. You "search the Scriptures," says Jesus (John 5:39), because they "bear witness about me." But in order to "have life," we must not "refuse to come to" Him (verse 40). Search the Word of God because "faith comes from hearing, and hearing through the word of Christ" (Rom. 10:17).

Instead of turning in any direction, we need to turn back. Back to the sources of Adventist spirituality. Back to the Bible and the Spirit of Prophecy. Preachers, evangelists, teachers, and theologians must faithfully transmit the biblical message, rather than transform it by changing it to suit cultural demands in an attempt to make the church user-friendly. There is no spiritual power in that. Again, power to transform people is not in the preacher or theologian, but in the Word of God alone!

The Danger of Extremes

The Seventh-day Adventist Church today is faced with twin theological, hence spiritual, dangers. The first is extreme Pharisaism—salvation on the basis of what one does. The second is extreme evangelicalism—salvation in spite of what one does. It is the destiny of the church to face danger in this world as it seeks to be faithful to its message and its mission. This is especially true of the church that believes it has the last message for a world poised on the brink of disaster, that believes lines are being drawn and forces being gathered for the final conflict over the eternal salvation of humanity. The enemy of biblical Christianity does not rest content with tempting persons regarding morality and ethics. He drives to the very heart of things, to the very doctrinal/spiritual center of the faith. He does not deny that humans are religious beings. Indeed, he depends on it, because he himself is a religious being, believing religiously in his role as perverter of the faith, destroyer of humankind, disrupter of history, the great liar and deceiver.

Neither does he deny God or attempt to prove He is nonexistent. Indeed, he believes in God. After all, God is the one with whom he is in mortal combat. He is not at war with a figment of imagination, with a nongod. He does not deny humanity's need to believe. He simply wants to be the center of that belief. His wickedness is most subtle and deadly in his distortion of biblical truth, mixing error with truth so that people are deceived concerning the most vital issue of all—the way of salvation. His method is to convince people to believe lies or at least half-truths, for a half-truth is as dangerous as an outright falsehood. A half-truth is not a half-lie; it is a lie. People will thus end up, unwittingly, outside the kingdom of God and find themselves trapped forever as citizens of Satan's domain. It is no wonder that those who finally discover the great deception only when it is too late weep and gnash their teeth in utter frustration, helplessness, and hopelessness. There are only three alternatives when it comes to the way of salvation. One of them is truth; the other two are not.

The first alternative is the belief that one is justified, saved, by what he or she does. Paul talks about this alternative in terms of "works of the law" (Gal. 2:16; 3:2, 5). He makes a distinction between law and works of the law. But nowhere does he say there is something wrong with God's law. Instead he calls it "holy and righteous and good" (Rom. 7:12). The danger is not the law itself, which is the "tutor" that leads the sinner to Christ (Gal. 3:24, NKJV), but the belief that one can be justified by doing the works of the law. In other words, the danger is in the belief that the unregenerate sinner can be justified by his own attempts at righteous obedience. The result, however, is extreme Pharisaism and a distorted conception of perfection as something attainable by effort, rather than by imputation to those who have faith in Christ. This view constitutes a legalistic understanding of salvation in which faith is in what one can accomplish by emulating Christ. It produces legalistic church members.

The second alternative is that one is justified, saved, in spite of what one does. This leads to the second danger we face today, extreme evangelicalism. On the basis of such Pauline statements as "It is for freedom that Christ has set us free" (Gal. 5:1, NIV), some take the position that in Christ they are now free to make decisions and choices that contradict the moral, ethical, and social aspects of biblical truth and doctrine. This view leads to licentiousness, which is a misuse of Christian freedom and produces licentious church members. When Paul indicates that the believer has been set free in Christ and must not again become a slave, he is being critical, not of God's law, but of sin. Set free from sin's power and its consequences, the believer does not succumb again. In Galatians 5:4 Paul says that anyone who seeks justification by doing the works of the law has been "cut . . . from Christ" and has fallen from grace. By the same token, one who walks "by the Spirit" will not "gratify the desires of the flesh" (verse 16, NIV). Is it conceivable that the Holy Spirit, partner with the Son at Sinai, at Calvary, and in the heavenly sanctuary, would lead the believer in ways contradictory to the commands of God? Even to say it is to reveal its insensibility and its inconsistency with God's own character. It is utterly amazing how our spiritual enemy clouds our vision so that we fail to see that the problem addressed in both Romans and Galatians is not with God's law but with God's people. If the problem is with the law, which commands and establishes limits, then the law must be changed or eliminated or at least rendered impotent by a "gospel" that frees people to live in sin. But there is no evidence of such views of salvation in the Scriptures. The real problem is with persons who do not—indeed, cannot—measure up to God's moral law, and thus need redemption, restoration, transformation, and victory by means of imputed justification and imparted righteousness. It is sinners who need to change, and there is ample evidence for this view of salvation in the Bible. The people to whom Paul addressed his letters had a problem with accepting salvation on God's terms rather than on their own. That's our problem too. Which brings us to the third alternative, the only one that has biblical validity and experiential authenticity.

The third alternative is that one is justified, saved, by what was done for the sinner on Calvary and by what is being done in the heavenly sanc-

tuary and by what is being done in the believer through the ministry of the
Holy Spirit and the indwelling Christ. This view is founded entirely upon
grace. Salvation is a gift of God, unmerited by the sinner and received by
faith. The reality of salvation reveals itself in the way the redeemed relate
to Christ and to other people. A dependent relationship with Jesus issues
in a loving relationship with others. To bear one another's burdens, says
Paul (see Gal. 6:2), is to fulfill the law of Christ, which means to put it into
practice, practicing righteousness (see 1 John 3:4-10). The gospel is not
without law nor without warning. "For the one who sows to his own flesh
will from the flesh reap corruption, but the one who sows to the Spirit will
from the Spirit reap eternal life" (Gal. 6:8).

The theological/spiritual imbalance represented by the first two alternatives can be seen with respect to the doctrine of the nature of Christ. In
the first instance the primary theological focus is on the humanity of Christ
to the point that He becomes more human than divine. He is seen primarily as the believer's example, rather than as his or her substitute. The consequence of this view is an overemphasis on what the believer does for his
or her own salvation and spiritual growth. Coupled with this view is the
idea that human beings are intrinsically good and that the gospel is limited
to providing him or her with a new perception about self. Obedience is
primary, and faith consists of belief that one can do what Christ did.

In the second instance the primary theological focus is on the divinity
of Christ to the point that He becomes more divine than human. He is
seen primarily as the believer's substitute, rather than his or her example.
The consequence of this view is the idea that the believer has no responsibility for his or her salvation and spiritual growth. Sanctification and
Christlikeness are seen as impossibilities. Coupled with this is the idea that
human beings are intrinsically evil and that the gospel is limited simply to
declaring them righteous, as though saying it's so makes it so. In this view
the gospel does not set the believer free from sin; it merely forgives sin.
Faith in what Christ has done is primary, and because all a person can do
is believe, obedience, therefore, is not essential.

We can experience a theology and a spirituality that is free of distor-
tions if we will maintain the kind of balance found in the counsel of Ellen
White regarding the nature of Christ:

"Christ in the weakness of humanity was to meet the temptations of
one possessing the powers of the higher nature that God had bestowed on
the angelic family. But Christ's humanity was united with divinity, and in
this strength [of the *union* between His humanity and divinity] He would
bear all the temptations that Satan could bring against Him, and yet keep
His soul untainted by sin."[28]

"In Christ, divinity and humanity were combined. Divinity was not degraded to humanity; divinity held its place, but humanity, by being united to divinity, withstood the fiercest test of temptations in the wilderness."[29]

In the face of the above two theological extremes, we must be defenders of biblical faith and of the balanced Adventist understanding of that faith, or the resultant spirituality will not be biblical or genuinely Adventist. The silent majority who trust fully in Jesus for salvation and who by His grace and the power of the Holy Spirit are living out that trust in the obedience of faith need to be heard from, so that our church can maintain the balance that both Scripture and the Spirit of Prophecy portray.

The "Pop" Gospel

Again and again in the writings of the apostle Paul we read the phrase "the gospel." Without a doubt it was the gospel that informed his own faith and drove his mission and ministry. So it should be for any person called by the Lord to Christian service, whether that service be the ordained ministry or the ministry into which every believer is baptized. Ever since I was first ordained, back in 1960,[30] and faced with the challenge to preach week after week, I have been thinking about the nature of "the gospel." All through the years I have wanted to know what the Bible teaches about "the gospel" so that I can preach it accurately and clearly, with conviction and passion.

The question of exactly what is "the gospel" was very much on my mind when I went to the Seventh-day Adventist Theological Seminary as a student in 1970. I thought I knew what it was by then. However, I was forced by circumstances to discover that what I had learned about the gospel in seven years of ministerial training and 10 years in ministry was not all there was to know. I didn't have all the answers to my question. Those of us who preach and teach "the gospel" want what we preach and teach to be biblical. We want it to be based on the Bible, informed by the Bible, true to the Bible, and growing out of our understanding of the Bible. It must grow out of the Bible itself and not out of some theologian's ideas or out of some popular system of theology. It may be interesting and informative to read what theologians have to say, but what they say should be of only incidental interest.

"What does the Bible say?" should be the question uppermost in the mind of the preacher and teacher, because when it comes to the matter of human salvation, only what God's Word says really matters. Does the gospel preached today hold out false hope to sinners? Does it tell them that they can have eternal life in spite of the fact that they so often are living in rebellion against God and what His Word teaches? Does the contemporary "pop" gospel encourage people to "accept" Jesus as Savior apart from any consideration of the obligation to obey Him as Lord of their lives? Does the "pop" gospel promise people deliverance from judgment, while at the same time failing to promise them victory over sin? Does the "pop" gospel, in fact, offer false security to those who succumb to the sins of the flesh and spurn the way of righteousness? Does the "pop" gospel separate faith from faithfulness? Does it proclaim that there is no such thing as obedience to the truth, a denial of 1 Peter 1:22, 23, which says that the believer is "purified . . . by . . . obedience to the truth" and that this is what it means to be "born again"? Does the "pop" gospel make no call for transformation, no moral, ethical demands on those who claim redemption? Has the "pop" gospel brought into being a whole generation of so-called believers whose behavior in no way distinguishes them from the unregenerate?

Recent statistics indicate there are more than 2 billion Christians in the world and that fully one third of Americans claim to be "born again." If that is so, where is the visible impact of these numbers in today's world? We ought to be able to see the evidence, but the sad fact is that in our own society shocking forms of open immorality are everyday fare. Outrageously immoral, crude, and lewd talk-show hosts are applauded and approved by vast numbers. Why not, if the pulpits of America offer eternal life apart from the necessity of obedience to divine authority? That kind of "pop" gospel perpetuates the wretchedness of the unconverted and is not without enthusiastic adherents who insist that behavior has no relationship to spirituality, that obedience is optional. These people howl the loudest when the biblical gospel is preached, yelling "legalism" when any suggestion is made that faith without obedience is no redeeming faith at all.

This is why Francis Schaeffer wrote in his last book, *The Great Evangelical Disaster,* that "much of evangelicalism has been accommodating to the destructive and ugly world spirit of our day." He wrote the book to help young Christians "stand courageously against this accommodation," and because "the last few generations have trampled upon the truth of the Bible and all that those truths have brought forth."[31] The apostle James asked, "What good is it, my brothers, if someone says he has faith but does not have works? Can that [kind of] faith save him?" (James 2:14). Nobody wants to be a legalist, so we not only cringe when the accusation is hurled at us—we are intimidated into silence or to the dumbing down of the biblical message. Let me ask you, Which is more authentic—a person's verbal testimony of faith in Christ or a daily demonstration of Christlikeness? To see just how serious this is from the perspective of the Word of God, let's read Paul's warning to anyone who tampers with the message of "the gospel." Here is his sharp warning to any preacher or teacher who corrupts it in any way:

"I am astonished that you are so quickly deserting him who called you in the grace of Christ and are turning to a different gospel—not that there is another one, but there are some who trouble you and want to distort the gospel of Christ. But even if we or an angel from heaven should preach to you a gospel contrary to the one we preached to you, let him be accursed" (Gal. 1:6–8).

Why such strong words from the great apostle? Because the biblical doctrine of salvation is at the heart of everything we preach and teach. No preacher or teacher can show anyone the way to eternal life, with confidence and assurance, with conviction and passion, without having "the gospel" right. Paul says that anyone who distorts "the gospel of Christ" has deserted the very One "who called you in the grace of Christ." So this is not simply an intellectual matter; it is a relational matter. There is a most intimate relationship between "the gospel" and the One "who called you." We cannot distort "the gospel" and yet claim a relationship with the Savior. Why? Because "the gospel" is "the gospel of Christ." We don't know Christ apart from "the gospel" message about Him. The implication is that if we preach or teach a message that is in any way distorted or "contrary to the one" that has been revealed in its fullness in Scripture, then the Christ it proclaims is a false Christ. A distorted message equals a distorted Christ. It is "contrary." A contradiction. Incompatible. In opposition. Completely different. Leading to an erroneous conclusion.

Any other message, says Paul, is "man's gospel" (Gal. 1:11). In contrast, "the gospel" (verse 11) that Paul preached he "received . . . through a revelation of Jesus Christ" Himself (verse 12), which is precisely why that gospel, and only that gospel, is trustworthy. Only that gospel can be relied upon to show us the right way, get us on the right way, and keep us on the right way. For that reason we need an unambiguous understanding of what Revelation 14:6 calls "an eternal gospel." The biblical fact is that "the gospel" is a call to discipleship—not just a call to believe, but a call to live the life of faith. It's not just an invitation to receive Christ, to make a decision. Jesus sets people free from sin's bondage. Free to follow Him. Free to become like Him. Free to serve Him. Yes, "the gospel" offers repentant sinners forgiveness of sin and eternal life, but at the same time it is a rebuke to those who are merely outwardly religious and whose lives do not give evidence of righteousness. Dietrich Bonhoeffer, writing to his Lutheran Church that had been preaching justification through faith since the Reformation, understood this and said:

"Cheap grace means the justification of sin without the justification of the sinner. . . . Cheap grace is the preaching of forgiveness without requiring repentance, baptism without Church discipline, communion without confession, absolution without contrition. Cheap grace is grace without discipleship, grace without the cross, grace without Jesus Christ, living and incarnate. . . . It is a fatal misunderstanding of Luther's action to suppose that his rediscovery of the gospel of pure grace offered a general dispensation from obedience to the command of Christ, or that it was the great discovery of the Reformation that God's forgiving grace automatically conferred upon the world both righteousness and holiness. . . . It was not the justification of sin but the justification of the sinner that drove Luther from the monastery back into the world. . . . In the depth of his misery, Luther had grasped by faith the free and unconditional forgiveness of all his sins. That experience taught him that this grace had cost him his very life, and must continue to cost him the same price day by day. So far from dispensing him from discipleship, this grace only made him a more earnest disciple. When he spoke of grace, Luther always implied as a corollary that it cost him his own life, the life which was now for the first time subjected to the absolute obedience of Christ. Only so could he speak of grace. Luther had said that grace alone can save; his followers took up his doctrine and repeated it word for word. But they left out its invariable corollary, the obligation of discipleship. . . . [Luther] always spoke as one who had been led by grace to the strictest following of Christ."[32]

Bonhoeffer was right, as was my Lutheran professor, who was fond of saying to his eager students, "Good works do not save you, but their absence will damn you." Some in contemporary evangelicalism, even a few in our own ranks who are critical of the Seventh-day Adventist Church, would have it join in preaching cheap grace and easy discipleship, holding that any consideration of sanctification and holiness is legalism. To them I say, "Let's put aside the false choice between grace and obedience, because they are not antithetical principles and realities of faith. The one (grace) makes the other (obedience) possible. Without grace, obedience is not possible. Without obedience, grace has failed to produce its fruit of righteousness. So let us stop using language that fractures the fabric of the church, weakens its mission, and confuses members by distorting the biblical message of salvation. When we use the phrase 'law and gospel,' let's mean law *and* gospel, not law *versus* gospel or gospel *versus* law. To throw out *sola scriptura* is to throw out belief in the power of grace to transform the sinner into a faithful and obedient child of God." In the Seventh-day Adventist Church I found the understanding of the gospel that Lutheranism, as well as other evangelical denominations, were abandoning in favor of ecumenism, the resolution of social issues, and the political establishment of the kingdom of God on earth. I found in the Adventist Church the saving faith of Christ and the commandments of God set forth as the two foci in the doctrine of justification/righteousness through faith and identified as the great truths of biblical Christianity and of the Protestant Reformation. There I found these truths rescued and placed within a larger framework of other Bible truths, such as the Sabbath, the sanctuary ministry of Christ, His return, and the message of judgment in Daniel 8 and Revelation 14, entrusted by God to this worldwide revival/reformation movement. I saw there these truths preached to the whole world with amazing results and without apology.

The gospel puts sinners on notice that Jesus wants them to turn not just from sin but from sinning, and take hold by faith of Christ's own righteousness. In every way the gospel is good news, but it is not pie in the sky when we die. It is not easy-believism. Jesus taught that the cost of following Him was high, the way narrow, and that few find it. He said: "Enter by the narrow gate. For the gate is wide and the way easy that leads to destruction, and those who enter by it are many. For the gate is narrow and the way is hard that leads to life, and those who find it are few" (Matt. 7:13, 14). He also said: "Not everyone who says to me, Lord, Lord, will enter the kingdom of heaven, but the one who does the will of my Father who is in heaven" (verse 21). If you listen to the "pop" gospel, saving faith is growing broader and more and more shallow. This "different gospel" promises salvation to anyone who simply believes facts about Jesus and claims eternal life, There is no need for inner transformation of character or a change in one's lifestyle, no surrender to the lordship of Christ.

The result? This distorted gospel represents justification without sanctification. If it continues to be proclaimed, it will have catastrophic consequences for the mission and the credibility of the church. It will produce a shallow and ineffective faith, a faith that cannot and will not stand when difficult times come. Not even prophesying or casting out demons in His name, said Jesus, are evidence of salvation apart from a life of obedience to the gospel (see Matt. 7:21-23). True biblical salvation is an ongoing process, the sanctifying work of the Holy Spirit by which we are "conformed to the image of His Son" (Rom. 8:29). How does one know that he or she is saved, a born-again child of God? How is one assured of salvation? By holding on to some experience, such as making a public decision for Jesus? Or is it by being aware of the Holy Spirit's transforming work in the inner being? The Bible says: "Examine yourselves, to see whether you are in the faith. Test yourselves" (2 Cor. 13:5). "Therefore, brothers, be all the more diligent to make your calling and election sure, for if you practice these qualities [faith, virtue, knowledge, self-control, steadfastness, godliness, brotherly affection, and love] you will never fall" (2 Peter 1:10). According to the Bible, the evidence of God's work in the believer's life is clear. "By this we know that we have come to know him [God], if we keep his commandments. Whoever says 'I know him' but does not keep his commandments is a liar and the truth is not in him" (1 John 2:3, 4). "By this it is evident who are the children of God, and who are the children of the devil: whoever does not practice righteousness is not of God" (1 John 3:10). Faith that does not result in righteous living is a dead faith; it is no faith at all. That's clear and unmistakable. Faith is a matter of the head, the heart, and the life. It is not a matter of rituals. In what might be considered an unlikely place, I found the following:

"There is a spiritual yearning in the human heart. It is part of our basic wiring. All of us want to be connected to God and to the supernatural world that we believe is out there. Traditional religions make demands upon us and insist that there are requirements to being a child of God; mainly, living as He would have us live. For many people today, these requirements are a bridge too far. They want the experience of faith, but are unwilling to pay the admission price. So they try to satisfy their supernatural appetite void with spiritual junk food. These faith substitutes can take a variety of forms and have become an American cottage industry.

"Some place rocks on their chakras, strike a few yoga positions, and try to channel the dead to feel spiritual. Others consult their horoscopes, in hopes that the stars will show them the way. There are runes, tarot cards, palm readers, and all manner of New Age quick fixes to get your faux spiritual groove on. Whatever the new trend—Buddhist chanting while barbecuing, yoga with your dog, etc.—it'll find a platform on *Good Morning America, Oprah,* or *Ellen.*"[33]

Laura Ingraham is a radio talk-show host, not a theologian, and a practicing Catholic to boot. You may not agree with many of her political or religious views, but you will have to admit that she's basically right in this analysis. Also, you would have to agree, as I do, that her critique of contemporary culture is devastatingly accurate.

During 60 years as a Christian I have observed significant changes within the Protestant churches. Most of the mainline Protestant churches in the United States have failed Christ and America by a gradual, almost imperceptible to their constituents, abandonment of the major Reformation principle of *sola scriptura*. This has been followed by an inevitable deterioration of attention to spiritual issues and an increased focus on social issues. The result has been drastic declines in membership, in seminary enrollments, and a consequent reduction in the availability of trained ministers. When the biblical message is preached (sin, repentance, conversion, surrender to Christ and His lordship, empowerment by the Holy Spirit and the indwelling Christ for obedience to God's command- ments, righteousness, walking in newness of life, justification and sanctifi- cation, and discipleship), inward transformation is the divinely intended result. People leave churches, or are not attracted to churches, when the message preached does not result in such transformation, when nothing happens. This situation is decried by some evangelicals, such as Donald G. Bloesch, who expresses his concern for "deepening the inner life," saying that "the spirituality current in fashion is being tied to movements of so- cial liberation."[34]

Bloesch pushes my theological/spiritual buttons when he says: "The principal conflict today . . . is between faith and unbelief, light and dark- ness, salvation and sin. When we recover this essential truth of the gospel, we shall then be able to march forth into the culture and wrestle with and overcome the principalities and powers. The church needs to rediscover its spiritual mission, which is to uphold the biblical message of salvation before the world." *I think he would agree with me that what is needed is a re- vival of the Reformation.* He continues: "The contemporary church is in a state of theological ferment . . . whereas the neo-orthodox theologians placed the accent upon Christ for us, the younger generation of students is asking whether Scripture does not give equal weight to Christ with us and Christ in us."[35] He proposes a theology of devotion in which sanctification follows justification, "since God makes righteous those whom he declares righteous," in which a major element is "the call to a victorious life."[36] He views the kingdom of God "not as the reclaimed world, certainly not as the secular city, nor as the institutional church, but as the community of the redeemed, the remnant of the faithful." Devotion to Jesus Christ, he says, is that which "separates us from the world in its sin as well as identi- fies us with the world in its suffering."[37] Multitudes are being deceived by a corrupted gospel, hearing that Christ will accept them just as they are and let them stay that way.

Here are the red flags as I see them. We cannot afford to abandon our members or our youth in academies and colleges, leaving them to the in- fluence of mysticism and Eastern or Mideastern religions. If we want spir- itual revival, it is not going to come about by pandering to our culture or by abandoning *sola scriptura*. Or by a focus on the cerebral without a har- monious focus also on the "inner being." Spiritual revival will come only when we reaffirm the sources that shape Adventist spirituality—the Bible and the Spirit of Prophecy. It will come only when we stop deceiving our- selves and open our eyes. When we doubt our doubts and believe our beliefs. When we preach, teach, and live the message that brought the Seventh-day Adventist Church into being in the first place.

Meditation

What is your "gut feeling" about the warnings regarding your spirituality that are discussed in this chapter? Why is it impossible to have a genuine Christian and Adventist experience apart from biblical truth? What do you think Paul means when he exhorts us to "examine yourselves, to see whether you are in the faith" (2 Cor. 13:5)?

---

[1] James Sundquist, *Who's Driving the Purpose Driven Church?* (Italics supplied.) Sundquist's major criticisms of Warren's theology are that Warren belittles sound doctrine; that he endorses "breath" prayers; that he promotes false teachers, such as Brother Lawrence (a Carmelite monk), Richard Foster (who also endorses "breath" prayer), Henri Nouwen (a Catholic priest who does not believe Jesus is the only way to God), and the psychologist Carl Jung (considered to be one of the "fathers" of Neo-Gnosticism and the New Age movement). Sundquist states, "Jung was a master at creating obscure, scientific-sounding concepts, usually adapted from occultic literature" (p. 250), and maintains that Jung's views undergird the theology of pastoral care in most mainstream denominations today. An example of Jung's pantheistic philosophy is "I have constantly to repeat that neither moral law nor the concept of God nor any religion has ever fallen down from outside, so to speak, from heaven, upon mankind, but *man has all this within him* from the beginning and therefore he creates it out of himself" (in James L. Hayward, Sr., *The Time of the End* [Harrisburg, Pa.: American Christian Ministries, 2009], p. 260).

[2] Quoted in Francis Schaeffer, *The God Who Is There* (Downers Grove, Ill.: InterVarsity Press, 1968), p. 18.

[3] The material in this section is adapted from my article in the *Journal of the Adventist Theological Society* 5, no. 2 (Autumn 1994): 6-18.

[4] *1987 Annual Council: General Actions*, p. 15.

[5] New York: Simon and Schuster, 1977.

[6] Thank God for the contemporary Adventist youth movement Generation of Youth for Christ (GYC), which has all the earmarks of genuine spiritual revival—focus on the study of the Bible, prayer, singing of traditional hymns, and sharing the faith in mission.

[7] Not much is heard about Hare Krishna today. Such interest has been largely replaced by the New Age and the emerging church, both of which embody forms of Catholic and Eastern mysticism.

[8] *Turning East*, p. 16.

[9] *Ibid.*, p. 20.

[10] *Ibid.*, p. 31.

[11] Sitting silently for long periods of time inhaling and exhaling, following his breath "into the world." Cox points out that in the Eastern Orthodox Church a mystical practice called hesychasm, which is an attempt to find "divine quietness," has been practiced for a long time.

[12] *Ibid.*, p. 65.

[13] *Ibid.*, p. 69.

[14] *Ibid.*, p. 73.

[15] *Ibid.*, p. 70.

[16] *Ibid.*, pp. 70, 71. Cox associates this with his perception of God's activity on the first Sabbath as breathing, suggesting that the passage in Genesis 2:2, 3 may mean that in depicting "God himself as one who ceases work and does nothing but breathe could suggest a

deeper and older stratum of spiritual consciousness which lies behind the passage itself" (p. 67). Thus he not only attempts to justify biblically the form of Buddhist meditation he adopted, but implies that it represents a more ancient spirituality than that of Genesis.

[17] *Ibid.*, p. 94. The relationship between the decline in church school attendance and the turn East should be alarming to Seventh-day Adventists, who operate the most extensive educational system among Protestants worldwide.

[18] This appears to be the most ridiculous rationale for turning East, because Eastern as well as Middle Eastern religious traditions have their own, often very radical and even abusive, forms of female suppression. One can understand this point of view when held by secularists, but it is very difficult to understand it when held by Protestants whose faith tradition confessedly rests on *sola scriptura*.

[19] *Ibid.*, pp. 102, 103.

[20] *Do the Right Thing*, p. 54.

[21] E. G. White, *The Great Controversy*, pp. 204, 205. (Italics supplied.)

[22] *Review and Herald*, Feb. 21, 1899.

[23] Called the historical-critical method, which posits that the Bible is a human product that came into being by an evolutionary process, and consequently the history it records cannot be assumed to be factual or reliable. "The presuppositions of the historical-critical method are based on a rationalism in which the Bible is treated like any other product of the human mind. The method requires practical atheism in order to function. This leads to the separation of the message of Scripture from the history in which it is embedded and through which it was transmitted. The method is not neutral. It is not unbiased. It leaves the student of the Bible with a choice, not between what God says and what people believe, but between what one theologian believes and another theologian believes. The method requires suspicion (called 'methodological doubt'); doubt begins to predominate over faith, and the biblical tradition itself is questioned from an increasingly secular base. For Adventists this would mean eventual, perhaps even inevitable, questioning of the remnant tradition and all that it implies about the Sabbath and the final events of history" (in C. Raymond Holmes, *The Tip of an Iceberg* [Berrien Springs, Mich.: Adventists Affirm and Pointer Publications, 1994], pp. 35, 36).

[24] A theological seminary of the Evangelical Lutheran Church in America (ELCA). Reported in the March/April 2006 issue of *Network News,* published by the Word Alone Network, which is a reform movement within the ELCA.

[25] It is this kind of thinking, on the part of the leaders of the Evangelical Lutheran Church in America, that made it possible for that church to approve the ordination of noncelibate gay clergy in August 2009. It was reported that after the vote the presiding bishop emotionally appealed for unity. But it is no use appealing for unity when the basis for such unity has been trashed. This kind of thinking also makes possible the creation and use of "Lutheran Prayer Beads," as reported in the *LSTC Epistle* (Fall 2009, pp. 14, 15), published by the Lutheran School of Theology at Chicago.

[26] *Luther's Works*, vol. 19, pp. 35-37.

[27] According to the *Catechism of the Catholic Church* (1994), it is in the liturgy (rituals, ceremonies) that the Holy Spirit "prepares the Church to encounter her Lord" (p. 284). "Every liturgical action . . . is an encounter between Christ and the Church" (p. 285). "Through the liturgy the inner man is rooted and grounded in 'the great love with which [the Father] loved us' in His beloved Son" (p. 279). Note, this rooting is not through faith but through liturgy. Also: "The liturgy . . . is the font from which all her [the Church's] power flows" (p. 279).

[28] *The Seventh-day Adventist Bible Commentary*, Ellen G. White Comments, vol. 7, p. 927.

[29] *Ibid.*, vol. 5, p. 1082.

[30] My Lutheran ordination took place in Fairport Harbor, Ohio, and my Adventist ordination at Andrews University, Berrien Springs, Michigan, a little more than 10 years later. I have tried unsuccessfully to convince conference administration that double ordination

ought to qualify for double salary and double vacations. Some have responded by saying that double ordination actually means double work!

[31] (Westchester, Ill.: Crossway Books, 1984), pp. 15, 29.

[32] *The Cost of Discipleship*, pp. 37–43.

[33] Laura Ingraham, *Power to the People* (Washington, D.C.: Regnery Publishing, Inc., 2007), pp. 298, 299.

[34] *The Crisis of Piety* (Colorado Springs, Colo.: Helmers and Howard, 1988), p. ix. At the time of writing, Bloesch was a professor of systematic theology at DuBuque Theological Seminary.

[35] *Ibid.*, p. 7.

[36] *Ibid.*, pp. 16, 17.

[37] *Ibid.*, pp. 17, 19.

Chapter 14

THE WAY TO GO

There are two major east-west highways in Michigan's Upper Peninsula, US 2 and M 28. I have traveled them often. They both pass through some very beautiful forested country. Sometimes those two highways go up or down hills. Sometimes they curve or go straight. In the summer there are often delays for road repairs, in which one has to wait for one-way traffic to pass. It is said facetiously that there are only two seasons in the UP—winter and road repair. One of the most impressive sights traveling east along US 2 is to make a curve and then burst upon the scene of pristine beaches along the northern shore of Lake Michigan. It is my favorite part of the trip from our town of Wakefield toward "Big Mac"— the Mackinac Bridge. Once in a while, but not very often, the road goes absolutely straight, like the section of M 28 between Shingleton and Seney. Yoopers, as residents of the UP are known, call it the Seney Stretch. That stretch of road is as straight as an arrow for 25 miles. You can almost drive it with your hands off the wheel.

Some spots along those roads are not so nice, with dead trees, burned-over sections, and occasionally some trash and roadkill scattered along the way. Then there are the ubiquitous deer, for which one must always be on the alert. They have the nasty habit of dashing out of the forest and running right into your vehicle. Frequently one confronts an intersection, where roads converge, and a decision is required as to which direction to take. Those who have a reliable map and diligently follow it without deviation won't get lost. But the journey is not over until the destination is reached. "I am sure of this," said Paul to the Philippians, "that he who began a good work *in you* will bring it to completion at the day of Jesus Christ" (Phil. 1:6). The spiritual road I travel is like those familiar UP roads. The important thing about the road one travels is not whether it is curvy or straight, bumpy or smooth, but that it takes you to the place you intend to go. You have to know where you are going. You have to know the way. And for that you need clear and unmistakable directions that you can depend on.

"We all need a guide through the many strait places in life as much as the sailor needs a pilot over the sandy bar or up the rocky river, and where is this guide to be found? We point you, dear brethren, to the Bible. Inspired of God, written by holy men, it points out with great clearness and precision the duties of both old and young. It elevates the mind, softens the heart, and imparts gladness and holy joy to the spirit. The Bible presents a perfect standard of character; it is an infallible guide under all circumstances, even to the end of the journey of life."[1]

The Destiny of God's People

The seminary in Chicago, where I received my Master of Divinity degree, publishes a quarterly alumni news magazine called *The Epistle*. A recent issue contained an article quoting the views of some theologians, one of whom was a classmate of mine at that seminary back in 1958-1960. He later became a professor in the Lutheran School of Theology in Chicago. He wrote, "We need a new image of what it means to be human." As I read that, my response was "No, we don't." We already have God's revealed image of what it means to be human made clear for us in the Bible. The question is: Do we believe it or not? My classmate also wrote, "We need to develop new rules for our social compact." Again, my response was "No, we don't." We already have God's rules for human social relationships in His written Word. They are called the Ten Commandments, the Sermon on the Mount, the inspired counsel of the Bible. Again, the question is: Do we believe them or not? When humankind has tried to develop their own "new rules," they have failed miserably.

My classmate further wrote, "The task today . . . is to start with the world as we best understand it and find paths leading toward God." Really? We should start with humanity's "best" understanding of the world to find paths to God? Once more, my response was negative. That path is a certain road to uncertainty, even deception. We already have been shown the path to God, in His Word—the only path that can be trusted to get us there. The word for it is *revelation*. It is God revealing Himself to us. It is His telling the story of how He has reached out to us, comes to us. The path to Him is His path to us! Once more, the question is: Do we believe it? Historically, Lutherans have insisted on that revealed path, at least until recently. I can say, on the basis of published official documents, that Seventh-day Adventists do insist on it,[2] for which I, for one, am profoundly grateful, as faith in the inspiration and authenticity of the written Word of God is the revelational foundation on which my own spirituality is based. Furthermore, we don't find God; He finds us. If He didn't, He would never be found. We find Him because He finds us.

The Bible is not the story of humankind seeking God, but of God revealing Himself to humankind. God takes the initiative. He inspired the Bible writers. He initiated the Incarnation. Joseph would never have known what was going on with Mary if God had not sent the angel Gabriel to explain it. Gabriel told Joseph the baby's name, Immanuel, "which means God with us" (Matt. 1:23). Gabriel told Mary, "The child to be born will be called holy—the Son of God" (Luke 1:35). Of course, she was mystified as to how that could possibly be. So the angel said, "For nothing will be impossible with God" (Luke 1:37). *For God,* not for human beings! This fits with divinity, with sovereign authority and power. These are not human ideas in humanity's imagined, and therefore uncertain and tragic, quest to find pathways to God. You and I can have hope because God acts, not because we have faith or perform certain rituals. The apostle Paul summarizes all of this in a marvelously concise and cohesive four verses, tucked away in one of the shortest books in the New Testament:

"For the grace of God has appeared, bringing salvation for all people, training us to renounce ungodliness and worldly passions, and to live self-controlled, upright, and godly lives in the present age, waiting for our blessed hope, the appearing of the glory of our great God and Savior Jesus Christ, who gave himself for us to redeem us from all lawlessness and to purify for himself a people for his own possession who are zealous for good works" (Titus 2:11-14).

"The grace of God has appeared." Paul doesn't say that the grace of God *first* appeared. It was there all along, all through Old Testament times. Just because the Old Testament was written in Hebrew does not mean it is exclusively for the Hebrews (Jews), any more than the New Testament is exclusively for the Greeks because it was written primarily in Greek. All through the Old Testament we are told that the people "found grace" in God. Noah and Joseph, for example, "found grace in the eyes of the Lord" (Gen. 6:8; 39:4). Renouncing ungodliness and living godly lives are our responses to the God who has appeared in Jesus to bring us salvation. The focal point of godly living is the blessed hope of another gracious appearing in which Jesus comes again. Meanwhile, His purified people are eager to do the good works He commands, empowers, authorizes, and commissions them to do.

The New Testament tells us that the grace of God was made manifest in Jesus Christ. Luke 2:40 says, "The child grew and became strong, filled with wisdom. And the grace of God was upon him." Jesus was born a baby in Bethlehem, but He didn't stay a baby. He grew up and became a man who fulfilled His destiny on Calvary and beyond. The Bible doesn't say very much about Jesus as a baby or about His childhood. The primary focus is on Jesus the man, what He did for us, is doing for us, and will accomplish in us. He was what the Father made Him to be. He said what the Father gave Him to say. He did what the Father wanted Him to do. When His work on earth was finished, the Father raised Him from the dead, and He went to glory, where now, as high priest, He continues His work for our salvation.

Pause with me for a moment while I tell the story of what happened on the road I travel when the truth of Jesus' ministry as high priest in the heavenly sanctuary penetrated my consciousness and by so doing began to contribute to the shaping of my spirituality. It happened one day in the spring of 1971, when I was sitting in the seminary library at Andrews University reading in the New Testament book of Hebrews concerning Jesus as high priest. In all my years of Bible study as a seminary student and as a preacher, I had never given that part of His ministry any attention at all. Though it was there in the Bible, it was all new to me. It certainly was not referenced during my seminary training in Chicago. I remember that I stopped reading and thought, *I have believed all along that since His ascension Jesus has been interceding with the Father for His redeemed people, but what does it really mean to intercede?* Then I prayed, *Lord, if You want me to teach and preach this, You will have to make it experiential—not just a doctrine, but part of my faith experience—for me, just as You did with Calvary's cross.* He answered my prayer right then and there. What I had never seen before suddenly became both doctrinally clear and experientially real. In an instant it became part of believing faith that I have a living Savior who is exercising, on a daily, moment-by-moment basis, His loving and gracious care for me from the heavenly sanctuary. There in the seminary library I experienced a renewed spiritual awakening. Talk about a deepening and broadening and enlarging of faith; it was like being reborn! The same can happen to you. Start with Hebrews 7-10. Read those chapters. Think about them. Pray over them. Chew on what they say to you. Ask such questions as: "What are high priests?" "What do they do?" "Of what significance is what they do?" "Why do they do what they do?" "Where in the Bible can I find background information that will help my understanding?" "Is it spiritually important to know this?" "Why is it important?" "What does this have to do with me, with my salvation?" "Is this just an invention of Seventh-day Adventists, or is it Bible truth?" "What *has* Jesus been doing in heaven since His ascension?" "Is what He is doing there somehow related to His second coming and the final judgment?" "Did His work for our salvation really end at the cross, or was something more necessary?" "What do we mean when we say that His work was 'finished' at Calvary?"

"Does 'finished' mean the end of His work?" "If Calvary was the end, then why the Ascension, the intercession, the Second Coming?" Keep chewing on questions like these, and God will provide answers that will thrill your heart, transforming your life and your faith experience.

This may be confusing for some, but the same Christ who ministers as high priest in the heavenly sanctuary (the transcendent Christ) is the Christ who indwells believers (the immanent Christ). Is this a contradiction? How can Christ the high priest be present in heaven and in the believer at the same time? The answer is twofold—by His Spirit and by faith. Shortly before His crucifixion and subsequent glorification, Jesus said concerning His promise of the Holy Spirit:

"I will ask the Father, and he will give you another Helper, to be with you forever, even the Spirit of truth, whom the world cannot receive, because it neither sees him nor knows him. You know him, for he dwells with you and will be in you. I will not leave you as orphans; I will come to you. Yet a little while and the world will see me no more, but you will see me. Because I live, you also will live. In that day you will know that I am in my Father, and you in me, and I in you" (John 14:16-20).

The Holy Spirit was not given on Pentecost until after Christ's glorification. Only the ascended and glorified Christ is able to be present in more than one place at the same time—in the heavenly sanctuary and also indwelling every believer by His Holy Spirit. His presence is also by faith in the truth of His revealed Word, which testifies to both realities. We can know that Christ is present in the heavenly sanctuary and in the believer, because the Bible tells us so. Remember, Christ is present in faith.

This simultaneous transcendent and immanent ministry of Christ would not be possible without the biblical truth concerning the Trinity, which is an essential component of the good news that is the gospel. It is highly significant, both theologically and spiritually, that John begins his Gospel with "In the beginning was the Word, and the Word was *with* God, and the Word *was* God. *He* was in the beginning with God" (John 1:1, 2). Here we have the truth of one God in two persons. But Jesus also promised the coming of "another Helper [advocate, counselor, comforter]" (John 14:16). Notice that it is "another," which means there are others who do the same thing. Who are they? God, the Father, and the Word, Jesus the Son, who was with the Father and who is also God. Who is this "another Helper"? It is "the Spirit of truth" (verse 17), "the Holy Spirit, whom the Father will send in my name, he will teach you all things and bring to your remembrance all that I have said to you" (verse 26). The Holy Spirit is "He"—a person. He will come "in my name," said Jesus. The Spirit, as Christ's personal representative, will teach and speak with

Christ's authority. Just as Jesus "came from the Father" and spoke with the Father's authority (John 16:28; 17:1-26). Jesus also said that "when the Helper comes, whom *I will send to you* from the Father, the Spirit of truth, *who proceeds from the Father,* he will bear witness about me" (John 15:26). So the testimony of Scripture is that the Holy Spirit is sent by *both* Father and Son. Here we have one God in three persons. Jesus, the Son, does the Father's will, and the Holy Spirit does the will of the Father and the Son. The Spirit will be "with you forever. . . . You know him, for he dwells with you and will be *in you*" (John 14:16, 17). Paul agreed with John and said, "God's love has been *poured into our hearts* through the Holy Spirit who has been given to us" (Rom. 5:5).

The ministry of the Holy Spirit leads us deeper and deeper into both the knowledge and the experience of God's love. If there were no Holy Spirit, we could not know the truth; nor could we enjoy the experience of a believing faith. I would have no spiritual story to tell, and neither would you. Jesus made us responsible for making "disciples of all nations," promising, "I am with you always, to the end of the age" (Matt. 28:19, 20). The Lord's last words to the apostles, just before His ascension, were "You will receive power when the Holy Spirit has come upon you, and you will be my witnesses" (Acts 1:8). Equipped, enabled, and empowered by the Holy Spirit, we are to tell the story of the Christ we know in the heavenly sanctuary and in the "inner being" by faith (Eph. 3:16). Other people come to that faith when that story is told.

By the way, some time ago I read an article in a magazine published by some dissident Adventists, in which the author said that she had to leave the Seventh-day Adventist Church in order to find Jesus. Thankfully, my experience has been the opposite: I have found Him in the Seventh-day Adventist Church. Now, let's return to the destiny of God's people.

John 1:14 tells us that "the Word became flesh and dwelt among us, and we have seen his glory, glory as of the only Son from the Father, full of grace and truth." Romans 1:5 says that in Jesus Christ "we have received grace." Jesus said to Paul, "My grace is sufficient for you, for my power is made perfect in weakness" (2 Cor. 12:9). Ephesians 1:7, 8 says that in Christ "we have redemption [have been bought back/restored] . . . according to the riches of his grace, which he lavished upon us." God is rich in grace. He has more than enough to go around. He doesn't waste it, but He doesn't withhold it, either. He lavishes it upon us. God's grace in Christ is rich, all-sufficient, and powerful enough to accomplish its purpose. What is that purpose? What does God intend the power of His grace to accomplish? It brings "salvation for all people." No one is left out. But what does "salvation" mean? What does it mean to be "saved," to be "redeemed," to be "born again"? All these are biblical figures of speech.

Salvation includes the forgiveness of sin and the promise of everlasting life because of Calvary. But salvation means more than forgiveness and eternal life. The Bible says that the grace of God that appeared in Jesus Christ, and that brings salvation to all people, trains us "to renounce ungodliness and worldly passions, and to live self-controlled, upright, and godly lives in the present age" (Titus 2:12). Not just someday in heaven, but now. Right here, where godliness is so badly needed. Here, where self-control is needed. Here, where uprightness is needed. Something good, by the grace of God, is supposed to happen to people who surrender in faith to the lordship of Christ. Jesus changes them, makes them new, transforms them. When we read passages such as this, we want to cry. Not whiny, pity-party tears, but the weeping that comes when we realize just how incomplete and unfinished we really are. The kind of tears that move us to pray, "Change my heart, O God, make it ever true. Change my heart, O God, may I be like you."

Faith in God's forgivingness makes human self-criticism possible. Why? Because we too have a destiny just like that of Jesus. What is that destiny? It is to "live godly lives in the present age." In order for that to be possible, God's grace needs to trains us to "renounce ungodliness." We are not supposed to remain spiritual babies, but to grow up into spiritual maturity and to fulfill our destiny. *Renounce* means to give up, to refuse to follow, ungodliness. Only the grace of God can empower us to do that. Our destiny is found in Him "who gave himself for us to redeem us from all lawlessness and to purify for himself a people for his own possession" (Titus 2:14).

Paul frequently used the word *salvation,* but in his letter to Titus he used the word *redeem,* which means "bought back, restored." It means that God in Christ not only put back together a broken relationship with the Father, but put us back together again. God, by His Holy Spirit, is actively engaged in restoring His image in fallen humankind. It is all of grace, but He doesn't do it without our cooperation. He does not force godliness upon us. The apostle says that He redeems us from *all* "lawlessness"—every bit of it. What is lawlessness? The biblical definition is found in 1 John 3:4: "Everyone who makes a practice of sinning also practices lawlessness; sin is lawlessness." Romans 4:15 says, "Where there is no law there is no transgression." What law? God's law, of course. Paul certainly is not speaking of human law, which changes with the times and can be amended, altered, and even abrogated. God's law is eternal, always the same, unchanging and unchangeable. Its perpetuity is precisely why it can be trusted to be just and not arbitrary, not random or capricious. God's grace redeems us from all lawlessness. The redeemed are empowered by grace to be law-abiding.

What does "all" refer to? Which commandment? Does it refer to only one or two? Jesus said to the rich young man, "If you would enter life, keep the commandments" (Matt. 19:17). Verses 18 and 19, which follow, indicate that He was speaking of God's moral law. In spite of what some may think, the Bible does not teach that Jesus did away with God's law. Jesus said, "If you love me, you will keep my commandments" (John 14:15), and "If you keep my commandments, you will abide in my love, just as I have kept my Father's commandments and abide in his love" (John 15:10). What happened at the cross? When Jesus died on Calvary, it was not God's law that was nailed to the cross, but the record of our sin, because we break His law every time we sin. Then Jesus said, "Therefore whoever relaxes one of the least of these commandments and teaches others to do the same will be called least in the kingdom of heaven, but whoever does them and teaches them will be called great in the kingdom of heaven. *For I tell you, unless your righteousness exceeds that of the scribes and Pharisees, you will never enter the kingdom of heaven*" (Matt. 5:19, 20).

"All" means all. Here is the destiny of God's people. Jesus gave Himself for us to "purify for himself a people for his own possession who are zealous for good works" (Titus 2:14). Isn't that good news? It's the best news we could ever hear. God does not leave us forgiven but living in sin. Because Christians are bound to Christ by faith, they obey the law, as Jesus does. Christ, the living Word, who is our authority, binds His redeemed people to God's law. His grace does not free us from observing His law; it frees us from those things that would keep us from observing it—the power of sin, the flesh, and the devil. God's grace is more powerful than these. Victory is ours in Christ. When the rich young ruler wanted to know the revealed will of God, what did Jesus say to him? He pointed to God's law: "You know the commandments" (Luke 18:20). When this text is understood correctly, the bottom line is that only the one who does the will of God can *remain* in communion with Jesus. "You know that he [Jesus] appeared to *take away* sins, and in him there is no sin. No one who abides in him *keeps on sinning*; no one who *keeps on sinning* has either seen him or known him. Little children, let no one deceive you" (1 John 3:5-7).

Yes, God's law can be, and often is, taught in such a way that suggests it cannot be fulfilled. Such teaching has no authority from Jesus. He said that no one will ever enter the kingdom of heaven unless their righteousness exceeds that of the Pharisees. But we have an advantage over the

Pharisees, in that our obedience to the law is perfect. How is that possible for imperfect people? Because between us and the law stands the One who has fulfilled it perfectly. We are faced with a law whose demands have already been satisfied in Christ. The righteousness it demands is already there. And that's what it means to be a people of His possession. This is the only way that the righteousness of Christians exceeds that of the Pharisees. And it is righteousness indeed, because from now on, believers in Christ will do the will of God and keep His law by the power of His grace alone.

Seventh-day Adventists understand that every area of their lives is under the rule of God. They are "Lutheran" in that they hold firmly to Luther's (and Paul's) understanding of justification by grace alone through faith alone. But they are also "Methodist" in that they hold to John Wesley's view that the believer is not wholly saved unless also cleansed of sin. The work of Christ for the sinner is twofold. He saves from the guilt and penalty of sin, but the rest of the gospel story is that He also saves from the power of sin to control and dominate the believer's life. Adventist Christians understand that God calls the forgiven sinner to "put off your old self, which belongs to your former manner of life" and to "put on the new self, created after the likeness of God in true righteousness and holiness" (Eph. 4:22-24). They understand that putting on "the Lord Jesus Christ" results in making "no provision for the flesh, to gratify its desires" (Rom. 13:14). They understand that to behold, reflect, "the glory of the Lord" means to be "transformed into the same image from one degree of glory to another," and that this transformation "comes from the Lord who is the Spirit," not from within themselves (2 Cor. 3:18). They also believe, and yearn to experience, that the Christian life is a victorious life, because the indwelling Christ and His Spirit alone empower them for successful warfare against all the forces of evil and darkness that are in the world. Although they understand that the Christian cannot arrive at absolute perfection in this life, they are convinced that the kind of spiritual maturity that reflects the glory and holiness of Christ can be experienced by His grace. They believe that God's people are to be recognized "by their fruits" and that, as Jesus said in His most famous sermon, "not everyone who says to me, 'Lord, Lord,' will enter the kingdom of heaven, but the one who does the will of my Father who is in heaven" (Matt. 7:16, 20, 21). The power is in His Word. The power is in His grace. Genuine Seventh-day Adventist Christians do not believe, as the mystics do, that people are justified because they become righteous; they believe people are justified because they are declared righteous in Christ. But those Adventist Christians also believe, on the authority of the Word of God, that the God who declares repentant sinners righteous also makes them righteous (see Rom. 5:19).

The second chapter of Titus ends like this: "These, then, are the things you should teach" (Titus 2:15, NIV). It is not enough to teach the law of God; by God's grace believers must learn how to obey it and be empowered to obey it. Why? Because otherwise it is only by the letter and not by the Spirit.

But Now

Some, but not all, of the most popular Christian writers of today have been saying that one of the most tragic, disturbing characteristics of contemporary Christianity is its failure to take the Bible seriously. This does not mean the Bible is not believed, at least in some sense, because even street surveys readily get affirmations of belief in the Bible. It has been said, and rightly so, that the church must be in the world, because it is the world that Jesus came to save, and the church is His instrument. The church is to be in the world, but the world is not to be in the church. There is a distinct difference. When the church does not take the Bible seriously, there develops a reluctance, even a resistance, to recognize and uphold biblical standards of the *trans*formed Christian life and spirituality. Many people, even some confessed Christians, belong to the cult of the open-minded. It's OK to be open-minded as long as the mind isn't open at both ends. Yes, we are called to look with compassion, pity, and loving concern at the world, which needs the healing power of the gospel. If we don't, we have no right to the name *Christian*. But at the same time, this rightful concern for the world must not be allowed to carry us to the point that we become so worldly-minded, so influenced by the ways of the world, that it becomes easy to compromise on Bible truth. Have you ever seen a church sign that says "Don't be so heavenly-minded that you are of no earthly good"? That's far from the situation today. "Don't be so earthly-minded that you are of no heavenly good" would be more accurate. It is the church that is called to bear witness to the world, not the other way around. The church is to confront the world and culture with the truth of the Word of God, not only by the spoken word but also by courageous and righteous living.

It's one thing to say that, but saying it is not the end of the matter. After it has been said, no great spiritual power, no great surge of redeeming grace, will be let loose in the world that we know until what has been said has been heard and then lived. Speaking of the early Christians, the Bible says that they "turned the world upside down" (Acts 17:6). When the downside is up, the world needs turning upside down. The early believers moved the world; they didn't let the world move them or mold them. "Do not be conformed to this world, but be transformed by the renewal of your mind," Paul admonished the believers at Rome (Rom. 12:2). This verse in *The New Testament in Modern English,* by Phillips, reads, "Don't let the world around you squeeze you into its own mould." One of the operating premises in the secular world of politics and government is that a compromise between conflicting points of view will produce the wisest judgment or resolution for any issue. But that premise does not apply with respect to the truth of God's revelation. God's Word is absolute; therefore, it *is* the wisest judgment and produces the best resolution when it is believed and lived.

In Romans 6:19-23 Paul reminds us that because there are vestiges of the natural human still clinging to us, we ought to be able to understand that to be slaves to sin results in death. We have to be open-minded, yes, but on the God-ward side. "Go, sell what you possess and give to the poor" (Matt. 19:21), Jesus said to the rich young man when he asked what he must do to be saved. Was Jesus saying he could earn salvation by giving away everything? The truth is, he could do nothing to earn salvation! What, then, was Jesus saying? He was saying that to follow Him means denying self. Paul reminds us that our service must be an undivided service. Jesus Himself said, "Whoever is not with me is against me" (Matt. 12:30). That sounds harsh. Did He really mean it? Yes, He did. From the Word comes the call to "present your members as slaves to righteousness leading to sanctification" (Rom. 6:19), as eagerly as we once offered them "to impurity and to lawlessness leading to more lawlessness."

That was tragically misunderstood by the man who came to an African mission compound with no legs, no arms, no ears, no eyes, and no tongue. He had tried to solve the problem of sin himself, using drastic means. He actually cut off his legs, so he couldn't go to the wrong places. He cut off his arms, so he couldn't steal. He cut off his ears, so he couldn't hear evil. He cut out his eyes, so he couldn't see evil and be tempted. He cut out his tongue, so he couldn't lie. But he discovered that he could still think. He didn't realize that it was his heart, his inner being, that needed to be washed clean and changed.[3]

There has to be newness of life before there can be any spiritual fruit, before we can follow the way of the Master without reservation. His will lies down the narrow way, the way least understood by the world, but it is the most spiritually profitable way for the believer and for the world. Paul's original hearers may have asked, "Why bother with this kind of exhortation?" In reply, he appeals to reason, intelligence, and faith that is tuned to spiritual truth because of union with Jesus. He says that while we were slaves to sin we were free in regard to righteousness. Slaves to sin care nothing about righteousness. But now that we have been set free from sin, by virtue of faith we are "slaves" (servants) of God. He asks, "But what fruit were you getting at that time from the things of which you are now ashamed?" Every action of ours has an ultimate result—either life or death.

Paul says that in our pagan days the ultimate result was death. "The end of those things is death." Death is all we get from conduct that now makes us blush to remember. Sin earns death. Spiritually speaking, today's generation is a dry-eyed generation. In its own eyes it is pure. Postmodernism says there is no such thing as sin. Sin is minimized until it is nothing to cry about. In such a time many join churches with their heads erect and wills unbroken. It all comes from the modern version of the Christian life as a glorified good time. Peter agreed with Paul:

"The time that is past suffices for doing what the Gentiles [unbelievers] want to do, living in sensuality, passions, drunkenness, orgies, drinking parties, and lawless idolatry. With respect to this they are surprised when you do not join them in the same flood of debauchery [especially if before you used to do it with them], and they malign you; but they will give account to him who is ready to judge the living and the dead. For this is why the gospel was preached even to those who are dead, that though judged in the flesh the way people are, they might live in the spirit the way God does" (1 Peter 4:3-6).

Peter prefaced this text by saying that although we are still in the body, "whoever has suffered in the flesh has ceased from sin" and lives for the rest of his life "no longer for human passions but for the will of God" (verses 1, 2). Peter and Paul are of one mind on this. We have a new Master. It's not just being made free from sin, but being made slaves, servants, of God.

Then comes the contrast that reveals the blessing, the result of a believing faith. To follow pagan impurity and wickedness is death, "but now that you have been set free from sin and have become slaves of God, the fruit you get leads to sanctification [holiness], and its end [destiny], eternal life" (Rom. 6:22). "But now" makes all the difference. Everything is changed. Once free from sin, we can be servants of God. The personal benefit is holiness, righteous living. The ultimate result is eternal life. The closer we walk with the Lord, the more complete becomes our consecration. What is weak is given strength. What is uncertain is given certainty. What is powerless is given power.

When the Lord exhorts us to dedicate our lives to Him, He adds also the element of separation. We are asked to present ourselves as a living sacrifice and to "be not conformed to this world, but be transformed by the renewal of your mind, that by testing you may discern what is the will of God, what is good and acceptable and perfect" (Rom. 12:2). If we love the world, the Bible says, the love of God is not in us (see 1 John 2:15). If the Bible does not mean separation from the paganism of our age, what then does it mean? We are not, the Word says, to fellowship with unfruitful works of darkness, but reprove them. We are to put on the Lord Jesus Christ and make no provision for the flesh, to satisfy its desires (see Rom. 13:14). The way to make no provision for the flesh is to put on Christ.

Our Lord made it plain that the world hated Him and that it would also hate us because we are not of the world, but have been chosen out of the world. Just because the mood of the age is frivolity and licentiousness, we dare not think that the way to advance the cause of Christ is to be jolly good fellows after the pattern of the world. The truth of the gospel cannot be revamped and streamlined to make it acceptable to natural humanity. We must square with the gospel to be saved. No other testimony is credible. Why all this? According to Will Allen Dromgoole:

> An old man, going a lone highway,
> Came at the evening cold and gray
> To a chasm vast and deep and wide
> Through which was flowing a sullen tide.
> The old man crossed in the twilight dim;
> The rapids held no fear for him.
> But he turned when safe on the other side
> And built a bridge to span the tide.
>
> "Old man," cried a fellow pilgrim near,
> "You're wasting your time in building here.
> Your journey will end with the closing day;
> You never again will pass this way.
> You have crossed the chasm deep and wide;
> Why build you this bridge at eventide?"
>
> The builder lifted his old gray head.
> "Good friend, in the path I have come," he said,
> "There follows after me today
> A youth whose feet must pass this way.
> This stream, which has been as naught to me,
> To that fair youth may a pitfall be.
> He too must cross in the twilight dim—
> Good friend, I am building this bridge for him."

Meditation

You have a spiritual story to tell. How about taking time to write it down for your children and grandchildren? If you have surrendered to the lordship of Christ, has something good happened to you, and can you describe it?

---

[1] E. G. White, *Testimonies for the Church*, vol. 5, p. 264. Ellen White's position on the Bible and its use is clear when she says, "Bring your evidences, clear and plain, from the Word of God" (*Selected Messages*, book 3, p. 29).

[2] Such as *Seventh-day Adventists Believe . . . A Biblical Exposition of Fundamental Doctrines* (Hagerstown, Md.: Review and Herald Pub. Assn., 2005); *Handbook of Seventh-day Adventist Theology;* and *Seventh-day Adventists Answer Questions on Doctrine* (Berrien Springs, Mich.: Andrews University Press, 2003).

[3] I do not recall where I first heard this particular story, so I am unable to credit a specific source.

Chapter 15

THE HEARTBEAT
OF THE CHURCH

Throughout these pages I have tried to demonstrate the importance of searching for an authentic Adventist spirituality within the Seventh-day Adventist tradition rather than elsewhere. I have also tried to demonstrate that this tradition has two distinct foci—the Bible and the Spirit of Prophecy, which shape Adventist spirituality and the Seventh-day Adventist Church's understanding of its mission as one of bringing folks into its fellowship (evangelism) and also keeping them in (nurture).

Worship is a major component in spiritual nurture. Corporate worship, which is the extension of personal devotion, sustains spiritual life in the same way that the heartbeat sustains physical life by pumping the blood that energizes muscles to perform their intrinsic functions. For Seventh-day Adventist Christians, who understand the spiritual meaning of the great controversy, there is no doubt as to the centrality of worship in the conflict between the kingdom of light and the kingdom of darkness. Its centrality is made crystal clear in the message of the angel calling the redeemed with a "loud voice" to "fear God and give him glory, because the hour of his judgment has come, and worship him who made heaven and earth, the sea and the springs of water" (Rev. 14:7). Both the Word of God and the Spirit of Prophecy make clear that a significant part of that corporate worship is the celebration of the Lord's Supper.

Another Step Along the Road

As an Adventist worshipper and former professor of worship, I believe that Adventist spirituality cannot really be understood or experienced apart from the meaning of, and participation in, the Lord's Supper. That's why an event that took place in the fall of 1970 had such spiritual importance for me. Still a Lutheran, I had enrolled in a course at Andrews University titled Prophetic Guidance, taught by Professor Thomas Blincoe. It consisted of an in-depth study of the life and ministry of Ellen White, as well as biblical prophecy and how it works. I recall reading three times the assignments in the Ellen White writings, which the other students, who were all Adventists, read once. A few weeks into the course, Blincoe approached me with a proposition I could not turn down. He offered to excuse me from the final exam if I would write a research paper on the topic "A Comparative Study of the Eucharistic Theology of Martin Luther, Ulrich Zwingli, John Calvin, and Ellen G. White." So I went to work and, as I worked, became convinced that Blincoe was led by the Holy Spirit in making his proposal.

I had to research the three Reformers' views, especially regarding the presence of Christ in the Lord's Supper. Luther and Zwingli were no problem, as I was already familiar with their views in light of their confrontation at Marburg, Germany in the fall of 1529.[1] Calvin was another matter. When it came to Ellen White, however, I discovered that she sensed a deeper meaning in the Lord's Supper than merely the symbolic. The attention of the three Reformers was focused primarily on the words of Jesus: "This is my body." Not so Ellen White's. What follows in this chapter are insights gleaned from my study of her book *The Desire of Ages*, chapters 71 and 72, together with a renewed look at Paul's statement in 1 Corinthians 11.

We Do What We Believe

Somewhere I heard the story of a frequent passenger on a ferryboat who noticed one day that the greasy smells that usually came from the engine room were gone. The oil that usually covered the deck had vanished. A gleaming engine that looked like new occupied the engine room. The dirty, smelly bilge water was replaced by cleanliness, beauty, and order. Then he noticed that the engineer had been replaced by an immaculate, elderly man who was sitting in the doorway to the engine room, reading a Bible. In his eyes was a look of wisdom, and he appeared to be at peace with the world. The passenger asked if he were responsible for cleaning up the old engine and, if so, how he was able to make an immaculate sanctuary out of such a dirty, smelly place.

A wonderful smile lit up the old man's face as he gave the answer that could solve most of life's problems for most people. "Sir," he said, nodding in the direction of the engine room, "It's like this—I got a glory!"

What could he have meant? This, perhaps: "The Word became flesh and made his dwelling among us. We have seen his glory, the glory of the one and only Son, who came from the Father, full of grace and truth" (John 1:14, NIV). Because he had "a glory," because he had Jesus, he had everything. To him, that meant making that old engine room the best on the river. He had discovered a great secret—that the only certain way out of the filth and misery of human life is to find a glory and then to give to that glory all the determination and strength that we would otherwise spend in hopeless despair.

If we understand the word *sacrament* as referring to "a religious act that is a sign or symbol of spiritual reality,"[2] we can certainly understand that man's action in cleaning up the engine room. For him, the scrubbing and cleaning and polishing was a religious act that was a sign of the spiritual reality of his faith in Christ. This story, together with 1 Corinthians 11:17-34, illuminates the truth that we do what we believe.

"But in the following instructions I do not commend you, because when you come together it is not for the better but for the worse. For, in the first place, when you come together as a church, I hear that there are divisions among you. And I believe it in part, for there must be factions among you in order that those who are genuine among you may be recognized. When you come together, it is not the Lord's supper that you eat. For in eating, each one goes ahead with his own meal. One goes hungry, another gets drunk. What! Do you not have houses to eat and drink in? Or do you despise the church of God and humiliate those who have nothing? What shall I say to you? Shall I commend you in this? No, I will not.

"For I received from the Lord what I also delivered to you, that the Lord Jesus on the night when he was betrayed took bread, and when he had given thanks, he broke it, and said, 'This is my body which is for you. Do this in remembrance of me.' In the same way also he took the cup, after supper, saying, 'This cup is the new covenant in my blood. Do this, as often as you drink it, in remembrance of me.' For as often as you eat this bread and drink the cup, you proclaim the Lord's death until he comes.

"Whoever, therefore, eats the bread or drinks the cup of the Lord in an unworthy manner will be guilty concerning the body and blood of the Lord. Let a person examine himself, then, and so eat of the bread and drink of the cup. For anyone who eats and drinks without discerning the body eats and drinks judgment on himself. That is why many of you are weak and ill, and some have died. But if we judged ourselves truly, we would not be judged. But when we are judged by the Lord, we are disciplined so that we may not be condemned along with the world.

"So then, my brothers, when you come together to eat, wait for one another—if anyone is hungry, let him eat at home—so that when you come together it will not be for judgment."

Before we consider the words of Jesus, which have attracted the most attention in this passage, we need to consider some other details that are usually passed over.

"All God's acts are consistent with all His attributes."[3] Should not that principle apply to those who believe in Him, who profess to being His followers? Of course! This principle is at the very heart of what Paul says about the celebration of the Lord's Supper. He makes it clear that what he says in 1 Corinthians 11 are "instructions." He is giving instructions, counsel, to the church, the body of Christ, as to how its members should behave when they "come together," that is to say, when they engage in fellowship gatherings, some of which include eating together, and especially when they celebrate the Lord's Supper. Paul makes it clear that when they do not behave according to his instructions, "it is not the Lord's Supper that you eat," and that if anyone participates "in an unworthy manner," he is "guilty concerning the body and blood of the Lord." "That is why," he said, "many of you are weak and ill, and some have died." Was he speaking of physical or spiritual sickness and death? His use of the word *judgment,* when he says that "anyone who eats and drinks without discerning the body eats and drinks judgment on himself," seems to indicate that he is speaking about spiritual sickness and death. And this is exactly what happens when a person does not follow up confession of faith with demonstration of faith, when one's actions are inconsistent with the faith confessed. The faith itself gets sick, weakens, and dies, if something isn't done about it. Of course, such a spiritual condition may, and often does, lead to physical sickness and even death.

This is why Paul instructs us to "let a person examine himself, then, and so eat of the bread and drink of the cup." We are to take a good look at ourselves to see if our actions are consistent with our profession. Why? Because that is where healing and restoration of spiritual health begins. Paul instructs us to examine, not the bread or the cup, but ourselves. If we judge ourselves truly, we will not be judged. On what basis do we examine ourselves? What is the criteria? Our feelings? Our own opinions? How many people are there in the world? How many opinions, then? How can such judgment be done "truly"? To speak in any sense of that which is "true" is to speak of something that conforms to a standard, to something that is accurate. In construction terms, to speak of the true means to identify the perfectly level, plumb, and/or square. Anything less is not "true." In order to judge ourselves truly, our judgment must be based on an absolute standard.

For the believer, one who would be expected to come to the Lord's table and eat the bread and drink the cup in a worthy manner, that absolute standard has to be the Word of God. Why? Because the judgment of God is involved, and He is just and righteous. He does not judge us unfairly or capriciously. Can human opinion be depended upon for justice, righteousness, and fairness? Paul said that "when we are judged by the

Lord, we are disciplined so that we may not be condemned along with the world." So on the basis of the Word of God we examine and judge ourselves, what we believe (truth itself), and whether or not we are "truly" living what we believe.

Have you ever wondered why this passage is preceded by 16 verses in which Paul talked about Christ's being the head of the husband, the husband the head of his wife, and about head coverings and long or short hair? I think Paul is illustrating the truth that we do what we believe. In these verses Paul is talking about relationships and about appearance—based upon the biblical principle that if Christ is the head, then He has something to say about how His body, the church, functions and behaves.

Fashion, the way we make ourselves appear outwardly, changes with times and culture. But isn't the human concern with such things indicative of the fact that we are aware that something is missing? that humanity has lost something? Losing our original clothing, a garment of light, we have been obsessed with dressing up to compensate outwardly for what is missing inwardly. The more we sense the inner void, the more we hang on the outward form. Unfortunately, the fashion industry is more concerned with sensuality than spirituality. It glorifies the body, not the inner being. Today what is called "dressing up" is really "dressing down," or not dressing at all. Because sin has unbalanced us, we can overdress as well as underdress. But should we compromise faith with indecent appearance or behavior? Christian beauty comes from the quality of life within, not from outward adornment. Absolutely nothing that we choose to wear can add to the beauty of a Christlike character. But it can detract from it. Christian beauty is not something that is put *on*. Rather, it is put *in*. There is a new glory, the glory of a new character and a new life that prompts us to do what we believe. Not to do what we believe is to be inconsistent. It is acting out of character, a denial of what we claim to be. If we profess to know the love and grace of God, we must prove it by doing what He tells us to do—eat the bread and drink the cup, and by so doing remember, bring to mind again and again, His broken body and shed blood on Calvary's cross.

Do This

Paul quoted the words of Jesus, "Do this in remembrance of me" (Luke 22:19, NKJV). Do what? Follow through on what you believe with action. If you believe that Jesus died for you on the cross, that His body was broken and His blood shed for you, then eat this bread and drink this cup as a visual reminder and testimony of your faith. Evidently we need such a striking reminder of exactly what Jesus did for us on the cross—a perceptual as well as a conceptual reminder, a whole-brain response.

Preaching is verbal, conceptual communication. Participation in the Lord's Supper, eating the bread and drinking the cup, is visual, perceptual communication. It is the difference between hearing, seeing, and acting out the gospel.

There are 10 references in the above passage that refer to eating and seven references to drinking. In the quotes from Jesus, twice He said, "Do this." Those facts should be very significant as we seek to understand what Paul is saying about the Lord's Supper. When the entire passage is taken into account, it becomes apparent that the focus is on action, on something done by the members of the body.

The first Lord's Supper in the upper room was pre-Calvary. The Crucifixion had not taken place yet, though it soon would. So Jesus helped the disciples with the meaning of His sacrifice, comparing it to broken bread and poured-out wine. The repetitive eating and drinking would constitute a dramatic remembrance of what He did on the cross. What *they* did, "as often" as they did it, would call to mind what *He* did. The Greek word *anamnesis*, translated "remembrance," has the same connotation as in "remember the Sabbath day," which occurs every seventh day in perpetuity. God established the Sabbath's repetitive nature, which was to be perpetuated by faithful observance. The perpetual, repetitive observance constitutes the "remembrance." The Lord does not tell us to "think this about the bread and the cup," but to "do this" in remembrance of Him.

Jesus said, "This *is* my body," and "This cup *is* the new covenant in my blood." What did He mean? One could wish that He had been more specific, more detailed. Did He mean that when those words are repeated in the Communion service, the saying of the words actually serves to change the bread into His real body and the wine into His real blood? That would be astounding! If He really meant that, why did He not say so? Did He mean that He is present in the bread and in the cup? If that is what He meant, why did He not say so? Did He mean that the bread and the cup are signs, symbols, of His presence? If that is what He meant, why did He not say "This bread is a sign of My presence"? I don't think these distinctions were on the Lord's mind at all. If they were, He would have been more specific. It is more likely that He was thinking about the faithfulness of His body, the church, with respect to its mission in the world, for which He would die on the morrow. His focus was more on "do this" than on "this is." When He washed the disciples' feet, He said, "If you know these things, blessed are you if you do them. I am not speaking of all of you; I know whom I have chosen. But the Scripture will be fulfilled, 'He who ate my bread has lifted his heel against me.' I am telling you this now, before it takes place, that when it does take place you may believe that I am he [your Lord and Teacher]" (John 13:17-19). His focus appears to be on the mission He was leaving them, to tell the whole world of what He would accomplish by His great sacrifice on the cross—*expiation,* which is putting an end to sin, as well as *propitiation,* which is to appease the wrath of God because of sin.[4]

I suppose it depends on our understanding of "is." That one little word has been the cause of intense theological thought and debate through the centuries, as well as the source of dispute and dissension. It was at the heart of the Reformation. In my opinion, it was because of the Catholic doctrine of transubstantiation, which had been held exclusively until the sixteenth century, that the focus of the Reformers was on the question of just *how* Christ is present in the bread and the cup of Communion. But that emphasis does not seem to be Paul's focus. His focus is on the eating and the drinking, on the "do this."

If, instead of *instructions,* Paul had used a word that could be translated "ideas" or "formula" or "concept" or "theory" or "precept" or even "recipe," we could legitimately conclude that Paul was developing a doctrine, a fundamental article of the faith that is to be believed, concerning the presence of Christ in the Lord's Supper. This is exactly what theologians have done down through the centuries. Based on the presuppositions they bring to this text, they make it say many different things—such as transubstantiation, consubstantiation, real presence, symbolic presence, spiritual presence, etc.—all words the Bible does not use.

The Presence of Christ

How Christ is present in the Lord's Supper was the essence of the controversy between Luther, Zwingli, and the other Reformers. Luther, a former Catholic priest, could not tear himself away from the idea that in some way Christ is present in the bread and the cup. He finally settled on the words *in* and *under.*[5] Luther certainly was right in his view that Christ could be present simultaneously in heaven and on earth by the Holy Spirit. There are ample Bible texts that support this view. Zwingli, on the other hand, held that Christ could not be present bodily in heaven and in the bread and cup at the same time. At the first Supper, He could not stand physically in the presence of the disciples and also say that He was in the bread and the cup. That made no sense to Zwingli or to Calvin. Zwingli also held that if the word "is" is to be taken literally, it would have been impossible for a Jew to accept, because for the Jew the idea of drinking blood was repugnant, and Jesus and the disciples were Jews. Thus Jesus would, could, never say or imply such a thing. Therefore, "is" has to mean "represents" or "stands for" or "in place of." The bread and the cup represent an event, Calvary, not a literal reenactment of Jesus' death.

I have a major problem with Luther's literal understanding of Jesus' phrase "this is," because he was hermeneutically inconsistent. By that I mean that Luther did not apply the same principle of interpretation to the fourth (Sabbath) commandment, the meaning of which is much more literally obvious than what Jesus said about His body and blood in the Eucharist. Also, Luther criticized Zwingli for appealing to natural human reason, although he himself appealed to natural law with respect to the observance of the Sabbath commandment.

Now let's take a close look at the Spirit of Prophecy. Let's begin with Ellen White's statements with respect to the footwashing that preceded the Lord's Supper, in John's Gospel.[6]

The Preparatory Service

The impact of Ellen White's words should be immediately obvious. She says that at the Passover supper "Jesus repeated His teaching by an *illustration* that impressed it forever on their [the disciples'] minds and hearts." The illustration was necessary because if the disciples "had been prepared to receive what He longed to impart [concerning His crucifixion the next day], they would have been saved from heartbreaking anguish, from disappointment and unbelief. But Jesus saw that they could not bear what He had to say." So He gave His disciples "an *example* they would never forget." He washed their feet, and something spiritually significant happened. "This action *opened the eyes of the disciples. Bitter shame and humiliation filled their hearts. They understood the unspoken rebuke and saw themselves in altogether a new light.*" It was "the *type* of a higher cleansing." When Peter initially refused to let Jesus wash his feet, he was "refusing the *higher cleansing included in* the lower. He was really rejecting his Lord." Notice that the higher cleansing was *included in* the lower.

The disciples "needed His cleansing grace," and when Jesus washed their feet, "He desired by that very act to *wash* the alienation, jealousy, and pride from their *hearts* [inner being]. *This was of far more consequence than the washing of their dusty feet. . . . Their hearts* must be cleansed." Pride and self-seeking "Jesus *washed away in washing their feet.*" We, too, "must come to Christ *for His cleansing grace. . . .* All our infirmity and defilement we must bring to Him. *He alone can wash us clean. . . .* I have given you *an example,* that ye should do as I have done to you," said Jesus. In His act of washing, "He imparted grace and significance to the service" and was "instituting a religious service. By the act of our Lord this humiliating ceremony *was made a consecrated ordinance.*" It is His "appointed preparation for the sacramental service" of Communion. He had "appointed the *memorial of His* humiliation to be first observed." It is meant to "clear away" misunderstandings and bring us out of our "selfishness" and "self-exaltation."

Is Jesus *present* when His followers wash each other's feet? "The holy Watcher from heaven *is present* at this season to make it one of soul searching, of conviction of sin, and of the blessed assurance of sins forgiven. Christ *in the fullness of His grace is there* to change the current of the thoughts that have been running in selfish channels. The Holy Spirit [who is also present] quickens the sensibilities of those who follow the example of their Lord." With this consciousness, "sins are confessed, they are forgiven. The subduing grace of Christ comes *into* the soul, and the love of Christ draws hearts together in a blessed unity." Ellen White concludes with this: "To those who receive the spirit of this service, it can *never become a mere ceremonial.*" Why not? Because "whenever this ordinance is *rightly celebrated*, the children of God are brought into a holy relationship, to help and bless each other." When is it *rightly* celebrated? When believers come conscious of Christ's presence and in an attitude of confession. When they come accepting His gracious forgiveness and the work of His Spirit in bringing about the effects of His subduing grace. When they are yielding to the transforming power of His grace.

Christ is present, not in the water, but in the washing. Subduing grace comes into the soul, because Christ and the Holy Spirit are present on that occasion in the fullness of cleansing grace, because Christ does something spiritually transforming for those that come in confession, *opening* their eyes to their true spiritual condition, *forgiving* and *washing* sin from their hearts, *changing* selfish thoughts, *quickening* their sensibilities. Because Christ is present and acts on behalf of the repentant, footwashing can never be simply a routine, formal act without deep spiritual significance. When we wash each other's feet, Jesus does something for us and in us. This is what Ellen White means when she says that the higher cleansing is *included* in the lower. Therefore, it can never be a mere example, memorial, or ceremony. She senses something deeper. If Christ is not present, and if nothing of a spiritual nature happens, then why should we bother?

The "Sacramental" Service

Yes, as was pointed out in the first chapter, Ellen White calls the Lord's Supper "the *sacramental* service," as well as an "ordinance."[7] The service itself is "the *memorial* of His [Christ's] great sacrifice." It points to the cross; therefore "the *ordinance* of the Lord's Supper was given to *commemorate* the great deliverance wrought out as the result of the death of Christ." The service is "the *means* [vehicle] by which His great work for us is to be kept

254   THE ROAD I TRAVEL

fresh in our minds." The celebration of the Supper is a visual reminder of Calvary, in which the bread and wine are the "emblems" that "Christ employs to *represent* His own unblemished sacrifice." Unfermented wine was used at the inaugural Supper, because "nothing corrupted by fermentation, the symbol of sin and death, could represent the 'Lamb without blemish and without spot.' 1 Peter 1:19." Christ and the Holy Spirit, together with angels, are present when the Lord's Supper is celebrated. Ellen White states unequivocally that "there are present messengers unseen by human eyes." That "heavenly angels also are present," and, most important, "Christ by the Holy Spirit is there" to *"set the seal* to His own ordinance . . . to *convict* and *soften* the *heart.* . . . He is waiting" for "the repentant, broken-hearted one. . . . He who washed the feet of Judas longs to *wash* every *heart* from the stain of sin." Christ in communion "meets His people, and *energizes* them by His presence." He is there "to *minister to His children,"* and all who come "with their faith fixed on Him [not on the bread and wine] will be greatly blessed." All who neglect to participate "will suffer loss." It is obvious that something of great spiritual significance happens when the Lord's Supper is celebrated and when those who celebrate it come in faith. They come "to meet with Christ." Ellen White does not attempt to explain the *how* of Christ's presence; she simply proclaims it.

What are the results? "With hearts *cleansed* by Christ's most precious blood, *in full consciousness of His presence,* although unseen, they are to hear His words, 'Peace I leave with you, My peace I give unto you: not as the world giveth, give I unto you.' John 14:27." The service speaks "to our *senses* of the love of God that has been expressed in our behalf," because "our senses need to be quickened to lay hold of the mystery of godliness. . . . As faith contemplates our Lord's great sacrifice, the soul [inner being] assimilates the spiritual life of Christ. That soul will *receive spiritual strength* from every Communion." Faith operates both conceptually and perceptually, and, as communicants receive the bread and wine, "symbolizing Christ's broken body and spilled blood," they *"in imagination* join in the scene of communion in the upper chamber." The Communion service "forms a living connection by which the believer is bound up with Christ, and thus bound up with the Father." The ultimate result is that "he who beholds the Savior's matchless love will be *elevated in thought, purified in heart, transformed in character.* He will go forth to be a light to the world, to reflect in some degree this mysterious love." The Lord's Supper was instituted by the Lord for the spiritual benefit and well-being of His own, for His body, the church. It is not the church's offering to Him. The celebration is truly "sacramental" in the sense that Christ is present and accomplishes these results for those who participate in believing faith.

Who is invited to the Supper? Who decides? "God has not left it with men to say who shall present themselves on these occasions. For who can read the heart? Who can distinguish the tares from the wheat?" No human being, no priest or minister, can make such an omniscient judgment. Then Ellen White quotes Paul's words (1 Cor. 11:27-29, KJV) in support of this view: "'Let a man examine himself, and so let him eat of that bread, and drink of that cup.' For 'whosoever shall eat this bread, and drink this cup of the Lord, unworthily, shall be guilty of the body and blood of the Lord.' 'He that eateth and drinketh unworthily, eateth and drinketh damnation to himself, not discerning the Lord's body.'" What do nonbelievers receive in the eating and drinking? Only judgment. Why? Because the body of Christ, the church, is not discerned, and they are not members of it, because of the absence of faith. Such individuals might be there in the flesh, but they are not present in spirit, are not part of the family of God.

The "body" means the church, which is the body of Christ. Paul uses the same Greek word for *body* in 1 Corinthians 12:27—"Now you are the body of Christ, and members individually" (NKJV). The corporate oneness of the church is both demonstrated and affirmed by the sharing of the common bread. Paul's teaching regarding union with Christ by faith is basic to his thinking. Christ dwells in the believers, and the believers are in Christ (see Rom. 8:10; Gal. 2:20; Col. 1:27; 2 Cor. 5:17). For the believers, this is not just an individual matter, because they are in the body of Christ by virtue of baptism into Christ; many are united in that body. Therefore, "just as the body is one and has many members, and all the members of the body, though many, are one body, so it is with Christ. For in one Spirit we were all baptized into one body—Jews or Greeks, slaves or free—and were all made to drink of one Spirit" (1 Cor. 12:12, 13). The reason the breaking of bread is sharing in the body of Christ is that "there is one bread, we who are many are one body, for we all partake of the one bread" (1 Cor.10:17). Ellen White captures this sublime truth in that marvelous statement near the end of her chapter on the Lord's Supper.

"To the death of Christ we owe even this earthly life. The bread we eat is the purchase of His broken body. The water we drink is bought by His spilled blood. Never one, saint or sinner, eats his daily food, but he is nourished by the body and the blood of Christ. The cross of Calvary is stamped on every loaf. It is reflected in every water spring. All this Christ has taught in appointing the emblems of His great sacrifice. The light shining from that Communion service in the upper chamber makes sacred the provisions for our daily life. The family board becomes as the table of our Lord, and every meal a sacrament." [8]

Eating and drinking without "discerning the body" means failing to recognize the church for what it is—the body of Christ in which He is present. Is He *really* present in His body, the church, and thus in the celebration of the Lord's Supper? This we believe, because the truth of that presence is rooted in Scripture and affirmed by the Spirit of Prophecy. Therefore Seventh-day Adventists, together with Luther, are able to confess the *real presence* of Christ in that celebration. However, the focus of His presence is not the bread and the cup, but the eating and the drinking. Ellen White supports Paul's consistent emphasis when it comes to the bread and wine themselves. They are the means by which the body and blood of Christ are shared in the celebration of the Lord's Supper, but they are not equated with them. Christ is present, not in the bread and wine, but in the eating and drinking. Just as in the footwashing, He is not present in the water, but in the washing. Thus Adventists are Melanchthonian in that Luther's colleague Philip Melanchthon found Christ's presence not in the bread and cup, but in the action of the celebration. This, too, as Luther would say, is an object of faith based on the words of Paul in 1 Corinthians 11. Those words are addressed not to the elements, but to the congregation. They do not cause Christ to be present; they alert the congregation as to the manner of its presence. Have the participants come in faith or not? These insights, thanks to the study proposal of Blincoe, were a major step along the spiritual road I travel and served to help show the way to transition from the Lutheran to the Adventist Church.

Something Is Supposed to Happen

Finally, the Communion service is eschatological in nature, for as Ellen White indicates, it "points to Christ's second coming. It was designed to keep this hope *vivid* in the minds of the disciples," for "in their tribulation they found comfort in the hope of their Lord's return." The eschatological dimension of the celebration is experienced when the believer in loving obedience, by God's grace, fulfills His commission to "go therefore and make disciples of all nations, baptizing them in the name of the Father and of the Son and of the Holy Spirit, teaching them to observe all that I have commanded you. And behold, I am with you always, to the end of the age" (Matt. 28:19, 20). The celebration depicts the joy of anticipation when God's faithful people will share in the marriage supper of the Lamb in His kingdom (Rev. 19:6-10). The church is an eschatological reality, God's remnant people worshipping in anticipation, saying, "Amen. Come, Lord Jesus!" (Rev. 22:20).

Did you know that 500 years ago people died for the Lord's Supper? In England, Protestants were burned at the stake because they rejected the Catholic dogma of the Mass. Later, Catholics were burned because they refused to renounce that dogma. It had become tradition that the church decided who was a heretic and deserving of death by burning. The one declared guilty was then turned over to secular authorities, who carried out the sentence. Why? Because it was believed that the church was supreme and the state an instrument of the church. Priests were considered superior to laypeople, which led to ecclesiastical totalitarianism. The fundamental issue in the sixteenth century was that of religious authority—church tradition or Scripture alone. It is still the issue!

How was it possible for the church to insist that a priest had the power to offer the sacrifice of Christ every day on the altar of a church, year after year, when the Bible says, "For the death he died he died to sin, *once* for all" (Rom. 6:10), and "He has no need . . . to offer sacrifices daily, first for his own sins and then for those of the people, since he did this *once* for all when he offered up himself" (Heb. 7:27)? According to the Bible, the central event of the Christian faith has already occurred in history—on Calvary—and it cannot, will not, need not, be repeated. No wonder some men were burned because they dared to translate the Bible into English. Men such as William Tyndale, who was condemned as a heretic by the church and burned by secular authorities on October 6, 1536. Why? Fear. Fear of what? Truth.

But while Calvary could not be repeated, it was to be remembered—memorialized. On the first such occasion, Jesus told His followers to "do this in remembrance of me" (Luke 22:19). Paul repeated those very words in his "instructions" concerning the celebration of what he called, for the first time, the "Lord's supper." It was not meant to be like any other supper. It was not a supper eaten by a people secure in this world, who have settled down comfortably in this life. It was meant for pilgrims, people that are on the way, who have great expectations and for whom the greatest events were still to come.

People who come to the Lord's Supper should eat it as the Israelites ate the Passover meal. "In this manner you shall eat it: with your belt fastened, your sandals on your feet, and your staff in your hand. And you shall eat it in haste" (Ex. 12:11), looking to the future and ready for a journey. Did that mean they were to eat without thinking? Of course not. It meant that they were not to settle down in the wilderness and pitch a permanent camp. The entire context of Paul's words concerning the Lord's Supper indicates that it is to be celebrated by a people on the move, an interim people, people who live and worship between the now and the not yet. The Lord's Supper uniquely links the past with the future. It serves not only to remind us of Calvary, but also to "proclaim the Lord's death until he comes." To "remember" in the Lord's Supper is not just to call to mind what He did on the cross, but also to bring to mind His promise to return. The eating and the drinking in the unity of faith vividly points to His return.

The apostle also calls our attention to a striking thing—the institution of the Supper took place in an atmosphere of betrayal. There were 12 with Jesus that night. Judas, one of them, was an erstwhile follower and an opportunist, whose convictions were just skin-deep. He was a despicably corrupt man, a false friend. When crises come, we usually find out who our friends really are—and just how loyal and true we are. Loyalty to Christ requires that we stick with Him and with His truth, though we may lose friends as a consequence. Anything less is disobedience and unfaithfulness, spiritual adultery. Once His truth is recognized, the disciple is obligated to follow the Master. Jesus said to His disciples, "My food is to do the will of him who sent me and to accomplish his work" (John 4:34). The implication is that this was their "food" as well. Nothing else matters. The celebration of the Supper is always an end-time crisis, an eschatological event, as it is celebrated on the threshold of Christ's return. For each of us it involves facing anew the decision that must be made in every encounter with the Lord Jesus Christ. Self-examination is required. Are we truly the friends of Christ? Or are we betrayers of everything He is, blasphemers of everything He has done for us? desecrators of His blood and sacrifice? What makes this decision so serious is that we are not just remembering something He did in the past; we are in the very presence of the One whose triumphant return is imminent. Judgment is next.

At the first Supper, Judas sat in the very presence of Christ and "brooded upon his own dark purposes, and cherished his sullen, revengeful thoughts."[9] With intense sadness Jesus looked at the disciples and said, "One of you shall betray me." They began to question, "Lord, is it I?" Judas alone sat mute. He knew. He did not need to ask. Finally, with all eyes on him, he asked, "Is it I, Rabbi?" (Matt. 26:25). It is sad, but true, that only a friend, not an enemy, can betray. This makes all the more serious the searching of heart and conscience when we come to the Lord's table. Surely Paul was thinking about Judas when he wrote, "If we judged ourselves truly, we would not be judged" (1 Cor. 11:31). Who on earth knows us better than we know ourselves? Just as the gospel that it illustrates, the Lord's Supper is for everyone. No one should be forbidden to come, because God is sovereign, and His work is done in any case—either judgment or conviction and a softening of heart.

So let us come in genuine repentance to the footwashing, and then with joy to the eating of the bread and the drinking of the cup. Come, letting God the Holy Spirit do His work of justification for us and sanctification in us. The Supper is not just a mysterious ritual. Something is supposed to happen, yes. But not to the bread and wine. It is not the bread and wine, but you and I, that need transformation. Let us remember, as the deacons hold out to us the bread and wine, that Jesus, our high priest, presents Himself and His blood before the throne of God in the heavenly sanctuary. It is the Lord's Supper, just as the Sabbath is the Lord's Day. We show our thankfulness for His grace and mercy by partaking of it, by observing it. From such a gathering and celebration we receive the spiritual strength and courage that we need for our mission in this world. That's what food does. To strive by the Spirit's power for the reunion in history of the body of Christ. If any church has an authentic ecumenical message and mission, it is the Seventh-day Adventist Church. The message God has given us to preach is designed by Him to do just that—unite His people in preparation for the return of Christ.

Yes, we worship God the Creator, conscious of His transcendence. But we also worship God the Redeemer, conscious of His immanence. Worship, as illustrated by its ritual (liturgy), is not just cerebral, involving our thoughts (worshipping in spirit and in *truth*). It is also experiential, involving the worshipper's inner being (worshipping in *spirit* and in truth), the essence of being human. Worship must be understood and practiced, ritually, in the light of Scripture and in light of the Seventh-day Adventist tradition (doctrine, theology, faith, mission, etc.), not culture. The true purpose of liturgy/ritual is not to control the worshipper's response, but to enable that response. Worship is meant to be repetitive, just like the Sabbath on which it takes place. Unfortunately, some have the opinion that repetition breeds overfamiliarity, so that appeal and purpose are lost. Is that really true? My experience has been the opposite. When the celebration of the Lord's Supper is accurately perceived to demonstrate/illustrate what is believed, the appeal is enhanced by repetition. It should become familiar. It is designed to become familiar and so contribute to the worshipper's developing spirituality. Not becoming familiar, I suspect, constitutes a major part of the contemporary bewilderment caused by a multiplicity of styles and forms of worship, some of which have been borrowed from other denominations without careful theological thought.

The body of Christ, the church, was intended to be a community of believers in which the crucified, risen, ascended Lord and High Priest is the very center and focus of its worship. After all, the goal of evangelism is to bring people to Christ so that He can transform them into worshippers. Worship, in turn, inspires and motivates evangelism. In this sense, worship is the heartbeat of the church.

One thing is certain: We can never claim to be wiser than Scripture.

Granted that there is an element of mystery to God's revelation and to the faith that rests on that Word, yet we are able to draw certain conclusions from biblical statements. "Mystery" does not mean "mystical." "Mystery" refers to a truth that can be known only by revelation, though it may not be fully understood, whereas "mystical" refers to the idea that one can have direct knowledge of God from subjective experience alone. The question is: Do we hear God speaking to us in and through the words of Scripture? If so, how, then, do we respond? We respond in the only way possible— by eating and drinking, by observing the "do this." By doing what we believe. Perhaps that should be enough for us.

One final word. It is not the bread and the cup that need to be consecrated, but those who do the eating and drinking. It is the church that needs consecration, so that its members can be broken bread and poured-out wine in the world for which Christ died. It is the body of Christ that is the true sacrament. The experience of Adventist spirituality is composed of just two basic things—faith in what God says in His Word and the doing of what God says in His Word. Check the blood pressure and the pulse!

Meditation

How do you prepare to participate in the Communion service? If you find it easy to skip church on Communion Sabbath, could it be because you know you would not be present in spirit? If so, what should be done about it?

---

[1] The meeting was called by Philip, landgrave of Hesse, who had become a Lutheran but was influenced by the views of Zwingli. The Turks were at the gates of Vienna, and Germany was on the brink of a religious war. The landgrave wanted desperately to find common ground between the Lutheran and the Reformed thinkers. Known as the Marburg Colloquy, the meeting failed to achieve the objective of compromise and unity. The controversy continued. Both Luther and Zwingli were convinced that they followed Scripture. For Luther, the Lord's Supper was a "means of grace," and for Zwingli, it was a "sign" of grace. For Luther, participation was "bodily eating," and for Zwingli, it was "spiritual eating." Luther took a very firm position that made it virtually impossible for him to recognize anyone as a brother in the faith who denied the real presence of Christ in the Supper. Zwingli was prepared to tolerate Luther's view, but Luther would not tolerate Zwingli's.

[2] *Webster's New Collegiate Dictionary* (Springfield, Mass.: G. & C. Merriam Co., 1976).

[3] *Adult Sabbath School Bible Study Guide,* Teacher's Edition (2003), p. 159.

[4] In 1 John 2:1, 2 and 4:8-10, references to the heavenly ministry of Christ, the term *propitiation* does not appear in the Revised Standard Version or *The New English Bible*. However, it does appear in the King James Version, the Revised Version, the New King James Version, and the English Standard Version. See also Romans 3:21-26 and Hebrews 2:17.

[5] The Augsburg Confession, Article X, says that "the true body and blood of Christ are really present in the Supper of our Lord under the form of bread and wine and are there

distributed and received." Luther's *Small Catechism* says, "Instituted by Christ himself, it is the true body and blood of our Lord Jesus Christ, under the bread and wine, given to us Christians to eat and drink." His *Large Catechism* says, "It is the true body and blood of the Lord Jesus Christ, in and under the bread and wine which we Christians are commanded by the Word of Christ to eat and drink."

[6] *The Desire of Ages*, pp. 642-651. (Italics supplied.)

[7] *Ibid.*, pp. 652-661. (Italics supplied.) We can assume that her definition of *sacrament* was based largely upon that of the 1828 edition of Webster's dictionary, which defines the word as "the solemn act or ceremony of commemorating the death of our Redeemer, in the use of bread and wine, as emblems of his flesh and blood." Also: "an outward and visible sign of inward and spiritual grace. . . . The bread and wine in the sacrament are significant of the body and blood of Christ." Also: "The sacrament is a representation of Christ's death, by such symbolic actions as he appointed." The word *sacrament* or its equivalent cannot be found anywhere in the Bible, except in the Latin Vulgate, where it is used for the Greek term *mystery*, in reference to the revelation of God in Christ—the gospel itself.

[8] *Ibid.*, p. 660.

[9] *Ibid.*, p. 653.

Chapter 16

REFLECTIONS

Retirement provides both the time and the opportunity for a special kind of reflection. One is able to take a break from the daily doing that makes up so much of life and to become more acutely aware of just how God has led in the past, which is what these pages really describe. Retirement allows one to look in a disciplined and, I trust, a perceptive way at the past in order to focus on being and becoming, as one's gaze shifts more sharply on the future. One cannot live in the past, no matter how meaningful and purposeful it may have been. One can live only in the present, as long as there is a present. It is from the present that one beholds the future, which, for the Christian, is shaped by promise and hope.

On God's Guidance

God's guidance in one's life must be understood and experienced as a twofold reality. God's guidance is effected by means of His written Word, together with the inward ministry of His Holy Spirit. One without the other is incomplete and leads to truncated knowledge and a distorted experience. This balanced guidance is necessary in order to avoid the extremes of fanaticism and religious fadism, which ultimately will not satisfy the deep inner needs for union and oneness with God and which will produce only bitter disappointment and delusion. In this regard, perhaps these are the two most relevant verses in the New Testament: "All Scripture is breathed out [inspired] by God and profitable for teaching, for reproof, for correction, and for training in righteousness, that the man of God may be competent, equipped for every good work" (2 Tim. 3:16, 17). What "teaching" is that? It is the instruction and consequent knowledge of God's revealed truth that includes doctrine, ethics, and morality. What is meant by "reproof . . . correction" and "training in righteousness"? It is the application of God's instruction, which we need so desperately in such a bewildering and directionless age. What is the purpose for this divine instruction and discipline? That we, His followers, be prepared with the spiritual substance that enables us to obediently follow His will—not just to believe His will, but to obey His will. Obedience is both the goal and the result of His teaching and training. In His Word, God shows us His will, and He is glorified when His followers obey it. In other words, He gets all the credit. Because He is a loving Father, He teaches us His will and His way, empowering us by His Spirit to walk in His will and His way. He will reveal His will and show His way for anyone who wants to know it and walk in it.

The believer is able to take comfort from the fact that sometimes God uses upheaval and distress to bring us to our senses. God told Jonah to go to the city of Nineveh and "call out against it" (Jonah 1:2), but Jonah refused and fled to Tarshish. Though God's direction was clear and unmistakable, Jonah went the wrong way. The crew of the ship on which he traveled threw him into the sea, and he ended up in the belly of a great fish. He repented of his disobedience, and the fish vomited him out "upon the dry land" (Jonah 2:10). Finally, he went to Nineveh as God had directed, and "the people of Nineveh believed God" (Jonah 3:5) and "turned from their evil way" (verse 10). When the apostle Paul went to Greece to preach the gospel in response to a night vision from God, he ended up in a Philippian jail. Later, when he went to Jerusalem, in response to the leading of the Spirit (see Acts 19:21), he encountered major trouble. The greatest example is that of Jesus, whose obedience to His Father's will took Him to Calvary's cross. The point? As one looks back on life, that which gives the most satisfaction is the knowledge of having done the right thing as God revealed the right thing, even though the road traveled was not without difficulty and challenge. Remember the story about Jesus and His disciples in a storm (see Matt. 8:23-27)? The good news that this story tells is that Jesus is with us in the boat and in the storm. That should be enough for us, because He is our protection. He not only shows us the way; He takes us all the way.

On the Adventist People of God

Adventist spirituality does not seek accommodation with non-Christian faiths nor with other Christian traditions that are in the process of abandoning *sola scriptura*. What Adventist Christians desire more than anything else is a spirituality in harmony with Scripture, confirmed and affirmed by the Spirit of Prophecy, which fortifies them for the demands of mission in the time of the end. Their heads are not in the clouds of doctrine and theology, with no awareness of what life is really like in an inhospitable world. Nor are their hearts buried in the sand of indifference to the desperate cries for direction and hope on the part of suffering humanity, as evidenced by a globe-encircling medical/health ministry, educational system, and patiently persistent evangelism. Someday the world will awake and discover these people of God living with a strong, unshakable faith in the midst of its chaos and brutality, who care about one another in an inviolate community that exists under the rule of God—the body of Christ in which evangelism and social concern are united in mission. Some will be irresistibly attracted by what they hear and see, and join the remnant people of God. Some will hate and falsely accuse and persecute them.

These people of God have been here, working, growing, witnessing, and waiting for the day that the eschatological Christ calls the world to pay attention. Do they struggle to maintain purity of doctrine and life? Are they tempted to abandon the tried and true for the current religious fad? Are they under pressure to adopt and incorporate in their worship the banal choruses and frothy songs that are so popular in contemporary culture, rejecting those doctrinally sound historical hymns that emerged out of Christianity's struggle for spiritual life, as humankind cast itself ever deeper into the sewer of immorality, greed, and oppression? Are they tempted to abandon the biblical principles of ethics and morality in response to cultural/social pressure? Does God have to periodically raise up voices to sound alarm and point the way? Yes. Adventism does not separate spirituality from doctrine; nor does it separate the "inner being" from the reality of life in the world.

Adventist spirituality is the combination of reading and study, involving rigorous analysis of what is read and studied, based on the framework of biblical truths and values, together with the perceptive ethical/moral application of those truths and values to life and experience. Adventists understand that spirituality is the shape into which they have been molded by the knowledge revealed through study of God's Word, impressed on their minds by the Holy Spirit and the indwelling Christ, learned in the practice of a believing faith, and experienced in the struggle to stay faithful in the midst of the conflict between the kingdom of light and the kingdom of darkness. It consists of the joy of knowing Him who is the way and the truth, together with the deep and abiding satisfaction of having taken the journey with the unmistakable guidance of the One who alone knows the way.

Spirituality is difficult to define because it is more of a process than a state. As such, it is made up of learning, purging, understanding, refining, enlarging, toughening, developing, deepening, wrestling, convicting, repenting, confirming, confessing, trusting, waiting, hoping, knowing, growing, yearning, anticipating, following, sharing, giving, crying, rejoicing, worshipping, serving, praying, praising, glorifying, obeying, enduring, maturing, training, and molding. All this, and more, comprises a *believing faith*. That's the way one is transformed into the likeness of Christ.

On Faith and Doctrine

The classical biblical definition of faith is that "faith is the assurance of things hoped for, the conviction of things not seen" (Heb. 11:1). According to this definition, faith has two basic characteristics: (1) assurance that produces confidence and certainty, and (2) conviction that produces determination to exercise a believing faith. We have confidence that what is hoped for, on the basis of God's promises, will come to pass. We have conviction concerning revealed reality, even without empirical proof. It is by "faith we understand that the universe was created by the word of God" (verse 3). *Faith* is a major word in the New Testament, which tells us that the righteous shall live by faith. That faith can be increased. That hearts are cleansed by faith. That believers are sanctified by faith. That sinners are justified through faith. That one can be weak in faith. That believers must stand firm in faith and walk by faith. That they must continue in faith and be established in the faith. That some will depart from the faith. That the faith must be shared. That believers petition God in faith. That they are guarded through faith. That the outcome of faith is salvation. That the genuineness of faith is tested. And that faith without works is dead.

When I put all of that from the Word of God together with my spiritual experience, I perceive that faith is the struggle to be believing. Such an experiential definition of faith may be unsatisfactory to the analytical proposition-prone mind. But I believe it to be accurate, at least, from the perspective of my own spirituality. I have observed that one can have a finely tuned doctrinal theology without having an experiential theology. During my ministry I have met people who wear the doctrinal truth they hold like a suit of impenetrable armor, which not only protects them from falsehood but also shields them from sensitive and meaningful human contact. Such protection does not reflect Christlikeness. Such believers are cold and heartless in demeanor, ready to debate and argue in a spirit of antagonism and meanness. It is possible to have right doctrine but wrong religion, if truth gets stuck in the head and never touches the heart. If one has a full head and an empty heart. My understanding has always been that God's truth is meant to soften the heart. As Ellen White so perceptively articulated when she pleaded:

"Why do you bring yourself with your coldness between the people and the truth, and so keep the truth from doing its work upon their *hearts*? Why do you go to the people with your *heart* as cold as an iron wedge, and expect to win souls to Christ? You want your lips touched with the living coal from off the heavenly altar. The influence of the truth is elevating and ennobling. The divine must combine with the human if you would make your way amid the moral darkness and the spiritual stagnation of the world."[1]

From my vantage point of 60 years as a Christian and 40 as an Adventist, I have to confess that not everything about the faith, and living that faith, has been settled. What I know intellectually about the faith, I really know after so many years, but I still have unanswered questions. One might think that to be disturbing, but, strangely enough, I am not in as much of a panic to find the answers as I once was. I have become content to live with my questions, because I suspect that many of them will not be answered on this side of the resurrection. For me, part of believing faith is being able to live with some unanswered questions. Also, at this stage on the spiritual road I travel, I have perceived a need to preserve some aspects of the "mystery" of the Christian faith of which Paul speaks in his Ephesian letter. Though it is "made known" by revelation (Eph. 3:3) into which "insight" (verse 4) is possible through the ministry of the Holy Spirit and which is brought "to light for everyone" (verse 9), it is, nevertheless, a mystery.

Understanding of this mystery does not come by way of education alone. It is hidden from human reason and can only be revealed. Paul speaks of the "mystery of Christ" (verse 4), which was understood by few people, yet preached among the Gentiles and accepted by many. For some reason I am not satisfied just with the explainable. My heart is most at ease when I allow for the unexplainable—more than simply allow for it, when I accept it as part of the whole package. During the years we lived in the Philippines, south of Manila, in beautiful Cavite province, I knew the scientific explanation for the volcanic formation of Mount Makiling and the magnificence of Laguna de Bay. But to watch the early-morning and late-evening sun playing on the water, on the canefields and coconut groves, on the deep-green slopes of that mountain, was to bask in the mystery of creation. The sheer beauty of it was far more compelling to my inner being than the scientific explanation. I did not need that explanation to enjoy the experience of what I was viewing. I have had the same sensation while driving through such states as Colorado, Arizona, Nevada, and Utah.

Making the substance of faith an intellectual matter alone is not satisfying for the inner being. In essence the Christian faith is a power to be experienced as much as it is a doctrinal system to be understood, believed, and defended. It is not the truth or its theological/doctrinal content that can be so troublesome to some folks, but why the presentation of it is often so cold, formal, and unfeeling. In this context I cannot resist quoting the following from Ellen White to Adventist ministers, in which she says that the object of preaching "is not to convey information alone, not merely to convince the intellect."[2] "The preaching of the Word should appeal to the intellect and should impart knowledge, *but* it should do *more* than this. *The words of the minister should reach the hearts of the hearers.*"[3]

It has taken a long time, but I have discovered that it is easier to believe the right doctrines than to live the Christian life. It is far easier to believe that Saturday is the true Sabbath than it is to enter into its observance, in spite of the costs that might impose. It is much easier not to smoke or drink alcoholic beverages than to relate in love to fellow human beings. Conformity is much easier than surrender of heart. Conformity is outward, while surrender is inward. Conformity has to do with appearances, while surrender has to do with essence. Conformity involves doing, while surrender involves being. The first has to do with a faith that believes, and the other with a believing faith.

Please do not misunderstand. It is critically important to believe biblical doctrine. But to speak of "the truth" and not be concerned about what is "true" is a contradiction in terms. When I speak about being able to live with unanswered questions, I am not talking about living with no questions. Nor am I speaking of a questioning faith in which everything is up for grabs and there are no answers, no absolutes. Nor am I speaking of a pluralistic kind of faith in which there is a smorgasbord from which to choose answers, all of which can be considered equally reliable. There are, after all, truths upon which we are to take our stand, to which we must hold firm, and that are of first importance (see 1 Cor. 15:1-3). To say there is no resurrection of the dead, in spite of the revelational evidence in terms of its apostolic proclamation, is to reject something "true." But all questions need not be answered in order for me to believe, to be content and at peace. I have concluded that this is the essence of faith. I am less inclined to search for answers than I was as a young believer. Let the mysteries, the unanswered questions, be what they are. My interest now is the exploration of the meaning of what I do know and am experiencing by faith. Perhaps that quest has been spurred on by the realization that there is not a great deal of time left in which to do it. Now, when I ask why it was necessary, in God's plan, to leave the Lutheran tradition and ministry for the Adventist, my focus is not on doctrine. That has long ago been settled for me. When it happened, doctrine was vital, as it had to be, and without it the transition could not have been made, nor should it have been made for any other reason, as it would not have had any truth basis. But now when I ask why, I am more interested in discovering the deep inner meaning that doctrinal truth is meant to produce, which is why I was ready to teach a course on spirituality. But even that was a tentative attempt to do so in a dialogical rather than monological format. I guess what I have been trying to express is that while doctrine may be a settled matter, the faith experience is never settled and is always moving, growing, deepening in awareness and meaning. Spirituality involves the truth basis, the dynamic faith experience, and the ethical/moral evidence—all of which make up the believer's own story.

On Holiness

Jesus came preaching what He called "the kingdom of heaven" (Matt. 4:17; 5:3, 10, 19, 20), and in the Sermon on the Mount (Matt. 5-7) He talked about the kind of life His disciples were to live in that kingdom. As I was reading through that sermon recently, my attention was arrested by how many times He used the word *Father*—17 times, according to the English Standard Version. Eleven instances refer to God as "your Father," four as "your heavenly Father," one as "our Father," and once Jesus refers to Him as "my Father."

The idea of God as "Father" is present in the Old Testament, but many of the references are to His power and His holiness, such as "Holy, holy, holy is the Lord of hosts; the whole earth is full of His glory" (Isa. 6:3). "Holy" sets Him apart. He is so holy that His "eyes are too pure to look on evil"; therefore, He "cannot tolerate wrongdoing" (Hab. 1:13, NIV).That holiness of God is reflected in the sermon when Jesus says, "Unless your righteousness exceeds that of the scribes and Pharisees, you will never enter the kingdom of heaven" (Matt. 5:20), and "You therefore must be perfect, as your heavenly Father is perfect" (verse 48).

The fatherhood of God is a major theme in the Sermon on the Mount. The sermon is full of a loving Father's instructions. Certainly Jesus knew that saving faith rests on the Father's justifying grace. But He also knew that such a faith understands that it is God's will that His redeemed people live in a manner that reveals the power of His grace, which demonstrates the Father's love. He knew that justification by grace and faithful obedience to the Father are not mutually exclusive. That they are not in conflict or opposed to each other, either doctrinally or experientially.

Justification by grace alone, received by faith alone, produces a believing faith that willingly and joyfully lets its "light shine before others, so that they might see your good works" (verse 16). He then says, "You will recognize them by their fruits. Are grapes gathered from thornbushes, or figs from thistles? So, every healthy tree bears good fruit, but the diseased tree bears bad fruit. A healthy tree *cannot* bear bad fruit, nor can a diseased tree bear good fruit" (Matt. 7:16-18). Is that not clear? If not, His next words are meant to remove any misunderstanding: "Not everyone who says to me, 'Lord, Lord,' will enter the kingdom of heaven, but the one who *does the will* of my Father who is in heaven" (verse 21). He underlines this by declaring that to those who claim to be saved by grace, but who do not do "the will of my Father," He will say "on that day . . . I never knew you; depart from me, you workers of lawlessness" (verses 21-23).

Throughout the sermon Jesus makes His point and application unmistakably clear. God's people are to bring "glory" to the Father by their "good works" (Matt. 5:16). They are to love and pray for their enemies, and by so doing demonstrate that they are truly the Father's children, who do not participate in the world's hatreds (see verses 44, 45). They are to be unobtrusively generous to the needy and will be rewarded by the Father (see Matt. 6:1-4). If they forgive others, the Father will forgive them (see verses 14, 15). When they seek first His kingdom and His righteousness, their heavenly Father will take care of their basic needs (see verses 25-34). He will give "good things to those who ask Him" (Matt. 7:7-11), and all who do "the will of my Father who is in heaven" will "enter the kingdom of heaven" (verses 21-23).

How is that possible for sinful, selfish, self-centered humans? The answer reveals the secret of the Fatherhood of God. The word *father* implies relationship. It is the son or daughter who can speak of a father. It is the son or daughter who knows what it means to have a father, and it is the father who knows what it means to have children. How is such a relationship with the heavenly Father established? There are only two ways that one can become a son or a daughter. One is by natural birth, and the other is by adoption. My two adopted children know me as their father. They know no other person as father, and they affectionately call me "Dad." From the day I first saw them as infants they have been my children. Nothing in this world could ever change that. They were not born to their mother and me; we made them our children by choice. We chose them. That's what adoption means, and that's the only way you and I can become children of God. He has chosen us and by so doing makes us His children. My children did not know it at the time, but when I adopted them, I not only accepted them as mine, I gave them myself. I gave them my fatherhood and everything that goes with it and that it implies. But if that relationship, established by choice, were to be maintained and nurtured, both father and children had to follow through on it.

Some folks think that every human being is a child of God simply by being born. But the Word of God teaches that "to all who did receive him [Jesus], who believed in his name, he gave the right to become children of God, who were born, not of blood nor of the will of the flesh nor of the will of man, but [born] of God" (John 1:12, 13). Paul said that in love "he [the Father] predestined us for adoption as sons through Jesus Christ, according to the purpose of his will, to the praise of his glorious grace, with which he has blessed us in the Beloved. In him we have redemption through his blood" (Eph. 1:5-7). And John wrote, "See what kind of love the Father has given to us [lavished on us], that we should be *called* children of God; and *so we are*" (1 John 3:1).

We are adopted by the Father, made children of God by faith in Jesus. What did that cost the Father? "God loved the world so much and so passionately that He willingly gave His only Son to suffer the cross and die, that whoever believes in Jesus should not perish but have eternal life" (John 3:16, paraphrase). It was not just the Son who suffered the cross, but the Father who sent the Son and who knew why the cross, was necessary. A true father suffers for his children, with his children, and he willingly suffers the pain they often cause him by their willfulness and disobedience, just as our heavenly Father does with us. He is a loving Father; we are part of His family and can come to Him unafraid, certain of His compassion and care. Jesus describes the marvelous truth of our relationship with our heavenly Father in this way:

"Ask, and it will be given to you; seek, and you will find; knock, and it will be opened to you. For everyone who asks receives, and the one who seeks finds, and to the one who knocks it will be opened. Or which one of you, if his son asks him for bread, will give him a stone? Or if he asks for a fish, will give him a serpent? If you, then, who are evil, know how to give good gifts to your children, how much more will your Father who is in heaven give good things to those who ask him!" (Matt. 7:7-11).

God's love for us is often misunderstood. For example, when Jesus says, "Enter by the narrow gate. For the gate is wide and the way is easy that leads to destruction, and those who enter by it are many" (Matt. 7:13), we ask, "If God loves me, why does the gate have to be narrow? Why not wide and easy?" Or when Jesus says, "If you forgive others their trespasses, your heavenly Father will also forgive you, but if you do not forgive others . . . neither will your Father forgive your trespasses" (Matt. 6:14, 15), we ask, "If God loves me, why doesn't He forgive me even though I don't forgive others?" Ellen White comments, "His [the believer's] words, his motives, his actions, may be misrepresented and falsified, but he does not mind it, because he has greater interests at stake."[4] What is that greater interest? The kingdom of heaven, which is not just an abstract idea but an earthly reality for which believers are to pray constantly, "Our Father in heaven, hallowed be your name. Your kingdom come, *your will be done*, on earth as it is in heaven" (verses 6:9, 10). The coming of God's kingdom involves the doing of His will on earth. Children do not always understand their parents, no matter how much a father or mother tries to explain or how careful and sound their instruction. What do good parents do then? They choose, as God does, to love their children, in spite of their inability or unwillingness to understand. Having said that, I need also to say that loving obedience is the fundamental characteristic of a child's relationship to his or her father and mother. Contrary to the contemporary view, it is not the parents' obligation to encourage their children to follow their own desires, no matter what they are or where they might lead. Children are truly free when they know to whom they belong, as Jesus exemplified— "Whoever has seen me has seen the Father" (John 14:9). Here is union, oneness, with the kind of life embodied in the will of God and made possible by His grace. "If you abide in my word," says Jesus, "you are truly my disciples." "If the Son sets you free [from sin and its power], you will be free indeed" (verse 36). Jesus' message is not one that abrogates dependence on, and subjection to, the Father's will. Rather, His message is that to abide in Him results in a new understanding, and experience, of such dependence and subjection, as defined by His Word.

True fatherhood demonstrates both love and authority. Neither is compromised for the sake of the other, which is what we find difficult to understand. God the Father loves us, but He will not compromise His truth, His will, His authority. He is always loving, always truthful, always just, at the same time. We have to understand the divine principles that are made so specific in the Sermon on the Mount, in order to appreciate that about the Father. That is precisely why the Father chose to show His love for "the world" by giving His Son to be crucified on the cross.

Jesus knew His destiny when He preached that sermon. If we had been there, we would have seen the earnestness and compassion on His face. We would have heard the love and authority in His voice. We would have been as "astonished" as were those who were there, "for he was teaching them as one who had authority" (Matt. 7:29), the authority of the heavenly Father's love. In the content and preaching of the Sermon on the Mount, we have the Father exercising His loving authority and kingdom rule, through His Son, making it plain by speaking in specifics, not generalities, on how His children are to live in His kingdom.

These "principles of His kingdom" are not debatable, not an agenda for discussion. This is the way it is. His intent was that those principles "would help them [His disciples] to comprehend its [the kingdom's] true nature."[5] In the light of this, what a comfort to know that "in the human heart He sees more than sin, more than misery. In His infinite wisdom and love He sees man's possibilities, the height to which he may attain. . . .

Living the life of the Life-giver, through faith in Him, everyone can reach the standard held up in His words."[6] "This subject," Ellen White says, "demands far more contemplation than it receives. Christians strike too low. They are content with a superficial spiritual experience, and therefore they have only the glimmerings of light, when . . . they might discern more clearly the wonderful perfection of Christ's humanity, which rises far above all human greatness, all human power. Christ's life is a revelation of what fallen human beings may become through union and fellowship with the divine nature."[7]

I happen to think that it is very significant that Jesus began His public ministry by preaching about holiness. When we speak about what God is doing *for* us, the focus is on justification. When we speak about what He is doing *in* us, the focus is on sanctification and the holiness (spirituality/character formation), which is the goal of redemption. The Bible says, "As obedient children, do not be conformed to the passions of your former ignorance, but as he who called you is holy, you also be holy in all your conduct, since it is written [Leviticus 11:44], 'You shall be holy, for I am holy'" (1 Peter 1:14-16). Holiness is about the health of the inner life.

I don't want to get into the seemingly endless argument about sinless perfection or perfectionism, because that argument is fruitless. It is fruitless because it ends in negativism, a denial of the power of grace and the indwelling Christ to transform the believer inwardly. Spiritual growth stops with this argument. How many times have you heard it said, or have said it yourself, that "we will always be sinners, always commit sins." The implication is that it is useless to spend time thinking about what the Bible says about holiness. But Jesus focuses on the positive, not the negative, on the possibilities (read the last quote by Ellen White again). Because He is just, He forgives sin, yes, but He also cleanses us "from all unrighteousness" (1 John 1:9). In other words, by His grace He remakes, transforms, us from the inside out.

Holiness is not a doctrine; it is a quality of character that only the Holy Spirit can produce. The question, then, is: How fully and completely are we surrendered to His ministry of sanctification? We cannot avoid sanctification, understood as growth in holiness, if we desire God's ultimate gift of eternal life. "But now that you have been set free from sin," said Paul, "and have become slaves of God [rather than slaves of sin], the fruit you get leads to sanctification and its end, eternal life" (Rom. 6:22). We have to describe spirituality in terms of what we are against (sin) and what we are for (holiness and righteousness). Holiness devoid of an ever-present attitude of repentance leads to spiritual pride, which is certainly not the goal of sanctification. Repentance is the response of a sensitive conscience that is, to borrow Luther's word, "captive" [bound] to the Word of God and determined, by God's grace, to follow His plan for holy living.

God's people, "in the last days," need more than the "appearance of godliness," as Paul admonishes the young preacher Timothy:

"But understand this, that in the last days there will come times of difficulty. For people will be lovers of self, lovers of money, proud, arrogant, abusive, disobedient to their parents, ungrateful, unholy, heartless, unappeasable [no matter what is done for them they are not satisfied], slanderous, without self-control, brutal, not loving good, treacherous, reckless, swollen with conceit, lovers of pleasure rather than lovers of God, having the appearance of godliness, but denying its power" (2 Tim. 3:1-5).

Denying the power of godliness to do what? Transform them from the inside out so that they are enabled not to *be* that kind of people, exhibiting such character traits. This is spiritual transformation.

When God the Holy Spirit works within us, He invites us to cooperate with Him. In order for us to do this with a sense of divine purpose and destiny, we need to be aware of His plan of operation and His will. The only way to perceive the nature and details of His plan and will is by the study, and meditation/contemplation, of His Word. Only when such study enables us to understand cognitively what God, the indwelling Christ and the Holy Spirit, are doing for us and in us, are we able to perceive what He enables us to do for Him. If we avoid the sources that inform, and form, a genuine Adventist spirituality, the temptation increases to experiment with others. "I am in great travail of soul for our people. We are living in the perils of the last days. A superficial faith results in a superficial experience," which, Ellen White implies, will not suffice for such a time.[8]

On Retirement by Faith

Facing retirement in 1994, I began to pray about it two years earlier. I had two questions in mind: Did the Lord want us to stay in Berrien Springs, Michigan, where we enjoyed the modest home we had designed and built with our own hands, or move elsewhere? If elsewhere, where, and why? The first question was answered, as an inner conviction grew that I didn't really want to hang around Andrews University. Preachers are a dime a dozen there. Don't get me wrong: the years on the faculty of the seminary were the highlight of my ministry. Andrews University was a wonderful place to work. I made many friends, and I loved the give and take with students and fellow faculty. I loved the daily challenge and the responsibility; I was eager every morning to find my way to the campus by

7:00 a.m. It would have been wonderful to continue to enjoy the academic environment, access to the library, special lecture series, musical events, and good preaching at Pioneer Memorial church. But the Lord had other plans.

The second question—where to retire—was answered in 1993. Our son lived in Denver, and our daughter lived in Orlando. Both places were appealing as major Adventist centers. Then there was the Upper Peninsula of Michigan, where we had built a cabin for winter skiing and summer vacations, just outside my wife's hometown of Wakefield. One day, while cleaning the garage, I was praying about where to retire and told the Lord that I needed some unmistakable direction. Doing what I had never done before, I promised that if He would see to the selling of our home, I would take that to indicate that He wanted us to move to the UP. Within a week the house was sold. I didn't advertise on the real estate market; a buyer approached me. I rejoiced in that obvious direction, because it was my inclination all along to go back to the UP, where I went to college and began ministry. I also had a burden on my heart for the people who live there.

Something else happened too. When the leadership of the Michigan Conference heard that we intended to retire to the Upper Peninsula, they asked me to serve as part-time "senior" pastor of the Bessemer congregation. It was then that I knew the answer to the "Why?" question, and the decision was affirmed and confirmed as a believing faith response to God's revealed will. Because of God's continued grace, demonstrated by the sensitivity and care of the Michigan Conference, my retirement has not been empty or bitter. Nor has it been placid or dull. After all, no one really retires from ministry, because the "call" is ontological, having more to do with being than with doing. In 1 Corinthians 1:1 Paul refers to himself as "called by the will of God to be an apostle of Christ Jesus." In many of his other letters he refers to himself as "an apostle"—not to do the work of an apostle, but to be one. He was always an apostle of Christ, waking or sleeping. At all times and in all places, no matter where he was, free or in prison, he was always an apostle of Christ. One who has been called by the Lord to ministry is always a minister of Christ, no matter where or how old that person may be. Ministry is what a minister is; it is a primary demonstration of the minister's spirituality. So ministry did not end for me when I left Andrews University to serve a small congregation in the UP of Michigan. The retirement years have been some of the most satisfying and rewarding of my life, and I am so grateful to the Lord. During the past 15 years the congregation has grown from a handful to almost 50 members. A new debt-free sanctuary has been built. "The Ark: Christian Child Care and Learning Center" was opened and now serves 40 children with a staff of eight. The congregation took a big step of faith, voting unanimously to once again operate a K-8 school. The school addition was built, and Bluff View Christian School opened its doors, also debt-free.

From October 23 to November 5, 1942, a decisive battle was fought between the British army led by General Bernard Montgomery, and the German/Italian forces, led by General Erwin Rommel, at a place called El Alamein in North Africa. After a long retreat across North Africa, the British achieved a dramatic victory at El Alamein and forced Rommel to retreat to Tunisia. It was a major turning point in the war. Of that victory Prime Minister Winston Churchill said to Parliament, "This is not the end, it is not even the beginning of the end. But it is, perhaps, the end of the beginning." That's the way I began to feel about retirement. Certainly, after so many years of meaningful ministry, one has to adjust to the idea. I recall having many negative thoughts as I saw retirees sitting in a shopping mall, watching the rest of humanity go by in its busyness. If that was retirement, I wanted no part of it. I wanted somehow to be useful and productive. Having lived and served by faith, I wanted to retire by faith. Hebrews 11 says: "By faith we understand"; "By faith Abel offered . . . a more acceptable sacrifice"; "And through his faith . . . he still speaks"; "By faith Enoch" "pleased God"; "By faith Noah . . . constructed an ark for the saving of his household"; "By faith Abraham obeyed" and "went"; "By faith [Abraham] went to live in the land of promise"; "By faith Abraham . . . offered up Isaac"; "By faith Joseph . . . made mention of the exodus"; "By faith Moses . . . was hidden . . . by his parents"; "By faith [Moses] left Egypt"; "By faith the people crossed the Red Sea," and more. So why not retire by faith?

By faith these individuals lived, acted, testified, obeyed the will of God, and accomplished significant things for Him. The Bible preserved the record of their achievements for us to read, so that we might have the same kind of faith. It is a catalog of accomplishments in the service of the Lord that is both inspiring and depressing. Inspiring because we too can look back and recall significant events and accomplishments. Depressing because retirement sometimes implies an end to service and significance. That's the way our culture has conditioned us. That's why the prospect of retirement is so traumatic for so many. All our lives we have been motivated to compete. Everything we do in terms of training supports that kind of preparation for life in a very competitive culture. Rewards are there for the achiever early on. The best performance in school gets the teacher's attention and the accolades. Grades reflect the level and significance of accomplishment, and the reward is equal to ability or determination. The sports hero gets the attention, as well as the academic achiever. The successful scientist, musician, doctor, lawyer, businessman, politician, gets the financial and celebrity rewards, because they have learned how to compete.

We have been conditioned to the idea that in order to find meaning and significance we must learn to compete, to beat out the other guy, to be better at whatever we do than anyone else. Being the best is the way to be noticed, the way to appreciation and significance. Usually when we meet each other, we ask, "What are you doing these days?" And we've learned to play the game with determination and skill, achieving one important goal after another, until suddenly there are no more goals. We discover—to our horror, perhaps—that we have fallen into the trap of identifying meaning with accomplishment. No wonder the prospect of retirement can be so traumatic, when we have allowed self-worth to be determined by doing. When the opportunities for accomplishment are over, we are terrified by the thought that our lives have lost meaning and value.

If my identity is determined by a job, a position, or a title, retirement can mean that I have become useless, unneeded, even unwanted. Income is sometimes drastically reduced. One is not "doing anything" of value for society, so he or she doesn't have to be rewarded. One goes on "pension" or "sustentation" or "Social Security." Webster's definition of *pension* has the connotation of dismissal. Because we have been conditioned to compete, the retiree often feels pushed aside, rejected, and ignored when he is no longer considered productive. However, retirees have a certain disruptive power. By their very presence they disturb a competitive society, which is inclined to keep them as hidden as possible. They remind society that it is fragile and fallible, that life does not go on forever, and that competition and achievement do not ultimately provide the meaning that makes life worth living. If we have been programmed to feel that to do nothing means worthlessness, how can our need for significance be met?

The question we face is not whether to retire, but whether to face it intentionally, to choose it as part of God's grace. Could it be that these words of Jesus to His disciples were meant for retirees in particular? "Truly, I say to you, unless you turn and become like children, you will never enter the kingdom of heaven" (Matt. 18:3). Could He be saying that we must end life in the way in which it was begun, with the innocence and trust of a child? With a child's open curiosity and simple joy in being alive?

We have a photo in our collection that is a treasure; it was taken by my wife during our trip to Finland in 1969. It is a photo of a small boy lying on his stomach in a field, closely examining a blade of grass with intense interest and pleasure. Could it be that a child's mind is yet open to the glory of simply being, at least before society begins to program that mind with competitiveness? Children don't have to explain themselves or justify their existence. Children seem to drink deeply of life; every day is a joy and adventure, filled with wonder and excitement. Do you remember what that was like? Perhaps that's why, as I grow older, I have become more observant of little children. I remember playing in the creek and what the clay felt like as I squeezed it between my small fingers. Is it impossible to recapture such delight, such simplicity, again?

One author has defined sin as "the arrogance of taking things for granted." I remember the resurrection I experienced when the Lord found me and I became a Christian. The sky was bluer, the grass greener, and I was given a love for people whom I had learned to hate. *I want that kind of resurrection again!* As we have lived by faith, worked by faith, served by faith, so we can retire by faith. Each day can be a new day, filled with God's grace and goodness. We can enjoy one day at a time, with each day bringing unscheduled challenges and blessings as gifts of grace from our loving Father who is certainly not finished with us yet. So retirement is not the beginning of the end, but the end of the beginning. The truth is that all of life is preparation for those retirement years, which are the frosting on the cake. During these years we can apply the wisdom that God and experience have given us, expressing unfettered the love of God in Christ. It is God's gift of grace to His own. Thanks to God, to the Michigan Conference, and to the members of the Bessemer congregation, I have been able to have the cake and eat it, too! I have been able to have the being and the doing. The retirement years are when the first and last—the childlikeness—come together. Pablo Picasso once observed that it takes a long time to become young. In this sense it is possible to refer to the "golden years" as a "second childhood."

Genesis 25:8 says that Abraham died "satisfied with life" (NASB). He was satisfied with his life, including its ups and downs, victories over sins, struggles and accomplishments. Best of all, he had been faithful to God in the long run. How many are there who enjoy the privilege of being satisfied with the life they have lived? Speaking of Abel, Enoch, Noah, Abraham, and Sarah, the author of Hebrews says:

"These all died in faith, not having received the things promised, but having seen them and greeted them from afar, and having acknowledged that they were strangers and exiles on the earth. For people who speak thus make it clear that they are seeking a homeland. If they had been thinking of that land from which they had gone out, they would have had opportunity to return. But as it is, they desire a better country, that is, a heavenly one. Therefore God is not ashamed to be called their God, for he has prepared for them a city" (Heb. 11:13-16).

Looking back on his life, David said, "I have been young, and now am old, yet I have not seen the righteous forsaken or his children begging for bread. He is ever lending generously, and his children become a blessing" (Ps. 37:25, 26). There are some wonderful promises in Psalm 34 for all retirees who exercise a believing faith: "The young lions suffer want and hunger; but those who seek the Lord lack no good thing" (verse 10). "The eyes of the Lord are toward the righteous and his ears toward their cry" (verse 15). "When the righteous cry for help, the Lord hears and delivers them out of all their troubles" (verse 17). "Many are the afflictions of the righteous, but the Lord delivers him out of them all. He keeps all his bones; not one of them is broken" (verses 19, 20).

On the Straight Course

The week before he died, I talked on the phone with my spiritual friend, Professor Walter Kukkonen. When our conversation was over, I began to make plans to visit him at his home in Minneapolis. I wanted to spend some time sitting at his feet again, while he explained the meaning of his last words to me, which were: "I have come to the conclusion that this [the Evangelical Lutheran Church in America] is a Christless church." That visit never happened, because a week later his son called with the news of his father's sudden death. He also informed me that his father had requested that I preach the sermon at his funeral. I had but two days to prepare. I was stunned and deeply moved by his request. It is unprecedented, after all, that he, a retired Lutheran seminary professor, should request a retired Seventh-day Adventist seminary professor to preach his funeral service. Still, given the things he had said to me over the years, I was not really surprised.

In that sermon I recalled that back in the mid–1980s I was able to arrange for him to give a lecture to the faculty and students of the Seventh-day Adventist Theological Seminary. After I had enjoyed the happy privilege of introducing him, he stepped to the lectern, looked over the assembly, and put everyone at ease by saying, "You don't look like Seventh-day Adventists. But then, I probably don't look like a Lutheran, either." I reminded the congregation that in 1958, writing about the factors that had shaped the Finnish Evangelical Lutheran Church, he had said: "The saving act of God is an *actus purus*, independent of man's merits or efforts, but it is not merely a forensic event, for it involves the individual in his relationship to God and his fellowmen. Sanctification, then, becomes the mirror which reflects justification, a sign of living faith. There is both the 'Christ for us' and the 'Christ in us.'"[9]

I called their attention to the fact that already, as a seminary professor and trainer of pastors, he was alarmed by the temptation to replace the indwelling Christ with sacramentalism and ritualism. I recalled his cryptic comment to a group of seminarians who were clamoring for the celebration of the Lord's Supper at every chapel service: "You can take Communion every hour on the hour until you burp, and it won't do you any good." He later said, "The primary sacrament of the Christian faith is the person of Jesus Christ. . . . Baptism and the Lord's Supper . . . are meaningful and effective only in union with Him as true man and true God." Then I read Romans 8:10, 11: "If Christ is in you, although the body is dead because of sin, the Spirit is life because of righteousness. If the Spirit of him who raised Jesus from the dead dwells in you, he who raised Christ Jesus from the dead will also give life to your mortal bodies through his Spirit who dwells in you." I followed that passage with Paul's words to the Colossians:

"Now I rejoice in my sufferings for your sake, and in my flesh I am filling up what is lacking in Christ's afflictions for the sake of his body, that is, the church, of which I became a minister according to the stewardship from God that was given to me for you, to make the word of God fully known, the mystery hidden for ages and generations but now revealed to his saints. To them God chose to make known how great among the Gentiles *are the riches of the glory of this mystery, which is Christ in you, the hope of glory.* Him [the Christ in you] we proclaim, warning everyone and teaching everyone with all wisdom, that we may present everyone mature in Christ. For this I toil, struggling with all his energy that he powerfully works within me" (Col. 1:24-29).

I told them that Walter Kukkonen gave me the greatest gift of all in 1969—the permission and freedom, in effect, to follow where Christ, who is the Way, was showing me the way. Then I quoted his last words to me, pointing out that we will never know exactly what he meant and that unfortunately (or perhaps fortunately), we will have to think about his words by ourselves, but not alone. Because "he who has an ear, let him hear what the Spirit says to the churches. To the one who conquers I will grant to eat of the tree of life, which is in the paradise of God" (Rev. 2:7). Near the end of his own book, in a section titled "Hope as the Corollary of Faith," he quotes the apostle Paul: "If only for this life we have hope in Christ, we are to be pitied more than all men" (1 Cor. 15:19, NIV).[10] Then he concludes with "The end-times are upon us, but not the end."

The stories of our spiritual journeys are really entwined, aren't they? Our roads may separate, but like his and mine they are parallel, rather than divergent, roads. What goes around comes around. As the Finns would say: "Let's covenant to stay on the *suora kurssi*—the straight course!"

On the Road Again

I am still traveling the road the Lord has assigned to me, and He continues to point the way. I am still studying the Bible and the Spirit of Prophecy, still growing, preaching, pastoring, thinking, praying, serving. The energy and alertness required to stay on that road has kept me alive, both physically and spiritually. Everything looks different from the long view, when one looks back as the end of the road approaches; when one is able to see the whole of it and not just the panorama of scenes as one passes through them. That's why I think I was a Seventh-day Adventist Christian at heart all along, though unaware of it.

I am a Seventh-day Adventist Christian because, as Luther put it, "my conscience is captive to the Word of God. . . . Here I stand; I can do no other. God help me." I understand conscience to be composed of both head and heart, conception of revealed truth and perception of its internal power and effect. My Lutheran friends, who are now faced with the challenge of being faithful to Scripture and the Reformation, will understand and appreciate that. I pray that my Adventist friends, who understand that the Reformation is not over, are determined to remain faithful to God's Word. My years as a Lutheran taught me that, and Adventism has affirmed it as a major factor of my own spirituality.

One final word. By God's grace I have "learned to understand by experience," to a degree at least, "what it means to have fellowship with Christ." And, it must be added, fellowship with those who are His own. As Sophocles said: "One must wait until the evening to see how splendid the day has been." The Lord has taught me patience when the road seemed obscure and uncertain. He did that by making me wait for Him to clear the way. I'm so glad I didn't miss the road and the journey. Along the way, at critical junctions, the right word came from the Word and from Spirit-led friends, speaking to both my head and my heart.

Meditation

What are your reflections as you think about your church, its message and mission, and as you contemplate your own spiritual journey and experience?

---

[1] Ellen G. White, in *Review and Herald*, June 11, 1889. (Italics supplied.)

[2] Ellen G. White, *The Voice in Speech and Song* (Boise, Idaho: Pacific Press Pub. Assn., 1988), p. 274.

[3] *Ibid.*, p. 272. (Italics supplied.)

[4] E. G. White, *Thoughts From the Mount of Blessing*, p. 32.

[5] *Ibid.*, p. 4.

[6] *Ibid.*, pp. vii, viii.

[7]Ellen G. White, *The Faith I Live By* (Washington, D.C.: Review and Herald Pub. Assn., 1958), p. 219.

[8]E. G. White, *Selected Messages*, book 2, p. 392.

[9]*The Lutheran Quarterly*, February 1958, p. 43.

[10]1984 edition.